THE COMMANDANT

ALSO BY IAN BAXTER

'Wolf' Hitler's Wartime Headquarters

Poland – The Eighteen Day Victory March

Panzers In North Africa

The Ardennes Offensive

The Western Campaign

The 12th SS Panzer-Division Hitlerjugend

The Waffen-SS on the Western Front

The Waffen-SS on the Eastern Front

The Red Army At Stalingrad

Elite German Forces of World War II

Armoured Warfare

German Tanks of War

Blitzkrieg

Panzer-Divisions At War

Hitler's Panzers

German Armoured Vehicles of World War Two

Last Two Years of the Waffen-SS At War

German Soldier Uniforms and Insignia

German Guns of the Third Reich

From Retreat to Defeat: The Last Years of the German Army At War 1943—1945

Operation Bagration – the Destruction of Army Group Centre

German Guns of the Third Reich

Rommel and the Afrika Korps

The Sixth Army and the Road to Stalingrad

Hitler's Eastern Front Headquarters 'Wolf's Lair' 1941—1945

U-Boat War 1939 – 1945

Last Years of the Panzerwaffe

Crushing of Poland – September 1939

THE
COMMANDANT

Rudolf Höss, the creator of Auschwitz

IAN BAXTER

Every effort has been made to contact the copyright holders of material reproduced in this text. In cases where these efforts have been unsuccessful, the copyright holders are asked to contact the publishers directly.

PUBLISHED IN 2008 BY MAVERICK HOUSE PUBLISHERS

Maverick House, Office 19, Dunboyne Business Park,
Dunboyne, Co. Meath, Ireland.
Maverick House Asia, Level 43, United Centre, 323 Silom Road,
Bangrak, Bangkok 10500, Thailand.

info@maverickhouse.com
http://www.maverickhouse.com

13 digit ISBN: 978-1-905379-50-7.
10 digit ISBN: 1-905379-50-1.

5 4 3 2 1

The paper used in this book comes from wood pulp of managed forests. For every tree felled at least one tree is planted, thereby renewing natural resources.

A CIP catalogue record for this book is available from the British Library.

Dedicated to my dear son Felix. I hope he and his generation ensure that history never repeats itself.

Contents

Acknowledgements

It is with the greatest pleasure that I would like to thank all those who helped make the writing of this book possible. In the USA, I would like to thank Charles Provan who supplied me with Eleonore Hodys' statement regarding her relationship with Rudolf Höss. In Washington, my thanks must go to the archivist Michlean L. Amir, and Caroline Waddell, the photo-reference co-ordinator of the United States Holocaust Museum.

In Poland, I would like to thank Wojciech Płosa and Dr Piotr Setkiewicz of the Auschwitz-Birkenau State Museum, both of whom supplied me with many invaluable photographs, documents and other important information relating to the Höss family and their residence. In Warsaw, my gratitude goes to Dr Zbigniew Nawrocki of the Institute of National Memory. In Krakow, I would like to offer sincere thanks to Michal Ostrowski, director of Auschwitz Tours. Michal not only helped organise my first visit to southern Poland, but he also provided answers to my endless stream of questions. Not only did he undertake some research of his own, contacting the old I.G. Farben chemical plant, which became known as F.Ch. Dwory in 1999, but he also translated numerous Polish documents for me. Another person I wish to thank is my Polish taxi-driver, Halina Kapka. Halina was endlessly helpful and patient. On most of my visits she drove me the one-hour journey from Krakow to Auschwitz. She would wait patiently for hours whilst I carried out my research, and then drive me back to Krakow later that day. Halina always took great interest in my project and went to great lengths to help me in any way she could. In fact, I owe my warmest thanks to her for my visit to the former Höss residence. During a trip to Poland with my friend Kevin Bowden, Halina drove us directly from Krakow airport to the perimeter of the Auschwitz camp and along the road where Höss's house is situated. To my surprise she suddenly stopped the car and brazenly walked up to the house. She knocked on the front door and somehow managed to convince the owner to give us unlimited access to his home, and for this Halina, words fail to express my gratitude.

In London, I am extremely grateful to Stephen Walton of the Document Department at the Imperial War Museum. I would also like to extend my gratitude to Marek Jaros, the photo archivist of the Wiener Library in London. I am also grateful to Laurence Rees, the creative director of history for the BBC. Mr Rees generously supplied me with a lot of documentary material that enabled me to gain a deeper understanding of Auschwitz. He not only corresponded with me but also allowed me to write letters to a number of people who featured in his acclaimed six-part documentary called 'Auschwitz'. I am also indebted to the staff of the Military Intelligence Corps Museum in Bedfordshire. In particular, my warmest thanks go to the archive historian, Major Alan Edwards, who supplied me with invaluable documents relating to Höss's arrest, and also took me on a personal tour of the Intelligence Corps Museum.

I would like to extend my gratitude to my friends Kevin Bowden and Chandran Sivaneson, both of whom visited Poland with me on two separate occasions. Not only were they extremely helpful with their support and advice but they were also infinitely patient as they followed me around Auschwitz and Birkenau.

Finally, I wish to thank Michelle for her support and tolerance on a subject that is evil and tragic in its content. It was with Michelle that I first journeyed to Auschwitz in January 2006. The temperature was 15 degrees below zero but the harsh weather conditions did not deter her from trudging through the thick snow and following my deep footprints around the Auschwitz complex. Standing on the grounds of the Birkenau camp, with the icy wind blowing in our faces, we could only imagine what it must have been like trying to survive a winter in Poland during World War Two.

Preface

Tackling the subject of the Holocaust had never really been my intention when I first started out in my long career in German military history. The subject had already received an overwhelming amount of attention. But throughout my various readings I found that many of the key figures behind the killings during this period remained shrouded in mystery. After much thought and deliberation I decided to immerse myself in a period of history that has left an indelible mark on the twentieth century and spawned endless research—yet is still so difficult to comprehend. Wading through a sea of books and other documentary material relating to the Holocaust, I found myself perpetually drawn to one particular concentration camp—that of Auschwitz. I was astonished at just how efficiently the Germans ran this enormous camp. Hundreds of thousands of Jews were transported here from all corners of Europe and executed in the specially constructed gas chambers. Such a barbaric system of mass murder made me wonder at man's capacity for evil. During my research I found that the perpetrators as a whole were not power-hungry sadists or the victims of brainwashing by propaganda—in my view, the majority of these people had made a conscious decision to perpetrate such evil. The individuals responsible for running the concentration camps varied in the severity with which they approached their jobs. There were the overtly brutal and ruthless commandants, like Amon Göth and Josef Kramer, who actually promoted the use of violence and terror. Then there were men like Rudolf Höss, the commandant of Auschwitz, who according to Whitney Harris, the American prosecutor who interrogated him during the Nuremberg trials, 'appeared normal... like a grocery clerk'.[1] Former prisoners confirmed this opinion, adding that he always appeared calm and collected. Yet he was ultimately responsible for the deaths of over 1.2 million people. It was this contradictory dual personality that I became increasingly drawn to. I began reading more about Höss, paying particular attention to his famous memoirs, which were written in a Polish prison and later published under the title *Commandant of Auschwitz*. I was intrigued by Höss and found that he was no mere robot blindly following orders; on the contrary, he was eager to adapt and improvise in order to excel at any task given to him.

Even after reading his memoirs, I was at first still somewhat reluctant to undertake a project relating to the Holocaust, let alone a figure as complex as Höss. Although I knew he was one of the largest mass murderers in history, I gradually began to uncover a more humane side of his personality and found that outside of the camp he was a quintessential family man. The more I read and learnt about this man, the more I felt compelled to offer up a new perspective on him.

Photographs show that Höss was average in appearance. He was of medium height, with searching eyes, a high forehead and a narrow mouth with thin lips. He was always well groomed, well mannered and carried himself in a dignified fashion. But it was his exceptional efficiency and organisational skills that made him far from average. He was a selfless and sentimental man in his private life, and harboured an ardent love for nature and music. But Höss was deeply dissatisfied with life at the Auschwitz camp. He had come to southern Poland to help build and take command of a small concentration camp for political prisoners and other so-called undesirables of the Reich. Never, not even in his wildest dreams, had he ever imagined that he would one day help build the largest mass-murder camp in the world. During his time at Dachau camp, he had found it difficult to watch beatings and other acts of brutality being inflicted on the prisoners. He had been selected to run the camp on account of the key psychological features he possessed: his loyalty to authority and his constant efforts towards self-mastery. Höss's initial abhorrence of the ill-treatment of prisoners subsided in time and he eventually became responsible for implementing such punishments. He came to see the beatings and murders as mere administrative procedures that were necessary if the camp was to operate efficiently.

I became fascinated with Höss's personal life and his ability to juggle the demands of his job as commandant with those of his role as a father and husband. I decided to take a closer look at life in the Höss villa—a rather imposing two-storey building situated on the corner of the main Auschwitz camp. Hedwig Höss called it her 'paradise'; however, behind closed doors life was generally far from paradisiacal. By late 1942, Höss was overworked and anxious, and frequently got drunk in the company of his wife, friends and associates.

In order to create a three-dimensional picture of life in the Höss household, I had to burrow deep to find the testimonies of those who had been employed in the villa. I relied heavily on published texts but I also managed to unearth several original manuscripts and other unpublished sources that provided me with valuable clues in my quest for the truth. I even managed to obtain a number of authentic, little-known diaries belonging to those who knew Höss personally, including, to my amazement, the 'Höss Family Visitors' Book', which listed the various guests who had been entertained at the villa or who had spent weekends there. Occasionally my research was hindered by misinterpretations and contradictions. In such cases, I was forced to weigh up the evidence myself and pass my own judgement on events. As a result, my research took me to Auschwitz several times. Here, I not only explored Auschwitz and its buildings but I also visited the museum archive, where I examined hundreds of documents and photographic material. I also gained access to the former Höss residence, which had been sold in the sixties.

I explored the whole of the two-storey house, much of which is still in its original condition. I inspected the attic, which was converted into servant quarters in 1942; this living space had small windows overlooking the commandant's office building and camp-administration offices. Descending the wooden stairs to the next floor, I found the bedrooms to be my main point of interest. I wondered what it must have been like to have had one's bedroom overlooking harrowing scenes of human degradation and suffering.

Much of the information I gathered at Auschwitz had already been widely published, but I had not visited the archives merely to obtain regurgitated information; I had come to reassess the facts and to walk in Höss's footsteps. I was determined to obtain a clearer picture of this man and thereby establish a new perspective on the commandant. Even before I began the arduous task of writing this book, I found it necessary to look at events from a fresh angle. Instead of being a mere spectator, I tried to imagine events as they would have unfolded before the eyes of Höss. Any information that he would not have been privy to does not appear in the pages of this book. By approaching the project in this way, I hope that his actions, opinions and motivations will provide a fresh basis for debate.

It is very easy to dismiss Höss as nothing more than a despicable monster. However, to picture him living a relatively normal family life at his villa is quite disturbing because it serves to humanise him. Identifying in any way with this man makes us worry that maybe we're not so different to Höss after all—perhaps given the right circumstances any one of us has the potential to do great evil.

My greatest challenge lay in unravelling Höss's complex character and understanding the circumstances that gave rise to his murderous career. He was undoubtedly an intriguing man, and at the end of his life he was quite willing to relate to his jailers the events that had transpired during his time as commandant of Auschwitz.

Höss's original memoirs, which are held at the Auschwitz museum, were written at the request of Jan Sehn, the prosecuting attorney for the Polish War Crimes Commission in Warsaw. His narration described camp regulations, the various personalities he encountered, and gave a detailed description of the implementation of the 'Final Solution'. The memoirs were principally written to assist Höss to remember the various events for his trial. However, while reading and researching the published memoirs and the original handwritten text, I began to question Höss's chronology of events. Throughout his narration he frequently misdated events, not because he was trying to deceive the reader but simply because he was unable to recall their correct sequence. He frequently attributes events that occurred in 1942 to the year 1941. One of the most controversial assertions he made was that SS-*Reichsführer* Heinrich Himmler made the decision to turn Auschwitz into a camp for the mass extermination of Jews in June 1941. On the witness stand he repeated his account of visiting Himmler in Berlin to discuss the plan. However, by June 1941 the plan to systematically exterminate the Jews was still several months away from conception. Höss's visit was therefore not to plan the genocide, but rather to discuss Auschwitz's development and to improve on its killing facilities. The meeting Höss refers to in his memoirs did not actually take place until a year later. With the help of documentary evidence, I tried as best I could to correct and re-date any other apparent memory lapses.

Despite the misinterpretations and erroneous information that crept into Höss's writings, his memoirs are, nonetheless, a unique document and have been invaluable to me in my attempts to unravel the mysteries of this man. I have used numerous extracts from the original memoirs to support my research. From the inception of this project, I tried to illuminate Höss as a human being, as opposed to a mere monster, who entered the realms of the SS order and fell blindly into a ruthless and barbaric career. He was without doubt a model SS soldier and a highly competent administrator, sacrificing everything, even his family life, to carry out the orders issued to him from Berlin. He devised killing methods that turned Auschwitz into the largest extermination centre of all time. But he paid a price for the success of the camp, and not by way of guilt for the terrible crimes against humanity that he had committed, but rather he became overburdened by the workload involved in overseeing such a mammoth operation. He received conflicting orders from his superiors, with the police headquarters, or the RSHA, repeatedly demanding that he increase the number of killings, while the SS Economic Office, or the WVHA, insisted that the prisoners be spared for slave labour.

From the beginning, the grand scale of the Auschwitz camp and the disposal of corpses proved problematic. Despite Höss's frequent bureaucratic protests during his time at Auschwitz, the camp was permanently overcrowded and there was a chronic shortage of building materials available for the expansion of the site. The building of the crematoria was delayed time and time again, leaving Höss to improvise in his disposal of the bodies.

During my research I found that Höss favoured the use of gas, not just because it was the most effective and efficient means of extermination, but because he believed it caused less psychological damage to the guards than killing prisoners by firing squad. Yet in spite of such concerns for his men, he generally looked upon many of them, and indeed many of his closest associates, as low-natured types who performed their duties in a careless or inefficient manner. He despised insubordination. On several occasions he received reports of SS men stumbling drunkenly around the camp and the crematoria while attractive female prisoners waited on them. He was determined to stamp out such behaviour.

Höss was far from being an exemplary leader himself though—he was guilty of numerous corruption charges. He regularly helped himself to the prisoners' confiscated belongings, pocketing such goods as food, clothing, diamonds, tapestries, silk, underwear and the finest champagne and cognac. He kept some of this loot for his own personal use and he sold the rest on the Polish black market, which was one of the largest in Europe.

The story of Höss, from his early beginnings to his time as commandant of Auschwitz, is a compelling narration. At times the tone of this book may sound somewhat detached, but from the outset I have been unwavering in my determination to assume Höss's perspective at all times. I hope that this book will become a valuable addition to Holocaust studies so that future generations can learn from the barbaric actions of this man and hopefully never repeat them.

Chapter I: Early Days

Rudolf Franz Ferdinand Höss was born into a strict Catholic family in Baden-Baden on 25 November 1900. His father, Franz Xavier, was a devoutly religious retired colonel of the German Army. He was a pedantically punctual man, who is said to have been strict, humourless and devoted to duty, order, and above all, discipline. In the confines of his own home his temper regularly flared up unpredictably. Höss's mother Pauline (née Speck), on the other hand, was a simple, modest and kindly woman. She tried her best to show sufficient affection towards her children to compensate for their father's reserved nature.

Höss's upbringing was very strict despite the fact that his father was often away travelling for months at a time. From an early age his social life revolved chiefly around the company of adults. As a child, he adapted well to his surroundings. He lived in an average house in the countryside, surrounded by farmland and farm buildings. Nearby was the Black Forest, with its tall pine trees, valleys, deep ravines and mountain slopes. He would often escape adult supervision to explore the forest. This lifestyle suited the young Höss. Although he had two younger sisters, he was a loner by nature and was far more interested in the animals that lived on the farm, especially the horses, than other children his own age.

When he was six years old his family relocated to an area close to the city of Mannheim. The move deeply saddened Höss and he desperately missed life in the countryside. However, on his seventh birthday his parents gave him a coal-black pony that he named Hans. According to Höss, he found renewed contentment with his new pet.

By now, Höss had started elementary school and was achieving good grades in most of his subjects. His moral conduct was regarded as satisfactory, his diligence above average, and he received very good results in religious instruction. His father hoped that he would go on to be ordained a priest and so the young Höss received most of his religious education at home. These years were an important formative phase in his character development. His father would sit with him for hours every evening, helping him with his homework and telling him stories about his travels abroad, to Africa in particular, with the missionary society to which he belonged. Höss was captivated by his father's stories and hoped to follow in his footsteps and become a missionary. On occasion, his father took him on pilgrimages across Germany, Switzerland and France. These trips further convinced Höss of his choice of vocation.

In spite of the strict Catholic doctrine that Höss's father enforced, the family lived a relatively happy life. His mother and sisters were openly affectionate, but much to his mother's disappointment, Höss himself was a very insular boy who found it difficult to express his emotions. He refused to share his problems, finding it difficult to confide in anyone. These problems spilled over into his school life and his peers considered him an awkward pupil. If Höss was wronged or antagonised in any way he could react quite violently and his classmates soon came to fear him. He wielded this sense of fear like a weapon and it undoubtedly contributed greatly to the development of his character.

When Höss was 14 years of age his father suddenly collapsed and died. His father's death had a significant impact on the young Höss, most notably by removing much of the parental pressure he had previously endured. In his father's absence, he assumed the role of man of the house, and this new level of responsibility signalled the end of his childhood.

In the same year that Höss's father died, Germany went to war. Höss watched as the newly enlisted young men from Mannheim left for the front, and months later he saw the first trainloads returning with the wounded. He was moved by these scenes and felt a great desire to make himself useful. He badgered his mother to let him volunteer at the Red Cross and she eventually relented.

The war, despite its brutality, transfixed Höss. He began to dream about becoming a soldier. The military life was already deeply ingrained in him as his family's history in the field dated back to 1870. Höss's grandfather had been killed heroically leading his regiment into action, and now Höss wanted to follow in his footsteps and join the army. His mother did her utmost to dissuade him and she urged him to fulfil his father's wishes and enter the priesthood. After much debate, Höss's stubbornness won out.

By 1916, with the help of a captain in the cavalry whom he had met while working for the Red Cross, Höss enlisted in the Reserve Unit of the 21st Reserve Squadron of the 2nd Baden Dragoon Regiment. Here, he saw action with the 6th Turkish Army on the Iranian front in Baghdad, Kutal-Amara, and Palestine. During his service his comrades considered him a committed, dutiful young soldier, who showed remarkable courage on the battlefield. In 1917 he became the youngest sergeant in the German Army. Following his promotion, he was sent on daring reconnaissance missions, during which he learned about the art of leadership and the importance of knowledge when commanding in difficult circumstances. He was injured during two such reconnaissance missions; once on 6 March 1917 and again in February 1918, when he was shot through the knee. He received the Iron Cross Second Class and the Iron Half Moon First Class in recognition of his bravery. On the second occasion that he was injured he spent time recuperating in a field hospital in Wilhelma, between Jerusalem and Jaffa.

As a soldier, he had a good relationship with his peers and he thoroughly enjoyed the camaraderie of the military. The majority of his comrades respected him and it seems that, for the most part, it could even be said that his character was quite liked. However, he seldom joined in any banter and his humourlessness made him an easy target for jokes. He often suppressed episodes of good-natured fun, especially when they were at his expense. Instead, he preferred to participate in serious conversations, but he never spoke about his friends or family. When he was not deep in conversation, he could often be found reading for hours on end in a corner of the dugout.

In 1918, Höss was discharged from the army and he returned to his defeated homeland. He was haunted by the scenes of human suffering he had witnessed during his service and his distress was compounded by the humiliation he felt over Germany's defeat. His faith had also been severely damaged by the traumatic experience of war and he became increasingly pessimistic about entering the priesthood.

His return to civilian life was further complicated by the death of his mother. She had died while he was in combat. The family homestead had been sold, and its belongings greedily pocketed by members of the family. Seething with anger, Höss informed one of his uncles that he no longer wished to become a priest. He donated his inheritance to his sisters and disassociated himself from the family.

* * * * *

A return to the lonely existence of his pre-war years held little appeal for Höss, especially now that he had neither a home nor money to his name. His future seemed bleak. Re-enlisting in the army appeared to be his only option so in January 1919 he travelled to East Prussia to sign up with an army *Freikorps* volunteer unit. He arrived in East Prussia, brimming with a sense of duty and pride, and enlisted in the East Prussian Volunteer Unit. However, on 13 September 1919 he left this unit to join the Rossbach *Freikorps*, named after its commander, *Leutnant* Gerhard Rossbach. The unit was composed of war veterans, students and adventurers, and was an active force in repressing communist revolts in Germany, and in the Baltic provinces of Prussia and of the former Russian Empire.

Joining a volunteer unit such as the *Freikorps* held great appeal for Höss. After the war, the climate in Germany had become one of political and ideological radicalisation. Many of the veterans were spurred on by their patriotism. The *Freikorps* were comrades of the front lines, and Höss shared with them the shame of surrender and a deep-rooted distrust of a homeland they believed was being taken over by Bolshevism. The Great War had generated a sense of solidarity amongst most of the volunteers of the *Freikorps*, but when they returned home in defeat they were devastated by the atmosphere of disintegration and collapsing morale that they encountered. Many of the soldiers found civilian life difficult and oppressive. This sense of defeat gave rise to new forms of aggressive nationalism, and resulted in various political movements and shifting alliances in many German towns and cities.

The German government regarded the *Freikorps* as a private army, and they often sought their assistance in the event of military, political or civil disturbances breaking out. But in reality, the *Freikorps* was a German paramilitary force that targeted opponents of German nationalism and militarism, particularly revolutionaries in Latvia and Germany, and including insurgents in Poland and Silesia.

The Rossbach *Freikorps* unit was assigned the mission of helping the Baltic Germans to re-establish their dominance in Latvia. According to Höss, the fighting he witnessed along the Latvian border was more brutal than any of the battles he had experienced during the war. For his services, he was awarded the Baltic Cross on 4 January 1920, and he continued to wear this medal for the rest of his life.

Over the next few years Höss continued fighting with the Rossbach *Freikorps*, and saw action in other theatres, including Upper Silesia, Mecklenburg and in the area of the Ruhr river. However, in mid-1921 the German government rendered the *Freikorps* an illegal organisation and Höss was reluctantly forced to change careers. He decided to move to Silesia and Schleswig-Holstein to study agriculture, and he became a member of a work team in Mecklenburg.

During this period, Germany plunged deeper and deeper into a maelstrom of civil unrest, and a string of extreme right-wing political parties were born. One of these parties was the National Socialist German Workers' Party, or the Nazi Party. Scores of volunteers from the now-banned *Freikorps* were Nazi sympathisers. Most of the veterans were idealistic activists who shared the Nazi vision of defending Germany from the destructive advances of Bolshevism. Unsurprisingly, these veterans, including Höss, responded with enthusiasm to the various announcements made by the Nazi Party, which condemned the Spartacists and called on every able-bodied veteran to join the party and support the mutiny.

On 22 October 1922, Höss joined what he considered to be the new brotherhood of the frontline fighters—the Nazi

Party. He was proud to show his fellow comrades his party membership card, number 3240. For Höss, joining the Nazi Party represented a kind of rebellion, but he was certainly not an anti-Semite by this time. Although the Nazi Party was undoubtedly anti-Jewish and saturated its movement with negative stereotypes of Jews, Höss initially considered this preoccupation with race to be of secondary importance. He was more interested in healing Germany of the national shame their defeat in the war had brought upon them, reversing the humiliation of Versailles, combating the threat of Communism and curbing the socialists. He saw himself as a martyr for a cause, of which Jews formed only a minor part.

* * * * *

Höss found life in the Nazi Party very fulfilling. He belonged to a large group of people who were united by their fear of Marxism and their devotion to restoring Germany to its rightful position of power in Europe. By day, Höss was just a regular farmer, but in the evenings he revelled in the company of his fellow party members and together they idolised their party leader, Adolf Hitler.

Surrounded by his old *Freikorps* peers and new Nazi Party comrades, Höss was spurred on by stories of crushing Bolshevism and resisting French occupation in the Ruhr, which they believed was winning applause from most patriotic nationalists throughout Germany. During these meetings Höss became increasingly drawn to one particular man called Martin Bormann. Like Höss, Bormann was ardently nationalistic, anti-Marxist, anti-parliamentarian and dedicated to a new order. Bormann had initially been a member of the *Freikorps* and had secured work as a goods inspector on the von Treuenfeld estate near Parchin. Bormann worked on the estate during the day, but at night he carried out sabotage operations against the French occupation troops. Although Höss recognised Bormann's less-illustrious qualities, namely his greed and unscrupulousness, he admired his dedication to preventing the Communist government from inflicting further destruction on German society. The party believed that Communist spies were lurking everywhere and they wished to expose them. The *Freikorps* and their successor organisations took it upon themselves to administer justice. Treachery was punishable by death and already many suspected traitors had been executed.

During the first half of 1923, Höss, Bormann and other accomplices were responsible for a number of political crimes. They called themselves the Union for Agricultural Professional Training, and were a prohibited successor-organisation to the banned Rossbach Labour Community, known by its comrades as the *Freikorps* 'Rossbach'. One incident happened in May 1923, when Höss and his comrades in the old *Freikorps* 'Rossbach' received a tip-off that an elementary schoolteacher, called Walter Kadow, had betrayed a proto-Nazi fighter by the name of Albert Leo Schlageter. The *Freikorps* and the Nazis considered Schlageter a key figure in the struggle against communism. During his time in the *Freikorps*, Schlageter took part in the Kapp Putsch as well as various other battles between military and communist factions throughout Germany. In 1922, Schlageter's *Freikorps* unit had merged with the Nazis in Upper Silesia, and during the occupation of the Ruhr in 1923 he led an illegal 'combat patrol' that had tried to resist the French occupying forces by means of sabotage. On 7 April 1923, the French arrested Schlageter. He was tried by court martial on 7 May and was condemned to death. On the morning of 26 May he was executed on the Golzheimer heath near Düsseldorf. He later became a heroic idol for the Nazis.

Höss was incensed by the execution of Schlageter, and he and Bormann decided that the traitor, Walter Kadow, deserved to be punished. Rumours and fake reports from the former *Freikorps* 'Rossbach' unit had led Höss to believe that Kadow was connected to the Schlageter affair. According to Bormann, Kadow, who had been his old schoolteacher, was a communist spy and this alone was reason enough to execute him.

On the night of 31 May 1923, having spent a number of hours drinking, Höss, Bormann and a comrade called Jurisch, together with other accomplices of the murder squad, planned Kadow's execution. During the early hours of 1 June, Kadow was abducted and taken into nearby woods, where the group beat him with branches and clubs. When they finally finished beating him, his throat was cut and a member of the group, who was allegedly drunk, finished him off with two bullets to the head.

For four long weeks Höss and his accomplices hoped that they might avoid implication in the brutal murder, but on 28 June they were finally arrested. Höss was formally arraigned at the local police station before being moved to a prison in Leipzig to await trial. Brooding in his small and uncomfortable cell he was convinced that he would not go to prison for his actions. He was confident that it was only a matter of time before the Nazi Party overthrew the Bavarian government in Munich and once they had seized control they would immediately release him from prison. Höss's legal representatives tried to convince him of the seriousness of his situation. The unstable and chaotic political circumstances that prevailed in Germany at the time were particularly disapproving of all nationalist movements, and Höss was told, in no uncertain terms, that he would face imprisonment, if not the death sentence, for his crime. When the reality of his situation finally sank in, Höss was utterly dejected. In November 1923, his morale plummeted even further when his hopes of being saved by his National Socialist comrades were shattered. The attempted putsch in Munich had been unsuccessful and its leader, Adolf Hitler, had been imprisoned.

On 12 March 1924, Höss's trial, known as the *Parchim Vehmgericht* murder trial, commenced, and over the course of three days evidence was presented to a court in Leipzig. Although the criminal justice system and its members favoured the political right, Höss was nonetheless sentenced to ten years' imprisonment. Bormann, for his part, was given only one year.

Höss's new residence in the Brandenburg Prison in East Prussia was very different to the prison he had left behind him in Leipzig. There, he had been allowed to freely receive both letters and parcels and could easily obtain newspapers, but the discipline in Brandenburg was much more rigid and rule-breaking was severely punished. In spite of the harsh restrictions imposed on him, Höss believed that prison life afforded him an invaluable insight into the 'thinking and psychology'[2] of the criminal mind. He considered himself a political prisoner, a martyr for a cause; in his eyes he had not bloodied his hands but had merely been an accomplice in a justified execution. He set himself apart from his fellow inmates who he believed deserved to be incarcerated for their crimes. While sitting alone in his cell, exercising in the courtyard, or just walking through the dormitories, Höss eavesdropped on the various mutterings of other convicts and watched with disgust as the homosexuals roamed the prison in search of potential partners. Höss regarded the majority of the inmates as social outcasts, and he therefore shunned their company, preferring to spend his time reading or reflecting on his life so far. Initially his incarceration had caused him a great amount of distress but he soon began to look more favourably on his new home. He found the regimental life similar to that of the army. He wrote:

I had been taught from a very young age to be obedient and thoroughly tidy and clean... I did not find it hard to accept the strict discipline of prison. I always carried out my duties. I completed the work given to me, and more or less to the satisfaction of the foreman. My cell was a model of neatness and cleanliness.[3]

In prison Höss prided himself on his unfaltering obedience. He considered himself a servant to the state; prison life was a form of therapy and the conditions he was made to endure would ultimately make him a better man. Over time he became accustomed to what he described as the crude language and low mentality of the prisoners and wardens alike.

Within two years he had grown accustomed to the primitive existence of prison life and he believed that he had gained a better understanding of those in authority. He often observed the guards in their dealings with other prisoners and noted with interest that the psychological abuse they used was often far more effective in breaking an inmate than any number of beatings with a truncheon. The litany of orders and regulations also 'crushed these serious-minded prisoners'.[4]

Höss developed a feeling of superiority over the jailers who had failed to break him mentally. He was modest and courteous at all times, particularly in the presence of the officials, and he was also unfailingly co-operative. He never resorted to violence or illegality. He continued to spend the majority of his time in the solitude of his cell, absorbed in books, magazines and letters that had been sent to him by friends.

Reading was an integral part of Höss's development as it was through literature that he first became interested in heredity and racial research, and in particular, Hitler's book *Mein Kampf*. He also read the works of Josef Goebbels, and Alfred Rosenberg's *The Myth of the Twentieth Century*. He acquired a deeper insight into Nazism and its accompanying rules of race, social efficiency and ideological conformity. He revelled in the Nazi theory of the laws of nature, the social Darwinist doctrine of survival of the fittest, and the belief that the weak go to the wall. He read about the struggles taking place between various different nations and races, and learnt about the struggle between the Aryans and the Jews. Although Höss may have agreed with some of the theories and ideas at the root of this struggle, the depth and virulence of his anti-Semitism had not yet become openly apparent to those who knew him. In fact, at this time he claimed to loathe the archaic, sadistic, almost pornographic anti-Semitism that had spread across Germany in various forms of propaganda. This frenzied propaganda, which was propagated by magazines like *Der Stürmer*, did not contribute to his hatred of Jews as it did for other more extreme National Socialists. By Nazi standards Höss wasn't yet a racist. He had joined the party for its revolutionary nature rather than any ideological reasons. Nonetheless, he gradually began to develop an interest in the future developments of the party and its violent opposition to the Jews. His fascination with the military and his pronounced German nationalism made him receptive to the Nazi racial ideology. Like so many other Catholics during this period, he had always been suspicious of Jews, but he was still capable of distinguishing between those he liked and those he disliked. However, during his time in prison he read a great deal of literature in which Jews were accused of conspiring against Germany, and he gradually became more and more fixated on the view of Jews as the enemy. Little by little he began to believe in the theory that the Great War had been lost due to an international Jewish conspiracy.

Having spent more than five years in prison, Höss believed that he had developed into a more mature and thoughtful individual who no longer posed a threat to authority. He was, in his view, a model prisoner. Nevertheless, in spite of good behaviour and strong recommendations for his early release, he was denied parole and remained in prison. He tried to safeguard himself from what he referred to as prison psychosis by reminding himself that he would one day be free and could resume civilian life as a farmer on his own land.

Höss was finally granted parole on 14 July 1928, having spent almost six years locked up in the Brandenburg Penitentiary. His governor told him that he was being released purely because a majority coalition between the extreme left and the extreme right had occurred in the Reichstag, which had resulted in the passing of a political amnesty act on 14 July 1928, freeing many political prisoners.

'The gift was given back to me', he later wrote. 'I was a free man at last.'[5]

Höss gathered his possessions and bid farewell to a handful of chess-playing petty criminals whom he considered relatively virtuous and friendly. Unabashed by his experiences, he left East Prussia, bound for Berlin, the capital of Germany. He vowed to never again become involved in activities that could result in the forfeiture of his freedom.

* * * * *

While still in prison, Höss had received a telegram from an old comrade inviting him to come and stay with him and his family; upon his release he travelled to Berlin to meet him. He spent ten days in the bustling capital, during which he gave much thought to his future. He decided to leave Berlin and pursue a career as an agricultural civil servant. However, within weeks of taking up this new position he resigned to join a farming community, called the Artamans, in Mecklenburg. He was eager to sever all associations with his old party comrades and to return to the healthy, secluded, rural lifestyle.

It was during the first few days of Höss's time with the young patriotic Artamans community that he met a young girl called Hedwig Hensel from Neukirch. The two began seeing one another and were later married in Neuhausen on 7 August 1929. Hedwig was an attractive girl with even features who dressed modestly. Although her relationship with Höss was sometimes strained due to his reserved nature, their marriage appeared outwardly very happy. Generally, Höss was not a difficult man to please. He was quiet and could be thoughtful in his dealings with others. However, he had high values and principles, and could be strict, distant, and occasionally irritable, especially when he felt others did not share his high standards. Although it saddened Hedwig when she was unable to share her deepest thoughts and emotions with Höss, their life together started out on a very happy note.

After more than two years of marriage Hedwig became pregnant. On 9 April 1932, she gave birth to a baby boy, whom they named Klaus. A year later, on 8 August 1933, Hedwig gave birth to a baby girl called Edeltraut. On 6 February 1935 another baby girl, Brigitte, was born. She was followed by a boy, Burling, on 1 May 1937. The deep affection Hedwig lacked with her husband she lavished on little Klaus, 'Kindi', 'Puppi' (Höss's pet names for Edeltraut and Brigitte) and Burling. Although Höss sometimes appeared detached and distant from the normal rigours of family life, he cared deeply about his family and they became the main bearing to his existence.

Whilst Höss was labouring hard on the land outside Mecklenburg, Germany was undergoing a series of dramatic changes. Adolf Hitler seized power in January 1933 and the Nazi Party went from strength to strength. Initially, Höss had little interest in the spread of Nazism or in rekindling his old revolutionary days as he was happy with his life on the land. However, this all changed when he met an old party comrade and fellow farmer, Heinrich Himmler. He had become acquainted with the bespectacled former chicken farmer between the years 1921 and 1922 when they were both working as couriers in the *Freikorps*; they met whilst visiting the protector and secret leader of the nationalist movement, General Ludendorff, at his house in Bavaria. Höss found Himmler dull, pedantic and humourless, but he had great respect for his thoroughness and efficiency. By 1929 he had risen through the ranks of the Nazi Party to become leader of Hitler's organisation of personal bodyguards—the SS. All prospective members were to be racially pure, physically fit, and above all, loyal and willing to obey and sacrifice their own lives for Hitler. By the early 1930s the SS had undoubtedly become a select body within the Nazi hierarchy, and Höss became increasingly interested in this band of soldiers. Himmler looked upon his old colleague as an ideal candidate for recruitment into the rapidly growing, racially ideological SS organisation. Although initially hesitant, Höss was won over by the status he stood to gain by entering the SS. Höss enjoyed his life as a farmer, but the opportunity to become part of an elite, well-disciplined organisation was ultimately far too alluring. He was also excited at the opportunity of becoming part of an organisation that promised to be instrumental in helping Germany recover from the series of set-backs it had recently suffered.

Finally, on 20 September, Höss decided to apply to the *Allgemeine* SS, which was part of the Nazi storm division, or the SA. He soon raised a group of mounted SS on the Sallentin estate in Pomerania. During an official visit to Stettin, Himmler inspected Höss's mounted SS and was greatly impressed. But Himmler had not travelled a long distance merely to admire the achievements of an old party comrade; he had come to recruit future SS soldiers. For some time now Himmler had been recruiting members of the old German elite. Through a tactful combination of pressure and adulation he eventually managed to lure Höss away from life on the farm and he signed him up as a full-time member of what was to become known as the black order of the new 'SS *Staat*'.

Initially, Höss enlisted in the 2nd battalion of the 5th SS Regiment, but in June 1934 he was transferred to the 10th battalion of the 9th *Allgemeine* SS Regiment. Within six months he had formally joined the SS guard battalion, which was assigned to one of the several concentration camps that had sprung up across Germany, called Dachau. He joined in the rank of an SS-*Unterscharführer* on 1 December. His unit had been formed earlier that year by SS-*Brigadeführer* Theodor Eicke, under the name Guard Unit Upper Bavaria. Eicke became commander of Dachau concentration camp in June 1933, and he went on to become a major figure in the SS. He was regarded as the architect, builder, and director of the concentration-camp system and he ruled it with an iron fist. He was stocky in appearance, and exuded an aura of raw, brutal energy.

Dachau was located on the grounds of an abandoned munitions factory near the medieval town of Dachau, ten miles northwest of Munich. It was the first concentration camp established by the National Socialist government, and Himmler described it as the first camp for political opponents considered a threat by the German government. Dachau was established on 20 March 1933 and it served as a prototype for the other concentration camps that followed. Its basic organisation, layout and construction were developed and ordered by Theodor Eicke.

Wearing his new black SS uniform, Höss arrived at Dachau in December 1934. When he drove through the large twin iron gates, which bore the inscription '*Arbeit Macht Frei*' ('Work Makes You Free'), he had no idea what lay ahead of him. Dachau was not like any prison Höss had ever encountered—the inmates had no idea how long their sentence would last and if indeed they would ever be free again. Höss was immediately struck by the strict and brutal regime the guards followed. Eicke's training had infused them with such resentment towards the prisoners that it made it easier for them to mete out severe punishments.

Höss's training at Dachau was intense and relentless. He learnt about which groups and individuals were considered enemies of the state, and he also underwent an in-depth indoctrination in SS philosophy and racial superiority. These ideological teachings were aimed at producing men who ardently believed in the new Aryan order. Copies of the racist newspaper, *Der Stürmer*, were often left in the SS barracks and in the camp canteen. Propaganda newspapers were deliberately pinned up in order to incite feelings of hatred towards the prisoners. Höss had already read these newspapers in prison and didn't feel compelled to read them again. However, he did notice that many of his fellow guards were highly susceptible to this anti-Semitic propaganda—the younger men in particular. Höss observed that once these guards had learnt the trade of brutality, and all compunction towards mankind had been obliterated, they fell under the absolute power of their commandant. In time, all of the guards in Dachau were indoctrinated into an almost fanatical determination to serve the SS with blind allegiance. Eicke invested each guard with life-and-death power over the inmates in the camp.

As an SS guard, Höss had the power to punish an inmate as severely as he saw fit. Initially, he found this responsibility quite difficult and he was repulsed by the sight of other guards using physical violence against the prisoners. The camp commandant inflicted various other measures of cruelty upon these hapless individuals. Prisoners were deprived of warm food for up to four days at a time and subjected to long periods of solitary confinement on a diet of bread and water. To supplement these harsh methods, Eicke introduced a daily routine of corporal punishment into prison life. Inmates received 25 strokes with the lash on the specific orders of the commandant and in the presence of assembled SS guards. In order to ensure that every SS officer, non-commissioned officer and SS guard was equally hardened towards the plight of the inmates, Eicke ordered the guards to routinely punish prisoners with the lash without showing the slightest sign of hesitation, sympathy, and above all, remorse.

Eicke indoctrinated his guards to hate Jews, immigrants, homosexuals and Jehovah's Witnesses. Höss was frequently present during the commandant's lectures on the groups that posed a threat to National Socialism. He instructed his guards to be especially brutal towards the Jews and to use whatever level of violence was necessary to keep them in check. Höss usually only saw the Jews at roll-calls as for the rest of the day they were generally shut away in sealed barracks.

Although Höss disliked the brutality of the camp, he was inspired by its strict discipline. He saw Dachau as a learning curve and believed that the training he was receiving would provide him with a crucial stepping stone to future success in the realms of the SS.

The acts of brutality continued to escalate during Höss's time as a guard in Dachau, but his desperation to climb the ranks soon began to outweigh his moral scruples. He became increasingly convinced that concentration camps were the most effective weapon National Socialism had to defend itself from its many enemies.

Höss became increasingly motivated by Eicke's success. He watched on as Eicke developed Dachau into a model detention centre, complete with various administration departments; there was a medical department, an administration pay office for the purchase of all supplies, another office to retain all the personal property surrendered by the inmates upon entering the camp, and a department for the production, repair and maintenance of the prisoners' uniforms.

Höss observed Eicke increase the camp's economic enterprises by using the inmates for free labour. Eicke expanded the camp and included a locksmith's shop, a saddlery, and a shoemaking and table shop. Höss recalled his period of incarceration in Leipzig prison where he had been put to work gluing paper bags together. He firmly believed that inmates gained a sense of discipline by working during their imprisonment, and this discipline would enable them to withstand the harsh environment of prison life. Eicke was also a great supporter of this theory. He believed that endless labour brought about a kind of spiritual freedom, and it was this belief that prompted him to inscribe '*Arbeit Macht Frei*' across the top of the main entrance gate to Dachau. The slogan itself was not new to the National Socialists, or indeed to Höss, but the idea of emblazoning it across the main gate greatly appealed to Eicke.

Höss's time in Dachau offered him status and a regular wage, and also a sense of belonging that he had yearned for since his revolutionary days in the *Freikorps*. Almost as soon as he arrived at Dachau his senior officers recognised his leadership potential. Eicke had already weeded out the SS men he regarded as unfit for concentration camp duty, whilst retaining SS officers, NCOs (non-commissioned officers), and enlisted men he considered reliable and disciplined. The commandant's SS cadre served him with blind allegiance. Promotions within the order were commonplace, especially for model SS men like Höss, and within a few months of arriving at Dachau he was made *blockführer*. He was promoted yet again in April 1936 to the role of *rapportführer*, which was the chief assistant to the commandant.

In a little over a year, Höss had secured his commanding officer's personal confidence and he looked destined for further responsibility and promotion. In June 1936 the new commandant of Dachau, Hans Loritz, recommended Höss for promotion, and on 13 September, he was promoted once again to the rank of SS-*Untersturmführer*—a rank he had aspired to since first arriving at the camp.

Höss's time in Dachau equipped him with a good understanding of the basic running of a concentration camp. He realised that the slightest sign of sympathy for the prisoners would not be tolerated by the SS. He was thus compelled to conceal any lingering feelings of compassion for the incarcerated and to follow Eicke's hard-line doctrine. However, unlike Eicke, Höss always appeared calm and collected and rarely denounced his enemies with anger or recrimination. Whereas for Eicke, and other high-ranking SS members, the crusade to rid Germany of enemies of the state was often personal, Höss's motivations were rooted in an ardent desire to be a member of a privileged order like the

SS. He was determined to carry out any orders issued to him with maximum efficiency.

* * * * *

On 1 August 1938, Höss was appointed adjutant of Sachsenhausen concentration camp. Sachsenhausen had been established in 1936 and was located near Berlin. Upon Höss's arrival at the camp the first thing he noticed was the infamous slogan 'Arbeit Macht Frei' emblazoned across the entrance gates to the camp. Höss soon found out that Eicke had set up his headquarters in this camp. He had become an inspector of concentration camps and had established a permanent concentration camp system that included camps such as Dachau, Sachsenhausen and Buchenwald. Eicke had based Sachsenhausen on the 'Dachau model' that he himself had created. Dachau's harsh disciplinary regulations, which included the death penalty and punishment by the whip, were administered alongside the general day to day mistreatment of prisoners. As with Dachau, solitary confinement, physical abuse and forced labour became standard practice.

The commandant of Sachsenhausen, SS-*Standartenführer* Baranowski, was possessed of the same level of fanaticism and elitism that Höss had witnessed in Dachau. Höss had come to realise that an imperviousness to human suffering was vital for all camp workers and he admired the lack of mercy Baranowski displayed towards the prisoners. Höss considered him a model commandant.

Life at Sachsenhausen was similar to Dachau, but Höss began to notice a gradual increase in the brutality of the guards and a corresponding rise in the death rate of inmates. He realised that the guards were clearly devoted to Eicke and willing to obey any order issued to them. A combination of careful indoctrination and enforced discipline established Sachsenhausen as a model camp of death and barbarity.

As an adjutant, Höss was responsible for ordering corporal punishments, and he was often obliged to attend these brutal gatherings alongside other staff members and service personnel. Outwardly, he was calm and composed, but occasionally he couldn't help but feel pity for the prisoners. He was aware, however, that Eicke would strongly disapprove of any such sympathy. After all, the specific purpose of enforced attendance at these beatings was to harden the guards. The pride Höss felt when he put on his black SS uniform and the Death's Head badge came at a high price. However, suppressing his inner emotions was not something he found difficult as he had been doing it all his life. He was loyal, tough and ambitious, and he refused to let his emotions compromise his position within the SS. He knew that he could quite easily order the punishment of a prisoner so long as he was not repeatedly forced to witness it being administered. His position in the SS meant everything to him and he was determined to prove to superiors like Eicke and Baranowski that no order or task was beyond his capabilities.

By the late 1930s, Nazi foreign policy had become increasingly aggressive. Eicke made it clear to his soldiers that the threat of war meant that the country needed greater internal security and so the SS would have to expand. This would also mean a greater influx of prisoners into the concentration camps. The SS-*Reichsführer* Heinrich Himmler had already envisaged such an expansion programme but his plans didn't involve Eicke. Although he would be allowed to retain command of the camps and the new SS-*Verfügungstruppe* (Special Service Troops), all policy matters concerning the *Totenkopfverbände* would be dealt with at the highest level by Himmler and the *Führer*, Adolf Hitler.

With new government policies in place and the prospect of a war against Poland looming, the Sachsenhausen guards adopted an increasingly barbaric attitude towards the prisoners. New slogans of hatred and discrimination were plastered around the camp with the aim of eradicating any remaining sympathy for the prisoners. The outbreak of war on 1 September 1939 had a huge impact on Höss's life.

> When the war came it was a major turning point in my life in the concentration camp. I could never quite imagine the atrocious tasks that would be assigned to the concentration camps during the course of this war.[6]

During the morning of 1 September, as German radios broadcast news of the triumphant wave of attacks across the Polish border, Höss received a phone call from the *Gestapo* informing him that a courier would shortly be delivering an order to him. He was told that a Communist had refused to perform his air-raid duties in the 'Junker aircraft factory in the city of Dessau'[7] and had consequently been arrested by the *Gestapo* and brought to Berlin for questioning. According to a new order passed by Himmler, all executions were to be carried out at the nearest concentration camp. When the accused arrived by car, handcuffed and flanked by two *Gestapo* officials, Höss informed him that he would be executed for his crime within the hour.

As the camp's adjutant, Höss was responsible for carrying out the execution. Eager to get the job over with, he quickly assembled three NCOs and led the condemned man to a pole. Höss gave the order to fire and the man was killed with a bullet to the head. The execution did nothing to desensitise Höss to the horror of cold-blooded murder; instead, he resolved that in future he would get someone else to carry out such dreadful orders for him. The outbreak of war meant that mass roundups would become increasingly frequent and overcrowding in the camps would worsen as a result, making such executions more regular occurrences. But the war did have certain positive effects on Höss's life. The defeat of Poland and the expansion of the SS meant that new career opportunities arose and his superiors seemed more than eager to see him climb the ranks.

Chapter II: *'Arbeit Macht Frei'*

Even before Germany's defeat of Poland, Hitler had made plans for the large-scale annexation of the doomed country. When victory came at the end of September 1939, the Germans acquired territory with a population of over 20 million, of whom 17 million were Poles and 675,000 were Germans. Hitler decided to incorporate large areas of Poland into the Reich and he set about clearing the Poles and Jews out of these areas and replacing them with German settlers. What followed was a period of more or less unrestrained terror in Poland, particularly in the incorporated territories. The areas which had not been integrated into the Reich had a population of some 11 million inhabitants and comprised the Polish province of Lublin and parts of the provinces of Warsaw and Krakow. From the summer of 1941, the Polish province of Lvov, also known as Eastern Galicia, which had been occupied by the USSR from 1939, was also excluded from Reich territory. Those areas of occupied Poland not annexed by Germany were placed under German administration and initially named the 'General Government of the Occupied

Polish Areas', but in 1940 this was shortened to the 'General Government'. The ultimate aim of the General Government was to ethnically cleanse the area of undesirables and those deemed enemies of the state, and to replace them with German colonists.

During the first cold months of 1940, the General Government was faced with the problem of how to accommodate thousands of homeless and penniless people in an area that was already overpopulated. Thousands of ethnic Germans were being drafted into the newly incorporated territories and they needed to be provided with suitable housing. The scale of the relocation was both enormous and highly chaotic.

By February, the relocation of Poles, Jews and ethnic Germans had become such an administrative nightmare that it was decided that the Jews should be forced to live in ghettos. This would both relieve the pressure on the resettlement programme, and also serve as a short-term solution to the growing Jewish problem. The Nazis hated and feared the Jews, with the Eastern Jews in particular believed to be carriers of diseases, so isolating them in ghettos seemed to be the most practical immediate solution.

Whilst plans were being drawn up for the creation of the ghettos, the SS announced that it would need to implement harsher policies in dealing with the threat of subversion by Polish nationalists and Jewish Bolshevists in the newly incorporated territories. By early 1940, the situation in the various detention centres and concentration camps had already become untenable due to new policies of arresting and detaining enemies of the state. News had already circulated through SS channels that government officials were demanding immediate expansion of the concentration camp system through the newly conquered territory of Poland. The German authorities quickly pressed forward, establishing camps in Poland where prisoners could be put to work as stonebreakers and construction workers on buildings and streets. It was intended that a percentage of Poles would be used as a slave-labour force, and the so-called 'quarantine camps' would be needed to suppress the local population. Initially, it was proposed that the quarantine camps would hold prisoners until they were ready to be sent to the various other concentration camps in the Reich. It soon became apparent that this proposal was totally impractical and it was decided that these camps would function as permanent prisons for all those unfortunate enough to be sent to them.

Between January and February of 1940, two commissions journeyed to southern Poland in search of suitable sites for the construction of concentration camps; the first was led by the *Schutzhaftlagerführer* of Sachsenhausen, SS-*Sturmbannführer* Walter Eisfeld, and the second was led by the new inspector of concentration camps, Richard Glücks. On 21 February, Glücks reported to the SS-*Reichsführer* in Berlin that the infantry and artillery barracks in the Zasole district of the town of Oswiecim would be suitable for construction. Himmler began negotiating with the German Army, who were in control of the former Polish military sites. Once the army had agreed to transfer the former Polish barracks, Himmler notified Sachsenhausen that another commission, led by the officer SS-*Hauptsturmführer* Rudolf Höss, was to be sent to the little town of Oswiecim. Höss was surprised and honoured to be chosen to lead this commission and he immediately began preparing for the trip.

Höss's five-man delegation undertook the long journey to Upper Silesia by car. As they drove through the countryside they spoke at length about the recent inspection reports that had been issued. During the journey they stopped off in the city of Breslau to confer with Erich von dem Bach-Zelewski's aide, Arpad Wigand. Wigand had already led his own commission to the former Polish barracks at Oswiecim in January and had pronounced the site suitable for development into a transit camp. Over lunch, Wigand advised his guests to take into account the fact that the site would serve both as a regional dumping ground for Polish political prisoners and as a holding pen for slave labour, allowing for the transfer of prisoners to camps in the west at a moment's notice. The camp, he said, had been conceived of by the *Reichsführer* as a quarantine camp for labour exchange. Höss and Wigand adjourned to the sitting room to discuss the size of the camp, and how best to accommodate some 10,000 prisoners.

* * * * *

The town of Oswiecim was situated in a remote corner of southwest Poland, about 35 miles west of the ancient city of Krakow, in a marshy valley where the Sola River flows into the Vistula. The town was virtually unheard of outside of Poland. Following the occupation of Germany, Oswiecim had been incorporated into the Reich together with Upper Silesia, and the German authorities had renamed the area Auschwitz. Prior to the war, the town's population had been approximately 12,000, almost 7,000 of whom were Jews. The surrounding countryside, which lies in the foothills of the Tatra Mountains, was often foggy and swampy; the winters were harsh, with the whole area buried in snow often as late as March or early April. In spring, the countryside came back to life and was very beautiful, especially when the warmer weather caused an array of wild flowers to spring up across the sprawling meadows. However, when Höss arrived in the town in mid-April 1940, the area did nothing to inspire him or his small committee of SS officers. The town's dreary buildings and hut-like dwellings reinforced his negative view of the land Germany intended to conquer. He wasn't surprised by the squalor in which the compliant Poles were living. Among those going about their business on the dusty, untended roads were men in high-crowned hats and kaftans. The soldiers had seen such men depicted in the anti-Semitic drawings that had been plastered on notice-boards, walls and lampposts across Germany. They were the enemy—the Jews. For some time now, hatred of the Jews had become almost akin to a religious creed, especially the hatred of Eastern Jews. For the time being, any malevolent thoughts the soldiers had on seeing the Jews would have to take second place to the more pressing problem of finding a suitable location for a quarantine camp.

Höss and his small commission arrived in the town on 18 April and stayed in a local hotel opposite the station. The former Polish barracks was only a five-minute drive from the town's main station. Upon arriving in Auschwitz, the commission immediately set out to inspect the site. They noted that the accommodation, which consisted of 8 two-storey and 14 single-storey brick barracks framing the north and south sides of a large exercise yard, could potentially be transformed into a prison camp with the addition of extra buildings. Although Auschwitz had a good railway connection, the area was still hidden from the outside world, making it the ideal location for a concentration camp. The fact that the water supply was polluted and that there were swarms of mosquitoes everywhere didn't discourage Höss and his delegation. They believed they would be able to transform the infested marshes along the Vistula and Sola rivers into a valuable outpost for the Reich. Armed with extensive reports on the area and hand-drawn sketches, the commission left the quiet town of Oswiecim the following day, bound for Berlin. When they arrived in the Reich capital, Höss and his committee attended a meeting with Glücks during which they discussed the suitability of the site. Glücks later paid Himmler a visit and reported that SS-*Hauptsturmführer* Rudolf Höss had pronounced the former Polish barracks in Oswiecim a suitable location for a camp. He quoted Höss, stating that the site would be hidden from the outside world, easily expandable and accessible by rail. The *Reichsführer* was happy with the report and instructed his Inspector of Concentration Camps to start preparing for construction.

A week later, on 27 April, Höss received word that Himmler had approved the plans for the Auschwitz site. It was agreed that it would house around 10,000 prisoners. SS-*Obersturmführer* Walter Eisfeld, on the other hand, who first visited the barracks in January, disagreed with Höss on the site's suitability. He warned the *Reichsführer* that not only would it be difficult to acquire the materials necessary to construct a fortified barracks, but the site's surrounding terrain would also pose additional problems. After much deliberation, Eisfeld decided to decline Himmler's offer of the commandant position in Auschwitz. Höss, however, was Glücks' next choice and after first submitting his name to Himmler, he asked Höss if he would accept the post. Höss could hardly believe his good fortune and delightedly welcomed the opportunity to showcase his organisational skills. On 4 May 1940, Höss was officially named commandant of the new camp. He wrote:

I had never quite expected being made a commandant so quickly, especially when there were senior protective custody camp commanders that had been waiting for some considerable time for the commandant's post to become available. My task was not a very easy one. In the shortest possible time I had to construct a transit camp for ten thousand prisoners, using the existing complex of buildings, which, though well constructed, had been completely neglected, and were swarming with vermin. From the point of view of hygiene, practically everything was lacking. I had been told in Oranienburg, before setting off, that I could not expect much help, and that I would have to rely largely on my own resources. In Poland I would find everything that had been unobtainable in Germany for years.[8]

Höss was given a budget of two million Reichsmark with which to build on to the existing 20 barracks and create a camp capable of accommodating 10,000 inmates. This generous allowance was to be spent on cleaning the existing barracks for the guards, rebuilding the two barracks outside the fence into offices and a hospital for the garrison, building a barracks for the *blockführer* at the gate, constructing eight guard towers around the perimeter of the camp, building a hayloft, installing a crematorium in the abandoned powder magazine building, and tidying the two-storey house on the edge of the existing camp in order to make it habitable for Höss and his family. While his new house was being prepared, Höss took up residence in a hotel overlooking the Auschwitz station. Here, he deliberated over plans for the construction of the camp and spent countless hours overseeing the developments.

Before construction could begin, Höss first needed to recruit a labour force. He asked the Reich Security Head Office, or the RSHA, to provide him with a labour team of political prisoners but they refused on the grounds that they did not want such prisoners working on the new site. Instead, *Rapportführer* Gerhard Palitzsch found 30 German criminals, who had been selected especially in Sachsenhausen, to fill the roles of supervisors, *Kapos* and blockmasters, and transported them to Auschwitz. The town council in Auschwitz was also required to provide the camp with a number of workers. The town's mayor gave Höss some 300 local Polish Jews, and under the close supervision of the newly recruited camp foremen, or *Kapos*, they escorted the Jews along the main road to their new place of work.

On 29 May, 39 Polish political prisoners, led by SS-*Untersturmführer* Beck, arrived at Auschwitz from Sachsenhausen. A consignment of barbed wire had been dispatched with the prisoners and the first temporary camp fence was to be made from a combination of this wire and some wood. When the prisoners had completed their work they were returned to Sachsenhausen.

Throughout May and early June construction work on the camp progressed slowly. A fence topped with second-hand barbed wire was installed around the perimeter of the camp, and construction on new buildings followed. At the entrance to Auschwitz, Höss installed a steel gate that had been forged in a hurriedly built workshop. Emblazoned across the top of the gate's frame was the inscription that Höss had liked so much at Dachau, 'Arbeit Macht Frei'. The gate, which survives to this day, was installed during the second half of July 1940. The inscription was the work of a Polish political prisoner called Jan Liwacz. Liwacz was a professional artsmith and had arrived at Auschwitz in the second transport sent from Wisnicz Prison on 20 June 1940. In Höss's mind the prisoners who passed through these gates were enemies of the state and their forced labour was a just punishment.

During the early phase of building additional guards were required. On 20 May, 15 SS men arrived from the Cavalry Unit stationed in Krakow and enlisted in the camp's guard garrison. In the month of June an additional 100 SS men were sent to reinforce the guard garrison, along with SS officers and SS NCOs of various ranks.

Construction work had only just commenced when Höss received a message from the Inspector of the Security Police and the Security Service headquarters in Breslau, impatiently enquiring when the camp would be ready to begin accepting prisoners. On 14 June, before Höss even had a chance to reply to this letter, a passenger train steamed into Auschwitz station from Tarnow Prison carrying 728 political prisoners. Höss was extremely irate at being sent prisoners when the camp was still far from completion. He redirected the train to the Polish Tobacco Monopoly, 400 yards from the main camp, and the prisoners were held there for three weeks. They were finally admitted to the main camp in July where they were subjected to a period of up to two weeks in quarantine. During this time they were forced to undergo so-called fitness exercises, which were really just a series of maltreatments, ranging from beatings to chicaneries and various other forms of torture.

From the very beginning, Höss intimated that the Auschwitz camp was to be modelled on Dachau but with a few small adjustments. He told his staff, which included Adjutant Josef Kramer, *Lagerführer* Karl Fritzsch, Deputy *Lagerführer* Franz Xaver Maier, and *Rapportführer* Gerhard Palitzsch, that some adjustments were to be made to the standard camp system.

> In order to harness all the available manpower to this task I had to ignore all concentration camp tradition and customs. If I was to get the maximum effort out of my officers and men, I had to set them a good example. When reveille sounded for the SS rankers, I must get out of bed. Before they started their day's work, I had already begun mine. It was late at night before I had finished. There were very few nights in Auschwitz when I could sleep undisturbed by telephone calls. If I wanted to get good and useful work out of the prisoners then, contrary to the usual and universal practice in concentration camps, they must be given better treatment. I assumed that I would succeed in both housing and feeding them better than other camps. Everything that, from my point of view, seemed wrong in the other camps, I wished to handle differently here.[9]

The construction of the camp was hampered by a shortage of building materials and other important provisions. Höss's budget would have undoubtedly covered all costs incurred by work in the camp, but there was simply very little for sale. The newly commissioned camp's 39-year-old architect, August Schlachter, and his deputy, Walter Urbanczyk, who had been entrusted with building the new construction office in the camp, found it almost impossible to obtain adequate supplies. Schlachter made repeated requests for help from Höss but he simply ignored the architect while he set about finding a solution.

Throughout July and early August, work continued at the camp, with the modification of the former powder magazine store commencing on 5 July. The new building was to primarily function as a crematorium but it would also serve for prisoner delousing purposes. Before the crematorium came into operation, those who died at the camp were transported to Gliwice and incinerated in the municipal crematorium. The conversion of the crematorium was undertaken with the full authorisation of the SS Construction Management. In fact, even before Höss took up his new post at Auschwitz the installation of a crematorium had already been decided upon. J.A. Topf & Sons of Erfurt, a company with a division specialising in the production and installation of crematorium furnaces, and which was headed by the chief engineer Kurt Prüfer, had been commissioned to carry out the preliminary drawings. The plans gave intricate details of the internal structure of the furnace. Schlachter gathered extensive information on the technology of the double-muffler system and the coke-heated furnace. He discussed this new equipment with Höss and the camp officials, and plans for its installation were agreed upon with SS headquarters in Berlin. Höss fully supported the construction of the crematorium at the camp. He considered the incineration of corpses to be the most hygienic alternative available to them.

Work on the crematorium got underway relatively quickly, considering the shortage of building materials at the camp. The installation consisted of an entrance on the northwest side of the building, and included a furnace room with two incinerators and a charnel house. The concrete roof was flat and the building was surrounded on three sides by earthen embankments, which had openings for the windows of the coke plant. There were two windows in the furnace room, which served to cool down the inside of the building following its use. An external chimney was constructed and was connected to the furnaces via underground flues. The entrance to the crematorium was camouflaged by a large concrete wall that contained two enormous wooden gates. In order to conceal the crematorium from view, a one-storey

SS hospital was constructed nearby, along with the camp workshops and the barracks of the Political Department.

While the former powder magazine store was being transformed into a crematorium, work continued on various other buildings both inside and outside of the camp. Building materials were still in short supply so Höss was forced to improvise. In July of that year, Tadeusz Wiejowski was the first inmate to successfully escape from the prison. He was aided by Polish civilians living in the area. In response to his escape, Höss wrote a letter to Glücks seeking permission to expel nearly all of the inhabitants of the western part of the town, where the camp was located. On 8 July 1940 and 1 April 1941, the SS expelled the residents of the western district of the town. On 8 March 1941, and from the 7th to the 12th of April 1941, further evacuations took place in several villages located at the confluence point of the Sola and Vistula rivers. The families were given a maximum of two hours to vacate their homes. Höss's soldiers then demolished the houses, keeping any useful materials for construction work in the camp. Around 150 Polish houses were adapted for the accommodation of local SS officers and their families. The building materials taken from these houses did not alleviate the overall problem, and Höss was compelled to personally drive across southern Poland, and even into the Sudetenland, in search of materials worth pilfering.

> I had to scrounge up cars and trucks and the necessary petrol. I had to drive as far as 100 kilometres to Zakopane and Rabka just to get some kettles for the prisoners' kitchen, and I had to go all the way to the Sudetenland for bed frames and straw sacks... Whenever I found depots of material that was needed urgently I simply carted it away without worrying about the formalities... I didn't even know where I could get 100 metres of barbed wire. So I just had to pilfer the badly needed barbed wire.[10]

On 17 August, two days after the first dispatch of inmates from Warsaw arrived at Auschwitz, a disgruntled Höss received a letter from the architect, Schlachter, outlining the significance of the shortage of building supplies. Without adequate materials, he said, the whole construction programme would eventually grind to a halt. A list of necessary items, such as nails, wood and fencing, was compiled and sent to Höss, who dispatched the list to the SS headquarters in Berlin. Several weeks went by without a reply, but in September Oswald Pohl, from the WVHA, paid a surprise visit to the camp.

Pohl intended that Auschwitz would play a fundamental role in the concentration camp system in Upper Silesia and he had high expectations of future economic success. He recognised that the camp's nearby sand and gravel pits could easily be incorporated into the SS-owned German Earth and Stone Works. In the meantime it was imperative that the camp be run efficiently and that the construction programme remained on track and within budget.

Höss's meeting with Pohl was cordial. As they walked around the camp, flanked by other staff members from the Economic Office, the commandant told Pohl about the shortage of building supplies and the consequent delays to construction. Pohl assured the commandant that he intended to rectify the problem and that he hoped to ultimately double the capacity of the prison by adding two-storey buildings to each of the 14 one-story barracks. Two weeks later, on 4 October, Berlin finally responded to the camp's repeated demands and the first trainloads of materials arrived at Auschwitz station.

The labour force in charge of building the camp lived and worked in appallingly bad conditions despite Höss's frequent inspections of the camp. Up until July 1941, aside from a small percentage of German criminals, nearly all of the prisoners in Auschwitz were non-Jewish Polish political prisoners. At that time, the number of Polish Jewish prisoners being sent to the camp was miniscule, as Jews and priests were automatically sent to a Penal Unit to be immediately murdered. In 1941, the majority of Polish priests were moved to KL Dachau.

By October, the inmates of Auschwitz consisted largely of members of the intelligentsia, the resistance and political prisoners. The entire population of the prison was struggling for survival and yet nothing was being done to alleviate the horrific living conditions. Under-equipped, lacking protective gear and malnourished, the plight of the inmates was further exacerbated by the constant barrage of mental and physical abuse they received from the guards. Höss was fully aware of the harsh regime his men enforced on the prisoners. Although he had no desire to watch *Kapos*, like Ernst Krankemann, whip and beat the inmates, he approved of the strict and brutal measures that he himself had implemented. He went about his daily business in the camp careful to conceal any hint of sympathy for the inmates. He knew that it was his responsibility as commandant to promote the same attitude that Eicke had cultivated at Dachau, regardless of his personal feelings on the matter. It was important that he demonstrate an unflinching authority to the whole of the camp—prisoners and guards alike.

The entire camp came under Höss's control and he was answerable only to his superiors in Berlin. He issued daily written orders to his SS officers, who then read out the orders to the prisoners during their morning roll-call. It was Höss's responsibility to issue punishments to any SS man caught breaking the rules. He also had the power to replace a member of staff at any given time.

Höss was assigned a building known as the 'commandant's office' which had been built between the years 1916 and 1919. The camp's pre-war buildings bore an outer coat of white plaster which was removed in the summer of 1941. Only two of the pre-war administration buildings were still standing, including the commandant's office. This large, imposing brick building generally handled matters concerning SS staff. All records, weapons and other important military equipment were stored here. Transport and communication matters were also controlled from the headquarters. The office was divided into a number of different sections: office supplies, communications office, judicial affairs, weapons, military supplies, and the engineer's office. Höss had his own personal office, as well as a boardroom where he and his staff gathered for meetings on Tuesday and Thursday mornings. Höss's adjutant was head of the commandant's office, and his deputy, who was always a non-commissioned officer, also served as the staff sergeant of the commandant's office.

The second most important office, after that of the commandant, was the adjutant's office. It was situated next door to the main commandant's office building, and it was here that SS-*Untersturmführer* Josef Kramer worked. Kramer was responsible for ensuring that Höss's orders were carried out. He was also accountable for various other orders, promotions, staff matters, issuance of passes and signing official letters. He often worked closely with Höss and regularly served as his deputy. He personally chaired the meetings that took place on Tuesdays and Thursdays every week and he was usually seated next to Höss.

Another department that opened in the camp in 1940, and which liaised with both the commandant's and the adjutant's offices, was the Political Department (or the *Gestapo* offices). This small building was constructed next to the newly built crematorium and primarily handled the population of the prison and dealt with any issues that arose with the SS staff. It maintained the registration records of new arrivals, as well as prison and investigation records. The Political Department was also responsible for torturing and executing prisoners; investigating corruption and fraud; tracking lost property, and arresting and prosecuting SS men accused of neglecting their duty or helping prisoners to escape. In fact, the Political Department played a crucial role in the running of the camp. The branch was so powerful that it even had the authority to bypass Höss and deal directly with SS headquarters in Berlin.

In 1940, SS-*Untersturmführer* Maximilian Grabner was head of the Political Department. He was answerable to the commandant, the RSHA and the WVHA. Grabner held a very powerful position in the camp; he was free to administer brutal policies of torture and execution without first consulting the commandant. In fact, a large percentage of the executions and acts of violence carried out at the camp were undertaken without Höss's knowledge. Höss was quite content to oversee the running of the camp and leave the subjugation of the prisoners to Grabner and his men.

Initially, Höss found Grabner a very nervous and sensitive individual.

> Whenever he made a mistake and it was pointed out to him, he always felt he was being picked on... Grabner was a hardworking person, but he was very absentminded and inconsistent. His greatest mistake was that he was too good-hearted to his comrades. Out of a false sense of camaraderie he often did not report the countless excesses and fights among the SS officers and men to protect them from punishment... In the beginning he was constantly at conflict with the camp officers. He never failed to stress the dominating role of his department as coming first, and he mixed this in with pure camp problems. But these differences were settled with his comrades during their drinking parties, which cemented the friendships all the stronger—much to the detriment of the camp Commandant![11]

Höss had a low opinion of many members of his staff, but he considered *Lagerführer* Karl Fritzsch to be a man of particularly limited intelligence.

> [I found him]... stubborn and always quarrelsome. He had to be right about all things. He wouldn't let anyone forget that he was an officer. The fact that he was my deputy made him

particularly proud. Right from the beginning I complained to the inspector of the concentration camps about Fritzsch because I knew enough about him when we were at Dachau together. His limited intelligence, his narrow-mindedness, and his stubbornness were reasons not to expect anything good from him. But Glücks ignored any complaints and said to try my luck for a while! And I later complained extensively; I was just as unsuccessful. 'Fritzsch was good enough for Auschwitz'.[12]

Rapportführer Gerhard Palitzsch was another man whom Höss did not fully trust. Although Palitzsch was considered an experienced officer, devoted to duty and adept at handling prisoners, Höss had his reservations about him from the beginning.

[I felt that] Palitzsch was lying to me and that he was two-faced. My feelings did not deceive me. Soon enough he was in league with Fritzsch and the second camp commander, Meier, and became very involved in their activities... Meier was also one of those warmly recommended by Glücks. Meier had been in Buchenwald, where he could not have remained a minute longer because of his loathsome behaviour. He was one of the creatures of Koch who participated in all kinds of truly disgusting things, a true gangster. Meier was only at Auschwitz a few months when I succeeded in uncovering enough evidence to find him guilty of serious black marketing and was able to hand him over to the SS courts. Glücks was really angry with me about this, because he thought that he would have to give an accounting of this to Himmler.[13]

Höss tried his best to conceal his doubts about the ability of several of the more prominent SS figures and he concentrated on investing his energy in the mammoth task of running the camp and completing the construction work.

* * * * *

One particular building Höss was keen to see completed was the house in which he and his family intended to reside. By the summer of 1940, the exterior of the house still needed to be painted but other than that it was ready. The residence, which was commonly known at the camp as the Höss 'villa', was a two-storey stucco building situated in the northeastern corner of the camp. The front of the building, with its large windows and small terrace, overlooked the Rajsko to Auschwitz road. There was a small untended garden at the front of the house, which was enclosed by a brick wall, and a gate opened on to the main entrance of the house. To the side of the building was a double gate and a driveway that allowed motor vehicles to access the property. On the opposite side of the house, a concrete flight of stairs led up to the tradesman's entrance. The garden was located at the side of the house and consisted of a number of trees and shrubbery that had been cultivated by the previous occupants. A barbed-wire fence had been erected around the perimeter of the house and garden in order to cordon them off from the main camp.

In November the fencing around the entire boundary of the camp was replaced by a three-metre-high concrete wall, topped with barbed wire. This new fencing was also installed at the rear and sides of the Höss villa, and together with a cluster of trees, the view of the camp was partially obscured. Höss was eager to conceal as much of the view of the camp as possible, and he made it known to his associates that he and his family wished to live in absolute privacy.

Inside, the villa consisted of two floors. The first two flights of stairs were concrete, whilst a third wooden stairs led up to a large attic. The house had ample space, but the absence of any radiators made it quite cold. When the Höss family arrived at the house in the summer of 1940, Hedwig immediately set about making the place as comfortable as possible for her husband and four children. She was excited at the prospect of buying furnishings for her new home.

It was not unusual for officers and their families to be requisitioned in houses like the villa. In fact, throughout the summer and early autumn of 1940 the more senior SS officers lived with their families in the 'Zone of Interest', which was roughly 40 square kilometres of depopulated land. The SS took up residency in the houses from which the locals had been evacuated. This area was located on the east side of the Sola River and was surrounded by a chain of watch towers.

The officers in the camp enjoyed a comfortable lifestyle, far superior to anything they could have hoped for had they been fighting on the frontline. A close-knit community developed amongst the camp's staff and their families; the guards' wives visited one another, gossiped, held afternoon tea parties, and invited their husbands along for evening drinks and dinner. As for the children, they attended private schools in Kattowitz and the surrounding areas, or alternatively the services of a governess were employed. When the children were not attending school they were looked after by domestic slaves, who cooked their meals and cleaned their nicely furnished homes. Initially, the vast majority of servants were female Polish teenagers who were employed as maids in the homes of the SS officers. It was an opportunity for these girls to avoid being deported to Germany for slave labour. All girls in occupied Poland who were over 14 years of age were forced to work under threat of death or admittance to the concentration camps. Later, from 1943 on, SS men employed the services of female German Jehovah's Witnesses in their homes. However, aside from the commandant, Polish political prisoners were not typically employed by SS officers. German families soon began to consider the Poles too inferior to make good servants and they worried that the Poles might even try to attack them. In spite of such fears, Höss himself employed a number of Polish servants at the villa and even advertised with a local employment agency, called Arbeitsampt, looking for a housekeeper. This agency was controlled by the occupiers and was responsible for providing workers for the German economy. Polish woman Aniela Bednarska was looking for work in the Auschwitz area at the time and registered herself with Arbeitsampt. She was offered the job of housekeeper in the Höss villa.

> I wasn't aware of who I would be working for. The name was completely unfamiliar to me at that time. It was the end of October 1940. It was only when I reported for work at the gate of the house that I realised I would be working for one of the SS men. I was then led to Kramer, who in turn led me to Höss. The house where Höss lived was the property of Soja, former sergeant of the Polish Army. Camp commandant Höss moved in after Soja had been evicted from the house in 1940. I was employed as housekeeper in the autumn of 1940. Höss was already there living with his family.[14]

According to Aniela Bednarska:

> [The living room had]...black furniture, a sofa, two armchairs, a table, two stools, and a standing lamp. There was Höss's study, which you could enter either from the living room or the dining room. The room was furnished with a big desk covered with a transparent plastic board under which he kept family pictures, two leather armchairs, a long narrow bookcase covering two walls and filled with books. One of its sections was locked. Höss kept cigarettes and Vodka there. The furniture was matt nut-brown, made by camp prisoners. The dining room was decorated with dark nut-brown furniture made in the camp, an unfolding table, six leather chairs, a glazed cupboard for glassware, a sideboard and a beautiful plant stand. The furniture was solid and tasteful. The parquet floor was covered with beautiful and expensive carpets, different colours in every room. There were beautiful curtains in the windows. The kitchen had white walls with white tiles, a big white cupboard where dishes were kept, a small cupboard for papers and brushes, and two white stools. There were three taps with running water for washing up. Next to the kitchen was the pantry. This was very well stocked and open... all the groceries were brought by the prisoners... The bathroom downstairs had white tiles, whilst upstairs it had light green. The main hall had a hanger

with a mirror covering the whole wall. From this hall there were stone stairs leading upstairs to four rooms. The first room was Mr and Mrs Höss's bedroom. The room had two dark nut-brown beds, a four-winged wardrobe made in the camp and used by Höss, a lighter wardrobe with glass doors used by Mrs Höss. There was also a sort of couch—hollowed and leather. Above the beds there was a big colourful oil painting depicting a bunch of field flowers. There were tile stoves in the rooms. Radiators were installed at the end of 1941 and they were hidden behind wooden boxes the same colour as the furniture. In the next room, above Höss's study, was the children's bedroom. The furniture was light and made with a bed net, a big light nut-brown wardrobe, a table, a chest of drawers and cream-coloured chairs. Above the kitchen and the pantry there was a separate room intended for the children to study and play. There was a dark table, hard chairs, a big, wide, blue couch and a large stand for books and toys. There was an enormous amount of toys in the room. The separate room above the black one was a guest room. There were two dark beds, a wardrobe and a set of shelves. All the walls were covered with light beige wallpaper with leaves of a darker shade... There were three basements and in one of them there was a laundry room. In the passageway there were two high water boilers... In the house I did all the housework—cleaning, laundering, ironing, cooking, and dishwashing.[15]

Höss ordered a prisoner called Mieczyslaw Koscielniak, who was a renowned Polish artist, to come to the villa and sort through and select the best art in the commandant's collection. According to Koscielniak, the artworks had been taken from the demolished Polish homes. He spent three days working in the Höss household and found the commandant and his family quite cordial.

Hedwig and her children were relatively content in their new surroundings in Auschwitz. During the early months, before the cold weather set in, Hedwig would often sit out in the garden, lovingly tending to her newly planted rose hedges and watching the children play. Höss occasionally took time out from his busy workload to spend with his wife in the garden. Such moments of leisure were rare though, and for the most part Höss was overworked and stressed about what he considered to be incompetent staff.

> Right from the beginning I was completely absorbed by my new assignment and my orders. In fact, I was obsessed. Every new problem that appeared lashed me on to even greater intensity. I didn't want this situation to get the best of me. My ambition would not permit it. I lived only for my work. It is easy to understand that because of the amount of these overall responsibilities I had little time for the prison camp or the prisoners. I had to leave the prisoners entirely in the hands of those thoroughly distasteful persons like Fritzsch, Meyer, Seidler, and Palitzsch, even though I knew that they were developing the prison camp contrary to my orders and instructions... My job was, and still remained, to finish the building and development of the camp.[16]

Whatever misgivings Höss had about his staff, he was still determined to create an atmosphere of unity and camaraderie within the camp. He held occasional meetings for the SS guards and their wives aimed at encouraging a sense of solidarity amongst the men. During these long meetings, food and wine was served and comrade songs were recited to the accompaniment of an accordion, trumpet player and pianist. These drunken and smoky meetings did nothing to encourage Höss's own feelings of camaraderie and he felt like he was participating in one big charade.

> The feelings of comradeship which had been a holy concept to me appeared to be a farce... I felt this because my old comrades so disappointed and deceived me. I did not want to have anything to do with them socially. I repeatedly began putting off going to such social events, and I was glad when I

could find a suitable excuse for my absence. This behaviour of mine was constantly thrown up to me by my comrades. In fact, Glücks himself pointed out several times that in Auschwitz there were no comradely ties between the commandant and the officers. I just couldn't do it anymore. I had been disappointed too much.[17]

At the beginning of October the first snow showers that fell on the camp did nothing to alleviate Höss's discontentment. Very little preparation had been made for the winter, but construction work carried on in spite of the plummeting temperatures. The inmates were forced to work in arctic conditions without adequate winter clothing or any other type of protection. They were sent out in icy rain and sleet showers and made to work from dawn till dusk every day. Oftentimes they went entire days without any break at all. Höss was determined that the construction of the main buildings would be completed by the end of the year regardless of the weather conditions. The successful escape of an inmate distracted him only temporarily. As a deterrent to other prisoners considering making a similar break for freedom, Höss punished the entire camp by making the prisoners stand at roll-call for 15 hours in heavy rain, sleet and subzero temperatures. Those still standing by the end of the roll-call were ordered to return to their barracks, and the following morning they were forced to work twice as hard.

* * * * *

In November, Höss was summoned to Berlin for a meeting with Himmler. Armed with a progress report on Auschwitz, he journeyed the 500 or so miles to Berlin. Upon his arrival, he found that a victorious atmosphere prevailed in the bustling city. The population were revelling in Germany's recent victories over Poland and France.

Höss had been acquainted with Himmler since his early days in the *Freikorps* and always found him calm, polite and well mannered. The meeting began with an informal chat, and Himmler asked Höss if his family were well. According to Höss, the *Reichsführer* never failed to make enquiries about the welfare of his family and he felt the question was genuine rather than just a case of being polite. Both men then turned their attention to more serious matters. The *Reichsführer* asked Höss to give him an oral report on the progress of the Auschwitz camp. Although Himmler had another pressing meeting scheduled that day, he allowed Höss to speak at length about each and every aspect of the camp. He went into great detail in describing the terrible conditions that prevailed at Auschwitz and the drastic need for action. He also highlighted the threat of an epidemic due to inadequate hygiene facilities. Himmler suddenly interrupted the commandant and curtly informed him that he was being too pessimistic. Höss was taken aback and decided that he should change tack. He produced various maps and diagrams of the camp and Himmler's anger immediately subsided and he became more animated. Conversation soon shifted from the running of the camp, the materials required for its completion and general concerns for hygiene, to Himmler's vision of ultimately turning Auschwitz into an experimental agricultural station. Himmler had a degree in agriculture so he and Höss shared a mutual love of farming. Himmler spoke passionately about his grand plans for Auschwitz.

> Every necessary agricultural and plant cultivation department had to be built. Cattle breeding of all types were to become important... The marshlands were to be drained and developed... He continued with his talk of agricultural planning even down to the smallest details, and ceased only when his adjutant called his attention to the fact that a very important person had been waiting for a long time to see him.[18]

The two men continued to pore over maps and plans as they discussed how best to relocate thousands of ethnic Germans and Poles. Himmler told Höss that the Germanization of Upper Silesia with agricultural workers formed the very core of his vision. He intended to use Polish labour in large agricultural enterprises that would build towns, villages, roads and draining ditches. Auschwitz, he declared, formed the crux of his plan. He would replace Polish farmsteads with well-managed German farms. Höss was enthralled by Himmler's vision. Being a farmer by trade, the possibility that Auschwitz could be developed into an agricultural empire excited him. These farms would embody German peasant culture, and a German settlement at Auschwitz would lay the historic foundations for generations of farmers to come. Various other farming villages would be established based on this model town of Germanization. The *Reichsführer* elaborated further, informing Höss that there would be a bell tower at the centre of these settlements, and it would be surrounded by a village hall, an inn, a school, a Hitler Youth Home, a kindergarten, and buildings for the local farmers. He intended to design the settlements in clusters; a principal village would lie at the centre of the cluster and satellite villages would border it. Concentrating the settlements in this way would encourage social cohesion and ultimately benefit both the farmers and the land.

Himmler considered himself the supreme architect of East Germany and he was confident that the areas within the expanded Reich would soon flourish with German settlers. The grubby little town of Auschwitz, which lay just outside of the General Government, had been claimed as German soil and would soon be transformed beyond all recognition.

Höss left Himmler's office in an optimistic mood. He spent the return journey to Auschwitz reflecting on his boss's vision for a centre of agricultural research. He knew that this was a highly ambitious dream, yet it appealed to him immensely. He was ideologically committed to the idea and hoped that if it came to fruition that he might be assigned control of it. However, given the ethnic and economic conditions in Upper Silesia he was conscious of the immense problems they would face in trying to remove the whole of the Polish population. If the Polish could not be removed altogether then the SS could at least continue to incarcerate the enemies of the New Order and use them for slave labour.

Upon Höss's return to the camp he took up where he had left off—overseeing construction and implementing the structures and principles necessary for the smooth-running of Auschwitz. With a New Year beckoning, he was determined to create an efficient operation in accordance with Himmler's original vision of a model camp.

By early December work was progressing nicely in spite of the harsh weather conditions that had descended on the camp. The wooden and barbed-wire fence that had previously surrounded the camp had been completely removed and replaced by a concrete wall. The prefabricated guard towers were on order with a firm and were due to arrive early the following year. The whole site, upon completion, was to have a kitchen, utility, storehouse, registration buildings, *blockführer's* office, commandant's office, camp administration offices, SS hospital, a fully operational crematorium, *Gestapo* offices and a medical block. It was also intended that 22 two-storey buildings would be converted into prisoner quarters. Plans were drafted and approved of for a prisoner hospital as well as offices and quarters for some of the camp's prisoners. The majority of these buildings were constructed in redbrick and ran in straight rows throughout the camp. Block numbers were assigned for identification purposes. The *Blockführer's* guardhouse, a wooden structure, was built just outside the main gate.

Most of the buildings planned for Auschwitz were intended to accommodate prisoners, guards and SS staff who ran the camp, and to satisfy the basic needs of these different groups. But there was one particular building that served an entirely different purpose and it was known as Block 13.* From the outside, this pre-war Polish garrison looked like any other redbrick building for the accommodation of prisoners. However, it was here that prisoners were punished or shot dead in either the courtyard of this building or in its washroom. Others were starved or killed by lethal injections to the heart. Prison cells were also specially constructed in the basement for holding prisoners for questioning. One of the most notorious members of the camp personnel in charge of running the block was SS-*Untersturmführer* Maximilian Grabner. He was responsible for deciding the fate of the prisoners held here. The unfortunate prisoners who were sentenced to death were first taken to the washrooms on the ground floor and ordered to strip naked. They were then hurriedly escorted to a secluded courtyard where they were shot dead against a brick wall. But it was not just the inmates of the camp who were tortured and executed at Block 13. The *Gestapo* informed Höss that Auschwitz was to host the police summary court for the Kattowitz area. This meant that Höss had no immediate control over Block 13—Poles arrested by the *Gestapo* could pass straight into the camp without registering and oftentimes without the commandant's knowledge. From January 1943, the summary court of the *Gestapo* carried out its sessions on the ground floor of Block 13. Police detainees—Polish civilians who were prisoners of the *Gestapo*—were sentenced to death in 90% of cases and faced immediate execution by shooting.

* * * * *

In spite of the daily tortures and deaths at Auschwitz, there were aspects of the concentration camp that were still run in a similar vein to the camp at Dachau. During the early days, inmates serving time at Auschwitz could actually be released

---

* In 1941 Block 13 was renamed Block 11.

by special order of the commandant. As long as they had been given a clean bill of health by the camp's doctor and they had signed a form stating that they had no complaints, they were allowed to leave as free men. However, prisoners were not set free on the grounds of a change in policy or a goodwill gesture. Höss had in fact been informed that the Red Cross and other institutions in the outside world, including representatives of the Pope, had voiced objections to the incarceration of various academics in the concentration camps. Höss called a meeting with his staff in order to discuss the matter. He reluctantly informed them that regular prisoner selections would have to take place. He added that when the time came to choose, prisoners who were deemed fit and healthy, and who had signed a form stating that they had no complaints against the camp authority, would be classed suitable for release.

But Höss strongly opposed the release of prisoners. He enjoyed the uncertainty that hung over their fates as it gave him an added sense of power. He himself had endured years of imprisonment and he enjoyed seeing how others coped with their incarceration. But the living conditions endured by the inmates in Auschwitz were far different to those in any state prison. Aside from the uncertainty of their sentence, the level of barbarity inflicted on the prisoners was so extreme that, for many, death represented a welcome release.

Höss continued to quell his moral scruples. He focused instead on running the camp and ensuring that the main buildings were ready by early 1941 to cope with the growing numbers of prisoners.

Chapter III: Year of Decisions

January 1941 opened with a series of important deliberations for Höss as Auschwitz entered into a new stage in its evolution. Although Himmler's bold plans guaranteed the camp a promising future, they also generated a large amount of extra work for Höss. Alongside the demands of overseeing construction and dealing with staff he considered incompetent, Höss now had the added burden of liaising with the Economic Office in Berlin about the new enterprising plans. One aspect of these plans had already been discussed during Pohl's visit in September, when the usefulness of Auschwitz's sand and gravel pits for the German Earth and Stone Works enterprise had been highlighted. An enterprise like this would be highly lucrative, so plans were put in place to enlarge the camp and prepare it for the accommodation of a permanent slave labour population.

The significance of the plans meant that more prisoners would need to be transported to Auschwitz as soon as possible. Already there were approximately 8,000 Polish inmates—a figure that was growing daily—but Höss was still behind schedule with the construction project and had neither the time nor the space to accommodate these new prisoners. He was already concerned that a typhus epidemic and other infectious diseases would break out in the camp. Since early October conditions had been deplorable and he could see the situation worsening if more building supplies could not be sourced.

Höss was beset by a never-ending series of problems during this period but his hard work did not go unnoticed by his superiors. On 30 January he was promoted to the rank of SS-*Sturmbannführer*. For the 40-year-old commandant the promotion was a great honour. His new rank temporarily lifted his spirits and infused him with a renewed sense of optimism. He saw his promotion as more than just a step-up in rank—it was proof that his hard work and willingness to serve had been recognised.

Over the coming weeks Höss's mood began to wane again. His huge workload and the general incompetence of his staff weighed heavily on his mind. On numerous occasions he tried to voice his concerns to Glücks, but like Himmler, Glücks wanted to hear nothing but positive reports on the camp.

In late February, Höss received word that the *Reichsführer* intended to visit Auschwitz that March. The disgruntled commandant had a litany of complaints for his boss but his first priority was to ensure that the camp was in satisfactory order for the visit. Inspector Glücks had in fact arrived at the camp at the end of February and was staying as a guest at the Höss villa. During his brief stay his conversations with Höss varied considerably. Glücks reiterated that the *Reichsführer* had taken a particular interest in Auschwitz. He told Höss that the camp would soon be transformed beyond all recognition and that Himmler's impending visit would probably be the most important one Höss would ever receive. Auschwitz's future depended in equal measure on the grandiose agricultural and industrial plans. Glücks was aware of Höss's frustrations with Auschwitz but he advised him to be co-operative and 'not to say anything that would irritate Himmler'.[19] Höss retorted that unfortunately he had nothing but negative feedback for Himmler.

On the afternoon of Saturday, 1 March, Himmler and his delegation arrived at Auschwitz. The camp's side gates, which were situated between the Höss villa and the commandant's office, were thrown open and the delegation made its way into the compound flanked by protective motorcycle combinations. Höss was there to greet the *Reichsführer* and his commission. Accompanying Himmler was the District Party Leader Bracht, Glücks, several governors, high-ranking SS officers, political leaders of Silesia and the leading corporate officers of the giant industrial chemical conglomerate, I.G. Farben, which was proposing the construction of a synthetic-rubber factory near Auschwitz. The *Reichsführer* had flown from Berlin to the industrial city of Gleiwitz, where he was met by the Provincial Governor Fritz Bracht, von dem Bach-Zelewski and Glücks. After lunch they made the half-hour journey to inspect Auschwitz; after that they planned on taking a tour of the local countryside with the commandant.

At the camp Höss wasted no time in showing Himmler, Bracht, Karl Wolff and the others around. Walking past the administration buildings, the crematorium and the prisoners' barracks, the officials witnessed firsthand the countless malnourished prisoners, their heads shaved and wearing tattered blue-and-white-striped uniforms, as they toiled under the supervision of the *Kapos*. The different groups of prisoners could be distinguished by their various coloured badges. The Polish political prisoners wore red triangular badges, containing the letter P. There was a small number of Polish Jews in the camp at the time and they wore a red and yellow triangle of the Star of David. The camp also contained approximately two hundred German criminals who wore a green triangular badge.

Höss guided his boss around Block 16 (known as Block 14 from 1941 onwards). The building had been specially prepared for Himmler's visit. Whereas the prisoners normally slept naked on straw mattresses on the ground, three-level bunk beds had been temporarily inserted. Most of the inmates were locked up for the duration of Himmler's visit. Only a small group of healthy-looking prisoners were left on show and they were given new clothes especially to impress Himmler.

The commandant briefed Himmler and the delegation on the general purpose of each building they inspected, and 'quietly pointed out the worst conditions, like the overcrowding, the lack of water, but he hardly listened to me.'[20]

Höss waited until he was alone in the car with Himmler and Erich von dem Bach-Zelewski before launching into a bitter diatribe on the conditions in the camp. Höss was confident that he could speak his mind with Himmler—he had done so numerous times before and had never faced any type of reprisal. Those acquainted with Höss, especially the higher authorities, knew that he was fully committed to the Nazi vision and wasn't criticising the ideology itself but rather how it was being implemented. As they toured the local countryside, Höss complained about the shortage of building materials, the lack of staff, and the problem posed by the continuous arrival of new prisoners when the camp was not yet complete. To Höss's surprise, Himmler sternly rebuked him.

> I want to hear no more about problems. For an SS officer there are no problems. When there are such problems, it's his job to see to them. How it's undertaken is your business, not mine.[21]

Höss and his entourage drew to a halt in a marshy tract of land in the district of Zasole. Equipped with maps and various architectural drawings of the land, Himmler casually announced that the area upon which they were standing had been selected as a potential site for a new camp. Auschwitz, he explained, was soon to be expanded and this patch of land had been designated for the construction of a huge satellite camp—more impressive than anything they had ever seen before. This new camp would accommodate a minimum of 100,000 prisoners. Höss was shocked, not least by the gargantuan plans, but by the considerable problems they posed. Fritz Bracht was quick to raise objections, as were several other officials, who spoke out about the drainage and sewage problems, not to mention the sizeable quantity of materials required by such a mammoth project. The site itself was situated on marshy land, with the ground only slightly higher than the Vistula and Sola rivers. This meant that rain, melting snow and floodwaters would neither drain into the river nor be absorbed back into the earth. But no amount of objections could dissuade Himmler and he simply replied:

Gentlemen, this project will be completed; my reasons for this are more important than your objections![22]

Himmler's proposal had not been officially agreed upon at this time but he was determined to set his ambitious plans in motion before the year was over. Höss returned to Auschwitz with a deep sense of anxiety over the new proposals. During dinner at the SS mess hall he was unable to shake off his mounting apprehension. After dinner, Himmler elaborated on his grandiose plans for the Auschwitz complex. He informed his bewildered audience that he not only proposed to establish a huge satellite camp but also intended to increase the capacity of Auschwitz from the current target of 10,000 inmates to a staggering 30,000. He said that such a transformation was imperative as the availability of slave labour was key to the continued development of the region. The *Reichsführer* envisioned bands of slave labour working on the dykes along the Sola and Vistula rivers and demolishing sites in the town to make way for new building developments. In order to undertake such developments, all Jewish and Polish residents living around the camp would be evicted and incarcerated in a camp in the neighbourhood of Auschwitz, where they would be used as unskilled construction workers. The evictions of the locals would free the town up for the influx of factory staff belonging to I.G. Farben—a massive new enterprise that Himmler was eager to see built in the area. Officials from this chemical cartel had accompanied Himmler to Auschwitz in order to decide whether or not a factory should be built in the area. I.G. Farben had been attracted by the vast pool of skilled and unskilled construction workers on offer in the concentration camps. It was estimated that between 8,000 and 12,000 men would be needed for the construction of the factory, and with the *Reichsführer's* plans to increase the pool of prisoners at Auschwitz to 30,000, the factory would have more than enough workers at their disposal. By expanding Auschwitz, Himmler not only stood to satisfy the I.G. Farben labour demand, but he would also be able to commit a further 10,000 inmates to his planned agricultural estate.

The *Reichsführer's* audacious plan to create a huge agricultural experimental centre was still pivotal to his overall vision for Auschwitz. He also made it known that he had no intention of abandoning his plans for the gravel and sand pit enterprise. He reassured Höss that the expansion of Auschwitz was imperative to the fruition of these enterprises and that in the long run the region would benefit immensely from such developments. It was for this reason, Himmler said, that the needs of I.G. Farben had to be given top priority. A site had already been chosen for a factory about two miles away. It would produce a synthetic rubber called Buna and inmates from Auschwitz would erect the building. Other construction workers from Germany would be brought in and accommodated in vacant homes in Auschwitz town. The town itself would be redeveloped, with schools and hospitals put in place to serve the German workers. Himmler also informed Höss that he intended to relocate a portion of the arms industry to Auschwitz.

Initially the proposals seemed ridiculously grandiose. Only months earlier Höss had been pillaging local towns and villages in search of building materials for the construction of a relatively small and unknown camp in southwest Poland. Now he was expected to construct what Himmler claimed would be the largest concentration camp in the Reich. The *Reichsführer* told the commandant that he would 'just have to make improvements as you go.'[23] Höss tried in vain to make Himmler see reason but he received a dismissive retort.

> Draining marshes and providing water supplies are a question of technology, which is a matter to be solved by the experts, but are not reasons for rejections... Epidemics will occur and must be ruthlessly fought against. But the camp categorically cannot be closed to new arrivals. My orders for police roundups must be continued. I do not acknowledge the difficulties in Auschwitz.[24]

Höss was not convinced by his boss, but he was steadfast in his commitment to the Auschwitz camp and he resolved to do his best to implement the plans.

Shortly before Himmler left Auschwitz, he visited the Höss family residence and met Hedwig and the children. All afternoon Höss had found the *Reichsführer* stubborn and unsympathetic, but as they approached the villa he suddenly reverted to his old charming and talkative self. Inside the house, Hedwig greeted Himmler warmly and he kissed the back of her hand in response. Hedwig directed her important guest into the living room, where he met the well-groomed children, Klaus, Edeltraut, Brigitte and the youngest of the family, Burling. Himmler took a seat on the black sofa and chatted familiarly with Hedwig and the children. According to the family gardener, Stanislaw Dubiel:

> [Himmler] spoke very warmly with Höss and his wife and took on his lap Höss's children, who called him 'Uncle Heini'... Such

scenes were captured on photographs that were later enlarged and hung on the walls of Höss's house.[25]

Hedwig found the *Reichsführer* easygoing and jovial, and she immediately warmed to his Bavarian mannerisms and dialect. Just before he departed, Himmler advised Höss that he should modernise and enlarge the house so that he could host important officials who visited the camp. Himmler considered the commandant's residence an integral part of any concentration camp. It was here that he rested and reflected on his day, devised new plans, met representatives, entertained family and friends, and preserved the family morals and values that were considered a fundamental part of German culture.

On 7 March, a week after the *Reichsführer's* visit, Höss took Professor Zunker and SS-*Sturmbannführer* Vogel on a tour of Auschwitz. They discussed how best to set about cultivating the thousands of acres of farmland that constituted Himmler's agricultural vision. They spent a number of hours touring the region and trying to find a solution to the problem of flooding around the Sola and Vistula rivers. They suggested various methods of improving the land, from reconstructing massive lakes and cleaning existing drainage systems, to laying nearly four million drainage pipes on 3,000 acres of farmland.

During the remaining weeks of March, Höss was once again immersed in the running of Auschwitz, and he found himself questioning the feasibility of the plans for the region. The company I.G. Farben was to the forefront of his mind. At a meeting held on 27 March, chaired by Höss and attended by Auschwitz officials and representatives of I.G. Farben, discussion focused on the potential advantages of a joint enterprise between I.G. Farben and the camp. The I.G. Farben engineers were curious to know how many prisoners the camp could promise them, but Höss was unable to give them the positive answer they were looking for. Unlike his boss, who had told them only what they wanted to hear, Höss refused to conceal the truth. He told them that at present he had difficulty enough in accommodating the existing prisoners, never mind drafting in more for the construction of the Buna factory. He explained that numerous problems prevented him from being able to house more inmates. Although, like the *Reichsführer*, he was eager to establish a prosperous business relationship with I.G. Farben, the shortage of raw materials was causing insurmountable accommodation problems at the camp. He tried to underline the seriousness of the situation by revealing that he had been forced to journey around the Polish countryside in search of building materials to pilfer. He suggested to the I.G. Farben representatives that if they could contribute a certain percentage of materials and resources to the extension of Auschwitz, it would help the camp solve the accommodation problems and ultimately benefit both parties.

Having heard the litany of difficulties the commandant was experiencing, the I.G. Farben representatives were somewhat more sympathetic. They said that they would go away and discuss amongst themselves how they wished to proceed. In the meantime, they were eager to agree upon a daily wage for the workers. Höss knew that this business arrangement could ultimately prove extremely lucrative for the SS, and 'the entire negotiations were conducted in cordial harmony'.[26]

[With either side]... wishing to assist each other in every way possible... I.G. Farben had agreed to pay a daily all-inclusive sum of 3 Reichsmark per unskilled worker and 4 Reichsmark per skilled worker, and work performance was estimated as being 75 per cent of that of a normal German worker.[27]

Höss promised that he would be able to provide at least 1,000 prisoners immediately and that this figure would increase as plans for the expansion of Auschwitz and the building of the satellite complex got underway. The inmates would construct the factory and later work in the plant following its completion. I.G. Farben vowed to give serious consideration to the proposal that they supply materials for the camp's expansion. Höss knew that the success of this partnership, and indeed the future of the Auschwitz camp, depended on this massive chemical conglomerate working in their favour.

* * * * *

In early April, construction of the Buna factory finally commenced. Höss ordered that every morning gangs of prison workers were to be sent from Auschwitz to the I.G. Farben plant in the village of Monowitz. Plans were already being drawn up for the construction of additional quarters for the inmates, as well as the construction of a bridge over the River Sola that would connect the camp to the factory. A narrow-gauge railway line was also under consideration as it would allow the inmates to be quickly transported back and forth from the plant.

The construction of this enterprise was an enormous undertaking, but true to the *Reichsführer's* word, Auschwitz's increased pool of labour ensured its rapid completion. The relationship between the SS and I.G. Farben blossomed, with both parties united by their desire to establish their own dominion in Auschwitz. The camp was central to these efforts and architects were drafted in to draw up plans for the expansion. Höss was apprehensive about this bold project and when he received a summons to visit Himmler in the SS headquarters in Berlin he couldn't help but wonder what grand new plans would be unveiled on this visit.

On 13 June, Höss arrived in the Reich capital and was introduced to the new chief of Office II of the SS Main Office Household and Buildings, Hans Kammler. SS-*Gruppenführer* Kammler, who was the head of Administrative Group C at WVHA, was responsible for construction work on behalf of the army, the SS and the police, including the construction of concentration camps and facilities for the armament industry. Kammler, an old *Freikorps* comrade and Nazi member, had been a qualified architect for some years now. The two men discussed at length the expansion of Auschwitz. Kammler revealed drawings of the planned site, and as previously agreed upon with the *Reichsführer*, the new camp was to accommodate 30,000 inmates. Construction was to get underway immediately on 30 two-storey barracks, which were to be extended as far as the station, housing for the commandant's staff and the officers, a delousing facility, a laundry, a storehouse for prisoners' belongings, and a large roll-call area flanked by an entrance pavilion. There were also plans for a camp for civilian employees and construction workers; new streets; an extensive new drainage and sewer system; a drinking-water installation; an SS private railway station and an SS settlement. Himmler's agricultural project was also being addressed and new villages, farmsteads and an agricultural estate, complete with barns and giant greenhouses, were all to be built.

The Auschwitz expansion project was very impressive on paper but the possibility of it translating into reality, with the already-existing pressures of building a new camp and meeting the Buna factory's labour demands, was in Höss's opinion very doubtful. But he kept his reservations hidden from his boss. In speaking about the design of the camp, the *Reichsführer* mentioned an area of land that lay to the rear of the site, close to both the hospital and the newly designed crematorium. He proposed that this tract of land serve a similar function to Block 11 and that the condemned be taken straight to this yard, stripped naked and executed. Their corpses would then be brought to the crematorium for incineration. The idea sounded good but Himmler added that a few adjustments would have to be made—he felt it would be more practical and efficient to run both the new and the old crematoria side by side, close to the back gate of the camp. He insisted that with increased efficiency Auschwitz would be able to handle a greater number of victims. Himmler told Höss that permanent crematoria, incineration sites and execution grounds of various designs were being installed at a number of other concentration camps. It was for this reason that he felt the need to discuss with Höss ways of making the execution facilities more sophisticated. Himmler emphasised the importance of carrying out these killings with the least amount of disorder and disturbance to the rest of the camp. An operation known as 14f13 was to be implemented, and all Jews who were chronically sick, mentally ill, or invalided would be selected for immediate removal from camp life.*

Himmler did not have to advise his loyal subordinate on how to handle these so-called 'removals' as he had confidence in Höss's ability to improvise. No matter how repugnant Höss may have found Himmler's order, he felt duty-bound to carry out his boss's command. He had spent his entire life following orders and he had long since ceased questioning them. He was determined to apply his innovation to the task at hand and thereby impress his superiors.

Höss returned to Auschwitz plagued by worries over construction work at the camp rather than the new task assigned to him. He felt completely dejected by the lack of support he was getting from his superiors and his unreliable colleagues. Höss wrote:

> Because of the general untrustworthiness that surrounded me, I became a different person in Auschwitz. Up to then I had always been ready to see the best in my fellow creatures, and especially

---

* 14f referred to the inspectorate of concentration camps, and 13 to the 'special treatment of sick and invalid Jewish male inmates'. The operation was otherwise known as Operation Invalid. Originally in 1939 the programme targeted ethnic Germans, but in 1940 it also began targeting Jews; mid-way through 1941 it broadened its scope once again to include concentration camp prisoners of various nationalities. A transport of 575 prisoners, the majority of whom were Polish, was sent from Auschwitz to Sonnenstein on 28 July 1941 and killed by lethal injection.

in my comrades, until I was convinced of the contrary. I had been badly let down by my naïvety. But in Auschwitz, where I found my so-called colleagues constantly going behind my back, and where each day I suffered fresh disappointments, I began to change. I became distrustful and highly suspicious, and saw only the worst in everyone... All human emotions were forced into the background.[28]

Höss realised that he was becoming increasingly distant and hardened towards his staff. The combination of his growing cynicism and an ever-increasing workload began to affect his home life too. He was returning to the villa later and later every evening, and usually in an irritable mood. Hedwig, or 'Mutz' as he sometimes liked to call her, tried to cheer him up and get him to relax. She occasionally organised parties even though she liked the camp's social life even less than Höss. During these gatherings, Höss relied on copious amounts of alcohol to escape the burden of his heavy workload. Under the influence of alcohol, Höss was much more talkative, and at times, even humorous. Those who knew him on a strictly social level found him in the main a polite, well-spoken man, but one who kept a close guard on his innermost feelings. By the summer of 1941 he had become exceptionally quiet and insular. His family were his only salvation, and although his sullenness made him difficult to live with, he was still very attentive, especially towards his children. The housekeeper of SS-*Untersturmführer* Georg Gussregen, who was soon to take command of the 2nd SS Sentry Company at Auschwitz, said of the commandant:

Höss was an ideal man at home. He loved his children. He liked to lie down on a couch with them in their room. He kissed and caressed them and spoke to them beautifully. However, he turned into a completely different person outside the house. He didn't speak to me at all. Frau Höss was the one who arranged everything. I was glad because I was really afraid of him. I was even scared of his voice. I was really happy when I finally got away from the house.[29]

Despite Höss's increasing detachment, he never neglected his duties at Auschwitz. However late he returned home from the camp at night, he was always fresh and ready for duty the following day. Every morning he would walk across to Department I, the commandant's office, and converse with his office secretaries, answer any urgent messages or telegrams and issue written orders to his subordinates. He regularly took letters, telegrams, telephone messages and other paperwork not classed as urgent, home to work on in his study. When he was not in the commandant's office or at home in his study, he was often seen strolling around the camp, ensuring that everything was running smoothly. He sometimes visited the prison barracks to converse with the officers and to ensure that his orders were being carried out.

* * * * *

Beneath Auschwitz's veneer of efficiency, the prisoners were forced to endure shocking living conditions. Most of the inmates were extremely emaciated and the prison hospital was overflowing with the sick. Höss's superiors instructed him that anyone unfit to work should immediately be removed from camp life and executed.

By the summer of 1941, the number of executions taking place at the camp had increased dramatically. Most of the victims were marched through the main gates and straight to Block 11 by the local *Gestapo*, but Höss was increasingly being asked to carry out the executions himself. On almost a daily basis the Security Police, or the RSHA in Berlin, sent messages to the camp listing which prisoners were to be hung or shot.

The Kattowitz military sessions were held at the camp every two to three weeks, with each trial lasting an average of five minutes. In 1941, Polish political prisoners, suspected of involvement in the resistance movement, along with Soviet POWs, were taken to either the courtyard of Block 11, the mortuary of the crematorium or the gravel pits surrounding the camp fence, and executed *en masse*.

Since September 1940, the Auschwitz crematorium had been working at a steady pace, burning the corpses of prisoners who had either starved to death, contracted a disease or been executed. Within weeks of it going into operation, the crematorium was burning two bodies at a time every 30-40 minutes. A single body could be inserted into each of the two retorts; Crematorium I eventually acquired a third retort. The crematorium was estimated to have an output of between 300 and 340 corpses every 24 hours. In direct response to the dramatic rise of the death rate in the camp, Höss decided to authorise the expansion of the crematorium, and he approached the SS New Construction Office with an urgent request for a second double-muffle incinerator. The second incinerator was fitted at a reduced cost owing to the fact that it was attached to the ventilator of the first. This incinerator doubled the daily number of cremations in the camp, yet it was still unable to handle the number of bodies amassing every day. In the summer heat the stench of rotting corpses was foul. Grabner requested that Schlachter, the camp's architect, install a more sophisticated ventilation system that would not only extract bad odours but would also introduce a fresh supply of air from outside of the building.

Although Höss did not regard the crematorium as his domain, he requested that he be kept up to date on its operation. He regularly broached the topic in meetings, outlining various ways of improving the crematoria's efficiency. He was conscious that as the destruction of Bolshevism began in earnest there would be an even more pressing need for an efficient camp crematorium.

On the morning of 22 June, Höss received word that a massive assembly of over three million German troops had attacked the Soviet Union and were victoriously forging ahead. In Höss's eyes Russia was a land ripe for plunder. He was firmly convinced that the Russians were an inferior race and had come to appreciate the Nazi theory about Communism and Judaism. Several days later reports of Russian Jews, Communist politicians and political commissars being treated harshly began to trickle back to Höss. Although Auschwitz remained a camp primarily for the accommodation of Polish prisoners, Höss received reports that the SS were actually weeding out commissars who had been found hiding in German Army POW camps, and several hundred of these Soviet prisoners were transported to Auschwitz in July. The guards at Auschwitz despised the Soviet POWs. They considered them to be at the bottom of the heap of prisoner groupings. Many of them were beaten and tortured, whilst some were shot in the gravel pits or were condemned to the cellars of Block 11. Here, they were locked in the dark cold cells and left to starve to death. Höss was present for the arrival of the first transport of Russian POWs.

> Following the arrival of the first Soviet transport and the departure of inmates to be killed under the aegis of the 14f13 programme, the camp physician began to experiment with more clinical methods of murder. Prisoners were injected with phenol, gasoline perhydrol, ether, and other substances, and after a number of trials phenol injections in the heart were found to be the most efficient.[30]

However, it was not just the Russian POWs who were killed in this manner.

> By orders of the RSHA, *Gestapo* chiefs were told to get in touch with me in respect of special prisoners whom the *Gestapo* had sent to concentration camps but whom they did not want, for political reasons, sentenced by special courts. Such prisoners were eliminated in a special way. I received lists on which

names of these persons were marked in red, from the *Gestapo* chief concerned or from the leader of the Political Department. In such cases I gave orders to the doctors concerned to carry out the necessary action. This was mostly done in the form of injections. Sometimes petrol injections were used. The doctors had to issue normal death certificates on orders from the RSHA naming some illness as the cause of death. These cases were limited to a small number of persons.[31]

The crematorium was struggling to keep pace with the ever-increasing death rate. During staff meetings, Höss discussed the inefficiency of certain methods of killing, such as starving, shooting, hanging or administering lethal injections to prisoners. He told his staff that in order to cleanse the camp of undesirables and those unfit for work, it was imperative that a more efficient killing method be devised.

Höss was aware of the euthanasia programme. In fact, the 14f13 programme had already been implemented in Auschwitz with positive results. Inmates had been removed from the camp and transported to special killing centres in Germany. The sick, chronically ill and physically disabled were loaded into vans that had been converted into gas chambers. These mobile chambers resembled shower rooms. After the last prisoner had been herded in, the airtight doors were slammed shut behind them. Bottled carbon monoxide was then released into the chambers, asphyxiating the trapped victims. Both Höss and his deputy, Fritzsch, were of the view that asphyxiation was the most effective means of exterminating prisoners and so they began to investigate implementing a large-scale facility at Auschwitz.

In late August, SS-*Obersturmbannführer* Adolf Eichmann, of the RSHA in Berlin, arrived at Auschwitz for a meeting with Höss. Eichmann was a Jewish-emigration specialist who was charged with managing the logistics of the mass deportation of Jews to ghettos and concentration camps in Nazi-occupied Eastern Europe. He had been sent to Auschwitz to discuss new deportation plans and to examine the camp's present facilities. Höss gave Eichmann a tour of the camp, after which they sat down to discuss business. Eichmann told Höss that the *Reichsführer* had sent him to Auschwitz to discuss the Jewish Question with him. Eichmann was aware of the plans for the new satellite camp that was soon to be constructed. During their conversation, he stressed that the *Reichsführer* wanted the SS to take care of the Jewish problem for once and for all. Preparations for the mass deportation of Jews were now underway, and it was believed that the excellent railway network in Auschwitz, coupled with the expansion programme of the camp, made it the most suitable camp for the accommodation of these new prisoners. Eichmann explained that the *Reichsführer* saw Auschwitz as the main hub of a huge semi-industrial complex. The Jewish prisoners would be sent to work at the various sub-camps in the surrounding area. Should their labour no longer be required or should they be deemed unfit for work, they would be transported back to Auschwitz and exterminated. Höss knew that at present the Auschwitz camp didn't have the facilities to handle such a massive influx of inmates and that a mammoth workload lay ahead of him. In the meantime, the Jews would remain in the ghettos and Eichmann would have to be patient.

Eichmann also spoke of the importance of designing an improved killing facility at the camp that would facilitate the extermination of greater numbers of inmates. Since early summer, Höss had known about the plans to systematically murder prisoners at Auschwitz. Initially, only the sick and disabled had been condemned, but Eichmann informed Höss that Himmler intended to implement a factory-like killing installation capable of exterminating anyone unfit for work or deemed a threat to the Reich. The list of enemies had lengthened, with anyone disliked by the *Reichsführer*, such as the Russian POWs, under threat. It was suggested that a killing experiment be conducted and that Russian POWs be used as guinea pigs. Although Höss loathed Russians, and was in favour of them being treated harshly, the prospect of killing them *en masse* did not sit comfortably with his conscience. However, once again his innate obedience and loyalty as an officer overshadowed his moral scruples and he focused instead on how best to carry out these cold-blooded murders.

* * * * *

During Höss's meeting with Eichmann, both men agreed that the carbon monoxide gas vans, whilst efficient, were far too expensive. *Lagerführer* Karl Fritzsch had previously suggested the use of hydro cyanide as an alternative, and Höss now proposed this idea to Eichmann. He told him that he was in the process of constructing a delousing installation at Auschwitz that could possibly double as a gas chamber; the lethal hydro cyanide could be used in these chambers. Eichmann approved of the idea and told Höss to instruct his deputy, who was in charge of the fumigation and disinfection process in the camp, to start experimenting with this new gas.

On 1 September, prior to Höss leaving Auschwitz on business, he ordered Fritzsch to commence the pilot experiments. Höss suspected that if the hydro cyanide was effective in killing infestations of insects, in sufficient doses it should also be able to kill what Höss saw as the human equivalent of such pests. Höss told his deputy that the orders had come from Berlin and were highly confidential. Eager to impress his superior, Fritzsch promised to commence the experiment without delay and to maintain secrecy at all costs.

Höss returned to Auschwitz a few days later and chaired a private meeting with his deputy during which they discussed the outcome of the experimental gassing. Six hundred newcomers to the camp had been selected as guinea pigs; there were 350 Soviet POWs and 250 sick Polish inmates who had been taken from the camp's hospital. Fritzsch told the commandant that, as planned, on 3 September he had conducted the first mass killing using crystallised prussic acid, which was sold in tins labelled 'Zyklon B'. He decided to stage the experiment in the basement of Block 11. He ensured that all areas of the basement, particularly the windows, were made airtight before removing the condemned from their sickbeds and hovels.

Under the cloak of darkness, he escorted the prisoners to Block 11 and herded them into the underground cells. He then slammed the door shut behind them and poured the Zyklon B crystals into the room. The execution lasted 48 hours in total. It took more than two days to air out the building and to transport the corpses to the already-overflowing crematorium. Neither the commandant nor his deputy were entirely happy with the results of the experiment. A more efficient method of dropping the Zyklon B into the room would have to be devised, and an alternative location to the less-than-ideal basement was also needed.

Fritzsch suggested that the camp's crematorium could be the perfect location. Not only did it have a flat roof but it could also be easily modified, with openings added to the roof to enable the insertion of the Zyklon B crystals. The morgue had recently been fitted with a powerful new ventilation system that would be more than capable of handling the poisonous gas. Höss gave orders for the immediate modification of the crematorium. Three square portholes, which were covered with wooden lids, were inserted into the flat roof. Within a few days of the modifications being made, 900 Russian soldiers were selected for a trial run of the gas chamber. This time Höss would be present and he hoped that the process would be quick and efficient.

Prior to the gassing, the area around the crematorium was sealed off and the windows of the SS infirmary were covered with blinds in order to obscure the view of the crematorium's roof. The crematorium forecourt was also closed off to all prisoners working in the camp so that the victims could get undressed in this area. From the sidelines of this forecourt, Höss and Fritzsch watched as victims were ordered to undress, before being herded into the gas chamber.

> The entire transport fit exactly in the room. The doors were closed and the gas poured in through the openings in the roof. How long the process lasted, I don't know, but for quite some time sounds could be heard. As the gas was thrown in some of them yelled 'Gas!' and a tremendous screaming and shoving started toward both doors, but the doors were able to withstand all the force.[32]

After the gassing the fans were turned on and the doors thrown open. Höss wrote:

> I really did not waste any thoughts about the killing of the Russian POWs... it was ordered and I had to carry it out.[33]

The procedure was a complete success, much to Höss's relief. The days of having to look his victims in the eye as he murdered them were over. The gas chambers allowed the SS to avoid what Höss termed a bloodbath. With a little innovation the guards would be able to dupe their victims into thinking they were going to be showered and disinfected in the crematorium. This deception meant that inmates would enter the gas chambers willingly. Overall, Höss believed this new method of killing would be far less stressful, both physically and psychologically, for the guards. He anticipated that subsequent transports of POWs would be killed in a similar manner, and his only concern was how to store and incinerate the huge number of corpses that would amass.

After the gassing, the corpses were stored in the laying room, the washing room and the morgue while awaiting cremation. The average waiting period was three to four days. The first successful mass killing saw 900 corpses awaiting incineration. From 16 September to 20 September the crematorium overflowed with bodies and the facility was stretched well beyond its normal limitations.

* * * * *

Towards the end of September, Höss received word that the German Army had captured an estimated three million Soviet prisoners. Some 100,000 of these prisoners were transferred from the army to the SS in the same month, with many of them earmarked for Auschwitz. Himmler ordered Hans Kammler, head of the Central SS Building Office, to inform the commandant that construction was to begin on the long-awaited POW camp adjacent to Auschwitz. It was proposed that the new camp would house the majority of these Soviet POWs and that living conditions would be so terrible that a large percentage of the prisoners would inevitably perish. During Himmler's visit the previous March, Höss had been displeased with these plans, but he now found the proposal increasingly attractive as it promised to reduce the problem of overcrowding.

The depopulated and dismantled village of Brzezinka was selected for the new camp. This marshy tract of land, which was surrounded by birch trees, was located nearly two miles west of the main camp. The SS had previously cleared the houses of this small village and relocated the inhabitants in anticipation of the land one day being required for construction purposes. The Germans had renamed the area Birkenau.

The task of designing Birkenau was left in the capable hands of two men: the newly appointed chief of the Auschwitz construction office, SS-*Hauptsturmführer* Karl Bischoff, and the 33-year-old architect, SS-*Rottenführer* Fritz Ertl. Their overall budget was to be 8.9 million Reichsmark, and the final camp was to accommodate approximately 97,000 prisoners. Birkenau would be divided into two sections, with the smaller part, which was capable of accommodating some 17,000 inmates, serving as a quarantine camp. Accommodation would be extremely overcrowded—initial plans for each barracks block showed that they would contain 550 inmates, however, this number was later amended to 744.

Two delousing stations were planned for the quarantine camp, as well as two kitchens, thirty barracks, five toilet barracks and five washrooms. The main part of the installation would be divided into twelve sections, each containing twelve barracks, one kitchen, one toilet barracks and one washroom. The inmates would be housed in 174 barracks; each barracks would be subdivided into 62 bays, and each bay would have a three-level bunk-bed system. The entire camp would cover some 80 hectares of land. Höss paid several visits to the site in an effort to get to grips with its vastness. As with the main Auschwitz camp, Höss was responsible for selecting inmates to build this new camp. Himmler's office confirmed that Russian POWs would be made available to Auschwitz. Höss wrote:

> From the onset I had my doubts as to whether these prisoners would be fit enough to work. I had already heard rumours that most of them were starving. It was probably going to be a thankless task of selecting the fittest.[34]

The military POW camp at Lamsdorf, known as Stalag VIII-B in Upper Silesia, began making preparations to send a transport of Russian prisoners directly to Auschwitz. Conditions inside the POW camp were appalling, with a large percentage of the prisoners reported to be severely malnourished. When Höss arrived at Lamsdorf in late September he was shocked to find that many of the prisoners had either starved to death or had died from illness. The remaining prisoners were huddled together on a small, square patch of land, living in squalid-looking huts that they had built out of earth. The distribution of food in the camp was completely irregular, resulting in the malnourishment of the prisoners. The inmates led a primitive existence, and Höss observed several men and women cooking half-rotten potatoes or turnips over fire pits in the ground. He wrote:

> Conditions were terrible. Their gaunt, lice-riddled bodies are being reduced to bones and the stench of death fills me with a sickening feeling in my stomach. But I had not visited these poor men to gloat and watch their death agonies before my eyes. I had come to Lamsdorf on important business to see my new work force that was supposed to help me construct my new assignment at Auschwitz. I was supposed to build the new camp with these half-dead prisoners, who barely had enough energy to stand up. According to the *Reichsführer's* orders, only the strong and able-bodied Russian POWs were to leave.[35]

One of the officers at Lamsdorf informed Höss that the best available prisoners had already been selected for transportation to Auschwitz. After inspecting these Russian POWs, Höss remained unconvinced. 'They were perfectly willing to work', he said, 'but were unable to accomplish anything because they were so weak.'[36]

In early October, Höss finally authorised the transportation order of his new Russian labour force. Those considered fit enough for the journey were rounded up and led to one side by SS guards, whilst those who were too weak were shot dead where they lay. The corpses were then dragged away by Polish prisoners and piled high to await disposal. In total, 10,000 Russian prisoners were to be marched from Lamsdorf to Auschwitz. The journey would prove too much for many of the prisoners, however, and hundreds died from thirst or exhaustion along the way. Höss was at the gates of the camp when the Russian transport finally arrived. He watched his new workforce being herded like cattle along the main road to Auschwitz. When the prisoners finally passed through the main gate of the camp they were directed into nine two-storey brick buildings located in the south part of the main camp.

A sign, reading 'Labour Camp for Prisoners of War', had been erected at the entrance to the POW camp. The prisoners were in a terrible physical condition when they arrived. Many were infested with lice and had to be stripped of their clothes and disinfected in a cold bath before being allowed into the camp.

Food shortages continued to be a problem for the Russian POWs in Auschwitz. Höss tried his best to increase their food rations but for many prisoners their emaciated bodies were simply unable to digest the food.

> They died like flies in front of me because of their weakened conditions or from the slightest illness, which their bodies could no longer fight off. I saw countless Russians die as they were swallowing turnips and potatoes. This was my workforce. How could I possibly get these poor souls to work for me and get the best results?[37]

On one occasion, while riding his horse outside of the camp's barbed-wire fence, Höss spotted a Russian man huddled behind a pile of stones while he chewed on a piece of bread. Höss watched as another man slowly crept up behind the starving prisoner and struck him across the head with a brick so that he could steal his meagre ration of food. Evidence of cannibalism presented itself on several other occasions. During the levelling of the land and the trench digging in the first section of Birkenau, soldiers discovered several corpses of Russians apparently beaten to death and partially eaten. The corpses had their flesh ripped open and parts of their internal organs missing, and had then been buried in the mud. Höss was shocked but he finally understood the puzzling absence of a number of inmates during roll-call.

Höss's Russian workforce was the source of a series of never-ending problems. Terrified of disappointing his superiors, Höss decided to increase the food rations of approximately 5,000 of these Russian prisoners. Trainloads of turnips were shunted into Auschwitz station in order to fatten up the half-starved men. Höss wrote:

> Everywhere the Russians walked around aimlessly, or they crawled around trying to find shelter when they found something edible to eat. They tried to force it down their throats, or they just quietly found a place to die. The entire railway complex was jammed because the turnips lay like a mountain on top of the railway tracks. The situation became much worse during the winter period. They could bear the cold but not the dampness and wearing clothes which were always wet.[38]

On another occasion, Höss was passing Auschwitz station in his car when he noticed a commotion.

> [Russians]... charged into nearby piles of potatoes stored next to a street on the other side of the railroad tracks. All in unison, they completely surprised the guards and ran right over them. The guards didn't know what to do. Luckily I saw this and was able to restore order. The Russians threw themselves into the piles of potatoes. It was almost impossible to tear these vultures away. Some of them died while digging into the pile; others died whilst chewing, their hands full of potatoes. They no longer exercised the slightest restraint towards each other.[39]

Rather than feeling pity for the starving prisoners, Höss took this scene as further proof that he was dealing with animals and he was completely disgusted by their behaviour.

The Russian POWs were put to work almost immediately after they arrived in Auschwitz. Those who were too weak to work were killed and disposed of in the crematorium, whilst the remaining prisoners were dragged from their barracks and marched the 40-minute journey to the Birkenau construction site. The existing village had to be dismantled before work could commence on the new camp. The prisoners weren't given any tools with which to demolish the houses, but were expected to pull the buildings down with their bare hands and build the barracks in the same way. They were forced to work in spite of the appallingly bad physical condition they were in. All day long they laboured in sub-zero temperatures. They began by levelling the ground, then drainage ditches were dug, and finally, the various brick barracks and prefabricated wooden horse stables were built. The speed of the work had been of utmost importance, and within 14 days the quarantine camp was completed.

Höss was kept up to date on the progress of the Birkenau project, and he visited the site regularly, either on horseback or in his motor vehicle. He often strolled around the camp, accompanied by site managers and guards, with whom he discussed the details of the programme. But it soon became apparent to Höss that the labour force had not been supplied with the appropriate building materials. A shortage of wood meant that the barracks had to be built from brick. During October and November most of the materials were taken from the debris of the demolition of Birkenau. Bischoff's original requirements had not been met. Höss and Bischoff's plans to complete the camp in the shortest time possible were also hindered by the high mortality rate. By the end of October, 1,255 Soviet prisoners had died. Reports of the high death rate concerned officials in the SS headquarters in Berlin as they viewed their labour force as a valuable commodity.

The death rate continued to rise, with inmates dying from starvation, illness and injuries, whilst others were executed by the guards. The situation worsened during the winter of 1941 with the death toll reaching new heights. The crematorium soon began to buckle under the pressure of its increased workload. During a meeting with Grabner and Schlachter, Höss was informed that the crematorium hadn't been built to serve such a large population and that it simply could not serve the POWs as well as the inmates in the main camp. Bischoff summoned the Topf engineer, Kurt Prüfer, who had supplied the main incineration facilities in Auschwitz. He arrived on Tuesday, 21 October, and began poring over plans, searching for a more efficient arrangement. He suggested that the crematorium combine three muffles in a single furnace. It was considered impractical to waste money building a crematorium on the Birkenau site if this camp was only to serve as short-term accommodation until Germany won the war with Russia. It was therefore agreed that a new crematorium should be built in the main camp alongside the existing crematorium.

* * * * *

Over the next few weeks, construction on the Birkenau site continued. The Soviet prisoners were forced to work for hours on end in freezing weather conditions. An outbreak of dysentery compounded their misery. They were not allowed to abandon their work to go to the toilet and so they often ended up soiling their own ragged clothes and having to work with faeces engrained on their emaciated bodies. At the end of November snow showers began to fall and the number of fatalities in the camp soared as the temperatures plummeted. The conditions were so dreadful that prisoners were actually dying on site. Concerned that the construction programme was in jeopardy, Höss sent an urgent report to Berlin informing them of the situation. Despite Höss's ominous account, Bischoff sent a report to Berlin assuring his superiors that in spite of the high death rate amongst the Soviet prisoners, a good deal of progress had been made at Birkenau. In fact, according to reports, Bischoff confirmed that in just over one month 140,000 cubic feet of earth was excavated, 1,600 concrete foundations were laid, 600 concrete posts with 100,000 feet of barbed wire were erected for the fence, and 86,000 cubic feet of brickwork was constructed using more than one million bricks.[40] Work on the actual barracks, however, was still progressing slowly. These buildings were to be predominantly built from wood. A German company had designed the standard army horsestable barracks and this had been dispatched to Auschwitz as a kit that could be easily erected and dismantled. It was claimed that these prefabricated wooden huts could be quickly assembled with just one carpenter leading a gang of 30 unskilled men. In total, 253 of these huts were assigned to Birkenau.

Towards the end of 1941 Höss witnessed Auschwitz transform from a quiet, backwater quarantine camp into one of the largest concentration camp systems in the Reich. In little more than a year, Auschwitz had evolved into a dual-function camp, with many of the inmates both living and working there. Höss's innovative skills had established an institution of efficient brutality. With an effective killing facility in place, more and more undesirables of the Reich could pass through the '*Arbeit Macht Frei*' gates, and be exterminated. The dramatic increase in the number of prisoners being directed to the camp had been the source of a lot of stress for Höss during the year, but the Birkenau camp relieved the problem of overcrowding. For the immediate future, the Soviet POWs were to serve as a valuable slave labour force, but once the Germans had won the war on the Eastern Front, the Russians could be disposed of and the Birkenau camp converted into a huge agricultural facility.

Chapter IV: Nemesis

At the beginning of 1942 the German Army faced a number of major disappointments in Russia. It became clear to Höss that *Operation Barbarossa*, the codename for the German invasion of the Soviet Union, had failed miserably, and that Germany would have to mobilise all of its resources in order to continue its war effort. With most able-bodied German men enlisted in the army, German industry was suffering from a dwindling pool of labour. The armament industry, which was pivotal to the war effort, was particularly undermanned, and as a result Russian slave labour came to be seen as too precious an asset to waste on camps like Auschwitz. All prisoners, including Russian POWs, were to be reassigned to the armament industry. Himmler's dream of amassing a vast Soviet labour force for his farming enterprise and construction programme in Auschwitz had to be postponed until the war in Russia was won. This change in policy would not affect the Birkenau POW camp, however, and construction proceeded as planned. In the absence of Russian POWs, Birkenau would be free to accommodate the Jews—who were now considered an even greater threat to the German nation.

Höss received regular reports on the policies being implemented against the Jews in the East, especially by members of the *Einsatzgruppen* (Operational Groups). Since the summer of 1941, Höss had been aware of Himmler's preparations for the mass deportation of Jews to the East. During the first cold weeks of January 1942, the commandant was still awaiting confirmation of any impending transports. By the end of the month, reports from Berlin confirmed that Himmler had sent a telegram to Glücks informing him that over 150,000 Jews were to be sent to the concentration camps. Though it was not specified at first how many Jews were to be dispatched to Auschwitz, Höss anticipated that the number would be significant.

The first shipment of Jews was a small transport from the Upper Silesian town of Bytom and it arrived in Auschwitz on 15 February 1942. The majority of the transport were elderly, and because they had already been deemed unfit for work they were immediately led to the camp's crematorium and killed.

Höss was concerned that by continuously sending scores of convicted criminals and unfit labourers to the crematorium, the already-overworked facility would buckle under the pressure. If they were to open Birkenau to a large influx of Jews then Auschwitz would undoubtedly have to improve its cremation facility. It had already been proposed that another crematorium be built in the base camp alongside the existing one. However, for Birkenau to really excel it would be far more beneficial to install a crematorium on site. Höss chaired a meeting with his staff concerning the proposal. If Jews were now to be shipped *en masse* to the concentration camps, then the camp would need the necessary equipment to dispose of those unable to work.

On Thursday, 27 February, Höss, SS architect Bischoff, and Kammler, held a meeting to discuss the pros and cons of constructing another crematorium at the base camp, or what was now being formally called '*Konzentrationslager* Auschwitz I'. During the meeting it was decided that plans for another crematorium at Auschwitz I would be relocated to the Birkenau camp. The plans had been drawn up the previous October and the crematorium was expected to arrive shortly. Höss announced that he had personally visited the camp in order to ascertain the perfect location for this facility. Scouring the far northwestern corner of the camp he had found an abandoned small brick cottage with a tiled roof. He settled on this cottage, known as Bunker I, and nicknamed 'the Little Red House', and resolved to have it converted as quickly as possible. Its windows and doors would be filled in with bricks, their edges sealed with felt in order to ensure they were airtight, and the interior gutted and divided into two rooms. The doors to both rooms were to have a sign placed over the entrance, reading '*Zur Desinfektion*' ('To Disinfection').

The crematorium at Birkenau was not burdened by the same problems as Auschwitz I. Those unfit for work could be quietly removed and exterminated in secrecy, causing the least amount of disturbance to the rest of the camp. Plans for the new facility at Bunker I were similar to those at the main camp but on a much grander scale.

Within a few weeks, work on Bunker I was completed and on 20 March the gas chamber was made operational. Höss received a communication from the RSHA in Berlin stating that a group of Jews from Upper Silesia, whom the SS authorities had pronounced unfit for work, had been selected for what was now being called 'special treatment'. Under the cover of darkness the Jews were transported directly to Birkenau. According to Höss:

> The transport was conducted by Aumeier and Palitzsch and some block leaders. They talked with the Jews about general topics, their qualifications and trades, with a view of misleading

them. On arrival at the 'Cottage', they were told to undress. At first they went calmly into the rooms where they were supposed to be disinfected. But some of them showed signs of panic. Immediately all the Jews still outside were pushed into the chambers and the doors screwed shut. At the first signs of unrest, those responsible were unobtrusively led behind the building and killed with a small-calibre gun, which was inaudible to the others. The presence and calm behaviour of the Special Detachment [*Sonderkommando*] served to reassure those who were worried or who suspected what was about to happen. A further calming effect was obtained by members of the Special Detachment accompanying them into the rooms and remaining there until the last moment, while an SS man also stood in the doorway until the end.[41]

Some of the elderly Jews began to panic as they were being led into the gas chambers, but aside from some minor scenes, Höss confirmed that the first gassing operation in Birkenau was a complete success. The majority of the Jews had calmly filed into 'the Little Red House' and no disruption had been caused to the normal operation of camp life. Though Höss had solved the problem of how to carry out the killings without attracting unwanted attention, there was still the outstanding problem of how to dispose of the corpses. With no crematorium in place on site, the best short-term solution was to bury the bodies in a nearby pit.

The first trainload of prisoners dispatched to Birkenau consisted of 999 German women, predominantly prostitutes and criminal prisoners, who had been deported from Ravensbrück camp. The second transport consisted of 999 able-bodied female Slovakian Jews. The train arrived in Auschwitz on 26 March 1942 and the Jews were unloaded just outside the station. For many of the prisoners who disembarked from the crammed cattle cars that day, the railway stop was very much like that of any other provincial railway station. Under the strict supervision of SS guards, *Kapos* and the local police, the prisoners were marched through the town of Auschwitz in the direction of the main camp. The SS ordered the Jews to run in groups of five. Those unable to run were simply gunned down on the spot. Birkenau was still under construction so Höss was forced to house the female Jews in the main camp, in ten specially adapted, walled-off barracks. The women were registered as Jewish political prisoners and were sent to a newly created sub-camp within Auschwitz. The following day the prisoners' heads were shaved and they were given old uniforms that had previously belonged to the Russian inmates. Nine thousand POWs had perished from hunger, illness, malnutrition and various other acts of brutality, so there was no shortage of uniforms for the new inmates. Housing the Slovakian Jews in the main camp proved an administrative nightmare for Höss. No proper preparations had been made for their arrival. The living conditions at the camp had greatly deteriorated and there were growing concerns that a typhus epidemic would break out.

Conditions at Birkenau were considerably worse than in the main camp. Birkenau had officially been in operation since early March and was now home to the remaining Soviet POWs, a number of German criminals, and 1,200 sick prisoners incarcerated in an area officially known as BA I—which had been designated for the accommodation of the Slovak transport.

That March, Birkenau camp turned into a quagmire. There was scarcely any water and practically no washing facilities and the weak and starving prisoners were living in absolute squalor. Despite these abysmal conditions, Höss was eager to send as many new prisoners to the camp as possible in order to alleviate the problem of overcrowding in Auschwitz I. The Birkenau site would soon be capable of accommodating thousands of inmates, a large percentage of whom would be Jews. All able-bodied Jews were considered valuable assets, whereas the unfit were quickly dispatched to Bunker I to receive 'special treatment'. Höss had been aware for some weeks now of new, harsher policies for dealing with the Jews. He received reports that other camps in Poland were under construction near the villages of Belzec, Sobibór and Treblinka, and they were to have their own crematoria. Jews would be the sole occupants of these camps. The future of these unfortunate people looked bleak.

* * * * *

During the spring of 1942, life for the Höss family was marred by Rudolf's ever-increasing workload. Hedwig had noticed that their relationship was gradually deteriorating and her husband was becoming more emotionally withdrawn by the day. With the children, however, Höss was as devoted and loving as ever. When he had a gap in his busy work schedule he was often seen cuddling the children and playing with them in their toy room. On warmer days he would sit in the garden with the family, watching the children run around the vegetable patch and between the conifers, shouting and screaming as they played. The villa's housekeeper, Aniela Bednarska, said of the garden:

> There was a garden shed. There were also two green plush couches and a round light table with chairs. The parquet floor was covered with a carpet. Under a wide window there was a long concrete flowerpot. On the walls of the house and the garden shed were pictures painted by Frau Höss's brother— Hentzel. They depicted views of the surroundings of Auschwitz, usually a castle and the Sola River.[42]

Höss often took his family down to the banks of the River Sola, which, depending on the season, was visible from the front window of the first floor of their house. At the river's edge, Hedwig would lay out a picnic and Höss would sometimes play in the water with the children. He enjoyed these precious moments with his family, but they only ever momentarily obscured the mammoth workload that awaited him back at the camp. Hedwig and the children were relatively content with life at Auschwitz. The staff employed at the villa were reliable and friendly, and they generally found that the children, with the exception of Klaus, were happy to see them. SS-*Untersturmführer* Georg Gussregen's housekeeper wrote, 'almost everything in the Höss house and garden was done by the prisoners'. She remembered little Klaus vividly.

> The boy was about ten years old... He was naughty and malicious. An SS man and a prisoner taught him to ride horses. He used to carry a small horsewhip and beat the prisoners at the house with it. He always sought the opportunity to kick or hit a prisoner.[43]

According to Höss's housekeeper Aniela Bednarska:

> Klaus was a great ignoramus, he had no interests. He went to schools in Auschwitz, Pszczyna, Kattowitz, but was expelled from all of them. His father gave him an accordion to arouse his interests, but Klaus wasn't interested even in music. He was the type of a future SS man. The rest of the children were calm, they used to hang around the prisoners and watch them work.[44]

Despite her loathing of Klaus, Aniela liked Hedwig and the rest of the children. She recalled that:

> Frau Höss's attitude towards me was loyal. In the beginning she tried to persuade me to sign the family guest book, but when I refused she never troubled me with it again.[45]

Hedwig was always very helpful around the house, particularly with the cooking.

> The food was simple, Frau Höss prepared it herself and I helped her. In her absence I did all the cooking on my own. The food wasn't rationed for me so I shared it with the prisoners. I was often hungry because of this.[46]

Aniela Bednarska also described Höss as a very loyal person.

> Höss was very loyal both towards me as housekeeper and to the gardeners. On his birthday, and on more important holidays, he would go to the garden and treat the gardeners with food from a basket he himself used to prepare, adding even a bottle of beer for each of them.[47]

Bronislaw Jaron, Roman Kwiatkowski, and Stanislaw Dubiel were all employed as gardeners at the house.* Dubiel had been in Auschwitz since November 1940. He wrote:

> [I]... worked as a gardener from almost the very beginning, first for *Lagerführer* Fritzsch, who occupied the post until the end of 1941, and then for his successor *Lagerführer* Aumeier, who took the post in early 1942, after Fritzsch had been transferred to Flossenbürg. On 6 April 1942 I was sent to the house of camp commandant Rudolf Höss... During the time when I was working in Höss's garden and household I had the opportunity to observe both him and his family... Frau Höss, for whom I used to grow the finest flowers both in the garden and the greenhouse, was never satisfied with what I was able to grow using the camp's resources. She used to send SS men to the house of Roman Kwiatkowski from Bedzin, a fellow prisoner working with me in the garden, to bring her the seeds and cuttings she had ordered. Sometimes Kwiatkowski's sons had to deliver her plants.[48]

Höss often visited the garden department in Rajsk to place orders with *Rottenführer* Hartung.

> [He would order]... thousands of pots, seeds, cuttings and vegetables as winter supplies. He did this in secret so the boss of the camp agricultural economy [director of the camp farm

---

* Bronislaw Jaron had been a biologist and professor of the Jagiellonian University in Krakow. He was taken to Block 11 and executed by firing squad on Good Friday, 3 April 1942.

SS-*Obersturmbannführer* Joachim] Caesar wouldn't find out. Every winter I had to organise with some friends 70 tonnes of coke to heat the house and especially the greenhouses.[49]

When Dubiel was working in the garden or inside the house, he saw Höss quite regularly.

Höss often used to come home during the day. Very often he went by horse or other means of transport around the whole area of the camp, checking everything. He was interested in everything that was going on in the camp. He spent minimal amounts of time in his office. Case records, which required his signature, were brought to his home. He often hosted various SS dignitaries at his home.[50]

Dubiel vividly remembered many of the guests who spent time at the villa.

Among Höss's guests were also *Obergruppenführer* Schmauser, and also a few times, I think five times, the boss of the Economics and Administrative Department of the SS—*Obergruppenführer* Pohl. The atmosphere was very cordial whenever Pohl visited Höss. You could see that they were very good friends. We had the impression that Höss gave Pohl some gifts. Höss and his wife held wonderful parties whenever someone visited them. At Frau Höss's command I was supposed to 'organise' the food they needed for this purpose. Before every party Frau Höss would tell me what she needed or she asked me to speak about it with Zofia, the cook. She never gave me any money or food cards which were normally required to purchase groceries. So I got in touch with my friend Adolf Maciejewski who was a *Kapo* in the food warehouse for prisoners and he in turn contacted me with the boss of his warehouse, SS-*Unterscharführer* Schybek, from whom I collected every week food rations for the women prisoners working in Höss's household.[51]

Although Dubiel considered his position as the Höss's gardener to be one of the best jobs in the camp, he lived in constant fear that one day he would be dragged from his sleeping quarters in the middle of the night and executed. In fact, his fears were very nearly realised, but according to Dubiel the commandant saved his life.

With 172 other prisoners I was taken out of the block to the office, from which we were to be directed to the yard of Block 11. Höss ordered them to release me so that I could come back to work. In the afternoon of the same day, Grabner came with Hessler and Höss's aide-de-camp to Höss's garden, where I was working, and demanded from Höss to give me away for execution. Höss and especially Frau Höss were strongly opposed to my execution and got their own way... Frau Höss often reminded me about the incident thus forcing me to be zealous in doing whatever she asked me to do... I'd like to stress that neither Höss nor his wife interceded for me. They were both fierce enemies of Poles and Jews. They hated everything that was Polish. Frau Höss often used to say to me that all Jews had to disappear from the globe, and there would even come a time for English Jews.[52]

According to Aniela Bednarska, the Höss villa also employed two German women called Eryka and Elfryda.

They were assigned by the Labour Service to have a six-month training in housekeeping and then to work another six months in the fields. They lived in the attic of the Höss house doing the same work as me. I was assigned a room in Zasole, in a house turned into a school for German children. After half a year, when the two German women left Auschwitz, I started living in the attic of the Höss's house, still having the flat in the school at my disposal. Stoves were altered in the house during my first year of work for Höss and the central heating was installed a year later. Rooms were fixed up in the attic and an arbour was built.[53]

Aniela also recalled another prisoner, named Wilhelm Kmak, who had worked at the Höss residence.

> He was a painter and came from Grybow, near Tarnow. He was very shrewd. He often used to come to Höss's house to paint the walls destroyed by the children who scratched and drew on them.[54]

Another employee at the villa, called Janina Szczurak, remembered Wilhelm Kmak quite clearly. She recalled that he often carried out his work painstakingly slowly and would implore the other staff not to prevent the children from drawing on the walls. Janina was a registered dressmaker who worked from home 'with the help of some of my apprentices'.[55] Hedwig paid a visit to Janina's flat to offer her employment at the villa.

> I don't know how she obtained my address but it was probably from the labour exchange where I was registered as a dressmaker... I did not know I was dealing with the wife of the concentration camp commandant at Auschwitz, but I could not refuse the offer. It was not until I was given the address I realised where it was. Initially I felt very frightened to go there alone, so one of my apprentices came along with me to make me feel safe... I often sewed for Frau Höss, and she would even make me do her ironing. When I used to finish my day's work and was returning home Angela [Aniela Bednarska], on Frau Höss's orders, would pick a bunch of flowers in the garden for me to take home... Frau Höss was loyal to us. She kept no strict watch over us when we were working in the house. The Höss's children, with the exception of Klaus, never minded us working there. They used to run about the garden playing and watch the prisoners working. One day they came to me and asked me to sew them armbands with badges similar to what the prisoners wore... Klaus put on the armband of a *Kapo*, and for the other children I sewed triangles of different colours on their clothes. The children were very happy, but as they ran about playing they met their father, who immediately tore off their badges

and took them inside. I was not punished but asked not to do it again.[56]

Of all the staff employed at the villa, Höss and Hedwig found the German Bible students, or Jehovah's Witnesses, to be the most trustworthy and caring. They were particularly impressed by the love and consideration they showed towards the children, and the children were clearly very fond of them in return. Höss was fascinated by the Jehovah's Witnesses and of all the prisoners in the camp he liked them the best. The first time he had come into contact with them was while he was working in the Sachsenhausen camp. A number of Jehovah's Witnesses had been incarcerated in the camp for refusing to enlist in the military. Höss found their religious beliefs intriguing and he marvelled at their ability to remain so calm and content in spite of the fate that awaited them. Many of the other SS officers shared Höss's fondness for the German Jehovah's Witnesses and they were considered the perfect house servants.

Aside from the Jehovah's Witnesses employed in the villa, Höss was particularly fond of another member of staff. Her name was Eleonore Hodys and her camp number was 223. She was an Austrian political prisoner who had arrived at Auschwitz in one of the first female transports. Her classification as a citizen of the German Reich meant that she was eligible to work as a servant for SS officers. In April she was offered a job in the villa. Eleonore remembered the first time she met Höss.

He [Höss] or the *Hauptsturmführer* Schwarz used to ask the newcomers if there were typists amongst them, whatever their profession. I gave mine as a helper of a pharmacy. The medical doctor Van Brodemann wanted to have me for the hospital. Höss then let secretary Langenfels give me a room all to myself in Block 4. A few days later I was ordered by *Obersturmführer* Mueller to the commandant's house because an artisan was wanted. I was received in the house by the commandant's wife, who in the hall showed me a carpet and asked me if I could mend it. I undertook the job and worked at it for two days. During this time I saw the commandant coming and going. He asked me if I were Hodys and then remarked that he would not normally employ a political prisoner in his house, but his wife had various jobs for me. I then prepared two tapestries, a tapestry cushion in silk, a car rug, and various blankets. I liked to work in the commandant's house, as far as keeping up of the entrance lists allowed me the time. I still spent the night in camp. As long as I worked in the house, I was fed there. I ate alone in a room and had the same food as the commandant. The food consisted of soup, entree, meat, vegetables, and pastries or cakes, fruit, salad and coffee. It was extremely good and compared favourably with the menu of a big hotel in peace time. The two Jewish tailor girls who worked in the house got the same food. These two girls worked from 1942 onwards.[57]

In time Höss began to show an increasing interest in Eleonore. He often visited her when he knew she was working and conversed with her in a warm and friendly manner— something he had never done with any of the other inmates in the camp. It wasn't long before Eleonore began to notice the attention the commandant was paying her.

It did not strike me at first but my fellow prisoners soon drove to my notice to the fact that the commandant was strikingly interested in me. The commandant had me called to him each time he came into the camp, or he came personally to the place where I worked. He talked of business, but laughed at the same time in a particular way. I answered in the same way because I must confess that I liked him as a man. Apart from the frequent business talks, he did all he could to favour me and make my detention much easier. In the first room which I occupied there were three other women. The commandant got to hear about my situation and ordered Aumeier to prepare a special room for me on the floor of Block 4. I could decorate this with my own furniture and real carpets. On weekends I got a furlough on parole and could also move about freely in the town of Auschwitz, and could stay out the night. In these cases I used to sleep in the buildings of the staff, outside the camp. The commandant also saw me often smoke, which was forbidden to prisoners, and never said anything. When I wanted to hide the cigarette, he told me not to trouble. I also got permission to have a personal cook and a maid for my personal needs ... On my birthday, a special feast was organised for me in the commandant's house. The people in the camp believed at first that I was related to the commandant and asked me about it. The commandant expressed his particular feelings for me for the first time in May 1942. His wife was out and I was in his villa, sitting by the radio. Without a word, he came over and kissed me. I was so surprised and frightened and ran away and locked myself in the toilet. There were too many obstacles between him and me on account of his position and the fact that he was married. From then on, I did not come to the commandant's house anymore. I reported myself as sick and tried to hide from him whenever he asked for me. Though he succeeded time and again in finding me, he never spoke about the kiss. I only ever visited the house twice more, by order.[58]

Höss found the rejection very humiliating, especially considering his rank and position and the fact that Eleonore was a prisoner. But it was not just with Eleonore that Höss was experiencing personal difficulties. His marriage to Hedwig had become strained, and he even suspected that she was having an affair. Aniela Bednarska recalled Hedwig being very friendly with a *Kapo* called Karol Böhner.

He was German and was always in the house, usually cleaning shoes or frying fish. He behaved freely and had no number or designation. He was Frau Höss's friend, therefore when Höss returned home unexpectedly one day and found them together in the garden there was an enormous row. Frau Höss managed to calm him down, but I never saw Böhner in the villa again. I know he was a canteen manager in a shoe factory in Chelmek. Frau Höss often went there when her husband was away.[59]

Whatever personal problems Höss was experiencing during the summer of 1942, he still managed to devote his undivided attention to the camp. In early June, he was summoned to Berlin for an important meeting with the *Reichsführer*. His adjutant, SS-*Obersturmführer* Edmund Brauning, was left in charge of Auschwitz I. Upon arriving at the SS headquarters in Berlin, Höss was admitted to Himmler's office. The two men exchanged the usual warm greetings and pleasantries, before conversation turned to more official matters. The *Reichsführer* informed Höss that he would have to begin preparing Auschwitz for the mass annihilation of Jews.

The *Führer* has ordered that the Jewish question be solved once and for all and that we, the SS, are to implement that order. The existing extermination centres in the East are not in a position to carry out the large actions which are anticipated. I have therefore earmarked Auschwitz for this purpose, both because of its good position as regards to communications and because the area can easily be isolated and camouflaged. At first I thought of calling in a senior officer for this job, but I have changed my mind... I have now decided to entrust this task to you. It is difficult and onerous and calls for complete devotion notwithstanding the difficulties that may arise. You will learn further details from *Sturmbannführer* Eichmann of the Reich Security Main Office who will call on you in the immediate future... You will treat this order as absolutely secret, even from your superiors. After you talk with Eichmann you will forward me the plans of the projected installations. The Jews are the sworn enemies of the German people and must be eradicated. Every Jew that we can lay our hands on is to be destroyed now during the war without exception. If we cannot now obliterate the biological basis of Jewry, the Jews will one day destroy the German people.[60]

While Höss was not surprised by the nature of Himmler's order, he was astounded by the magnitude of what was expected of him. He wrote:

> I did not have the slightest idea of their scale or consequences. It was certainly an extraordinary and monstrous order. Nevertheless the reasons behind the extermination programme seemed to me right. I did not reflect on it at the time: I had been given an order and I had to carry it out. Whether this mass extermination of the Jews was necessary or not was something on which I could not allow myself to form an opinion, for I lacked the necessary breadth of view. If the *Führer* had himself given the order for the 'final solution of the Jewish question', then, for a veteran National Socialist, and even more so for an SS officer, there could be no question of considering its merits. 'The *Führer* commands, we follow' was never a mere phrase or slogan. It was meant in bitter earnest.[61]

Höss had known for some time now the fate that awaited the Jews. He had even prophesised on a number of occasions in the past that the Jews would one day disappear from Europe. Höss may have been loyal to his superiors, but he was also a pragmatist. Taking into account the scarcity of transport in the Reich, moving millions of Jews East for no other reason than to murder them seemed extreme. This plan seemed all the more senseless considering the fact that German industry was crying out for manpower. However, Höss saw Himmler's decree as binding and he felt compelled to put his own personal feelings on the matter aside. The possibility that he could actually stop and question an order was not something that had ever occurred to him. As part of the phalanx of the SS, he had been trained to blindly follow all orders issued to him. Yet he had taken his training one step further than that of the stereotypical automatous SS soldier. Since the summer of 1941, Höss had been using his innovation to improve upon the efficiency of the Auschwitz camp, and he had helped to implement the gas chambers that had revolutionised mass executions. He was relieved that the experiment involving the Soviet POWs had been a success and that the gas chambers could now be used for the mass extermination of the Jews.

Höss returned to Auschwitz in his new role as an executive recruit for the mass murder of Jews. He knew that his orders from Himmler were barbaric and it was for that reason that they were to remain strictly confidential. Any lingering feelings of compassion would have to be quelled if he was to carry out his orders. He looked on the extermination of the Jews as merely another administrative procedure. He saw his position in the camp as being similar to that of a factory director, charged with cataloguing the quality of materials before they could be processed through the plant. Glücks and Himmler requested that Höss maintain careful records of all that happened in the camp and that he send them regular progress reports.

* * * * *

Höss invested every ounce of his energy into making Auschwitz a success. He had been assigned a gargantuan task but he knew that if he succeeded his prize would be further praise and respect from his superiors.

Höss didn't utter a single word about his secret meeting with the *Reichsführer* to Hedwig. Although his family had been indoctrinated to hate Jews, the concept of mass murder would have shocked most anti-Semites. Höss was determined to carry on as normal at the villa. He tried to compartmentalise his life and thereby prevent the daily horrors of the camp from spilling over into his private life. He regularly brought stacks of paperwork home with him, but for the most part he kept as much distance as possible between his life as commandant and that of a loving husband and father.

No sooner had Höss returned from Berlin than he was making preparations for further gassings. Mass murder quickly became a part of his daily routine. He maintained regular contact with Eichmann, who was already arranging for the deportation of Jewish families to unknown destinations in the East. Those unfit for work were weeded out from the able-bodied and sent to Belzec camp to be gassed under the 14f13 programme. Höss was informed that Bunker I was to continue to function in a similar manner to the crematorium in the main camp. Those convicted by the *Gestapo* summary court were executed in the main camp at the 'wall of death', a cement wall covered in tar, which lay in the courtyard between Blocks 10 and 11.

Throughout the spring and summer, Bunker I, together with Crematorium I in the main camp, continued to operate, disposing of convicted criminals and those unfit for work. On 11 June, Crematorium I was used to gas a group of prisoners who had attempted the first mass escape from the camp. According to *Lagerführer* Aumeier, a number of prisoners from a penal company that had been responsible for digging the drainage ditches at Birkenau, charged at the SS guards and attempted to overpower them and escape through a fence. Although nine succeeded, thirteen were shot on the spot. The remaining prisoners were herded together and driven back into the camp. The enraged Aumeier proceeded to shoot 17 of them in cold blood; SS-*Hauptsturmführer* Franz Hössler shot a further three. In an effort to discourage other prisoners from making similar escape attempts, Höss decided to severely punish the remaining inmates of the penal company—he ordered that an additional 20 be executed at Block 11, and the remaining 320 inmates were marched off to Crematoria I

Whilst the corpses of the inmates from the penal company were being incinerated, Höss contemplated the future of Birkenau's killing facility. During early June, Bunker I had been used to kill an ever-increasing number of prisoners but Höss was still not satisfied with its efficiency. Höss called a meeting with SS-*Sturmbannführer* Karl Bischoff and other members of the Auschwitz Construction Office, to discuss plans to convert a second cottage, known as the 'Little White House', into what was termed 'a bathing facility for special actions'. At the end of June this peaceful-looking house, which became known as Bunker II, commenced operation. The interior of the cottage comprised four narrow gas chambers. With an improved ventilation system and a killing capacity of around 1,200 people at a time, Höss was sure that Birkenau would now be more efficient than ever before. Further Jewish transports were earmarked for Auschwitz as the finishing touches were applied to Bunker II. Höss appeared visibly more confident in front of his staff. He felt that yet again his hard work and initiative had paid off, and he hoped that his efforts would attract the recognition of his superiors.

On 4 July the first transport of Jews, numbering approximately one thousand, arrived at Birkenau and was submitted for selection. Höss was present for their arrival, along with SS-*Sturmbannführer Lagerführer* Hans Aumeier and his new adjutant SS-*Hauptsturmführer* Robert Karl Ludwig Mulka. The transport was unloaded at the side of the road near the entrance to Birkenau. Aumeier wrote:

> Upon arrival of the transport, the prisoners were divided by male and female. Those children up to the age of 14 stayed with their mother in the women's camp, and those over 14 years old with their fathers in the men's camp. [62]

In total, 108 able-bodied women and 264 able-bodied men were selected for work, and the remaining 638 people were sent to the barracks where they were ordered to undress before continuing on to the gas chambers. Höss wrote:

> In front of the farmhouse they all had to undress behind specially erected screens. On the doors were the inscriptions 'Disinfection Room'. The SS subalterns on duty had the order to tell these people, with the help of interpreters, that they should take proper care of their belongings so that they might

find them again immediately after de-lousing. These measures were intended to avoid any disquiet.[63]

The majority of the time no such incidents occurred.

> It was most important that when they arrived the entire procedure of undressing should take place in an atmosphere of the greatest possible calm. People reluctant to undress were helped by those that had already undressed, or by men of the *Sonderkommando*.[64]

The victims were told that they were being sent to bathe and delouse. Once they had been crammed inside the gas chamber and the doors closed behind them, SS-*Unterscharführer* Moll, wearing a special white protective suit and gasmask, poured the saturated Zyklon B pellets into the chamber through a small vent, and then waited roughly 25 minutes for the desperate screams of those fighting for their lives to subside. During the procedure, SS surgeons and an SS hospital orderly were on standby with oxygen apparatuses to revive the guards in the event of any of them inhaling toxic levels of the gases. Once the guards were certain that all the victims in the chamber were dead, the doors and windows were thrown open and the rooms were ventilated. The tangled corpses were later removed for disposal by the *Sonderkommandos*.

Höss regularly oversaw the arrival of transports to the camp, and he became morbidly fascinated with the process. He watched as the selections were carried out at the unloading ramps and witnessed firsthand the harrowing scenes of families being pried apart as the men were separated from the women and children.

> [I saw how the]... *Sonderkommando* lied to them and how they emphasised these lies with convincing words and gestures... The women tried to hide their babies because they thought the disinfection process would harm their infants. The little children cried mostly because of the unusual setting in which

they were being undressed. But after their mothers or the *Sonderkommando* encouraged them, they calmed down and continued playing, teasing each other, clutching a toy as they went into the gas chamber… I watched how some women who suspected or knew what was happening, even with the fear of death all over their faces, still managed enough strength to play with their children and to talk to them lovingly. Once a woman with four children, all holding each other by the hand to help the smallest ones over the rough ground, passed by me very slowly. She stepped very close to me and whispered, pointing to her four children, 'How can you murder these beautiful, darling children? Don't you have any heart?'[65]

This incident clearly affected Höss but he was careful to conceal his emotions. He perfected a look of cold indifference as he watched each procession solemnly march to their deaths. Occasionally, a wave of panic might wash over the prisoners and distressing scenes would break out. People would start screaming uncontrollably while they were undressing, clutching at their hair and pulling lumps of it out. Höss described how they handled such outbursts.

They were led behind the farmhouse and killed by a bullet in the back of the neck from a small-calibre pistol. Sometimes, as the *Sonderkommando* were leaving the room, the women realised their fate and began hurling all kinds of curses at us. As the doors were being shut, I saw a woman trying to shove her children out of the chamber, crying out, 'Why don't you at least let my precious children live?' There were many heartbreaking scenes like this which affected all who were present.[66]

Höss felt he had to prove to the guards that he was willing to be 'present at whatever task I ordered my men to perform'.[67] He wrote:

I had to experience the mass murder and to coldly watch it without any regard for the doubts which uprooted my deepest inner feelings.[68]

It was inevitable that such harrowing scenes would eventually take their toll on the commandant. From the time of the first mass extermination at the camp he became increasingly distant and unhappy. Not only had he been given the deplorable task of annihilation, but he was also expected to organise the burials of all those killed in Bunker I and II. He knew that burying the bodies was an impractical method of disposal but for the time being he had no other alternative. Literally thousands of bodies from both cottages were disposed of in this manner. They were loaded onto carts and the *Sonderkommandos* pushed them to the pits along special railway tracks. Powdered lime was scattered over the bodies as they lay in the pits and they were then covered over with soil.

* * * * *

In July, Höss was informed that the *Reichsführer* was preparing to make an important visit to the Auschwitz camp. The news of his visit was received with a mixture of apprehension and tension. Höss did not intend to tell his boss about the threat of a typhus outbreak that currently hung over the camp, so he instructed his guards to conceal the unsanitary conditions as best they could. In preparation for Himmler's visit, Höss ensured that the main camp was in order and that the able-bodied prisoners were given new uniforms to make them look more presentable.

On the day of the visit, the camp's orchestra awaited the *Reichsführer* at the main gate. Höss journeyed to the Kattowitz airfield where he was met by *Gauleiter* Fritz Bracht and Higher SS and Police Leader, Ernst-Heinrich Schmauser. Together, they awaited the arrival of Himmler's flight from the Friedrichsruh airport in Lötzen, East Prussia. When he landed, Höss and the rest of the entourage boarded a heavily protected motorcade for the one-hour return journey to Auschwitz. As the cars approached the camp, the orchestra began playing the 'Triumph March' from Verdi's *Aida*. Himmler seemed very impressed with the music and stood listening to the band for a few moments before continuing on with Höss and his entourage, which included the architect Kammler, for a meeting in the officers' club. During the meeting, Höss showed Himmler maps and diagrams of the camps and gave him a progress report on the present conditions at Auschwitz-Birkenau. After the meeting, Himmler, Höss and the rest of the entourage took a tour of the main camp, which had changed considerably since the *Reichsführer's* last visit in March 1941.

Later, they visited the farms and soil-enrichment projects, the dam-building site, the laboratories and the surrounding farms. In fact, over the course of a couple of hours they toured 25 square miles of the Auschwitz Zone of Interest. One place that they visited, which had not been included in Himmler's appointment book, was Birkenau. Standing at the entrance to the camp, the *Reichsführer* requested a situation report on the whole area, including plans of the layout of the swamp-reclamation and water projects. He also demanded to see a report on the Birkenau expansion project.

By July, the Birkenau site had been completely transformed, with several drainage ditches already completed and many of the barracks assembled. But the camp still resembled a building site. Construction of the first sector, known as BI, which was intended for the accommodation of 20,000 inmates, was finished. Adjacent to this area, and still under construction, were sectors II and III. These sectors would soon be capable of accommodating more than 60,000 prisoners. Although Himmler remained silent during the tour of the site, he was clearly impressed. He showed particular interest in the drainage and sewage works that gangs of emaciated inmates were in the process of constructing. Walking around the site he could see for himself the terrible overcrowding of the barracks and the primitive conditions the prisoners were forced to endure. He took the time to watch the prisoners at work and to inspect the kitchens and sick bays. In the overcrowded sick bays, where conditions were at their worst, the camp doctor admitted to Himmler that the health of many of the previously able-bodied prisoners was rapidly deteriorating and the spread of disease was spiralling out of control. Whether bad planning, poor design or sheer incompetence was to blame, the sewage and washing facilities needed to be improved upon rapidly before disease wiped out the few remaining fit inmates.

As they continued their tour of the camp, Höss emphasised the difficulties he was facing in acquiring construction materials. But Himmler snapped at the commandant, accusing him of suffering from a profanely negative attitude. He curtly warned him that he didn't want to hear any more complaints. As commandant, it was his job to overcome any problems that arose.

Having inspected the Birkenau camp, Himmler announced the second important reason for his visit—he wished to witness the process of 'special treatment' in operation. Early that summer the *Reichsführer* had assumed direct control of the RSHA and he was determined to demonstrate a high level of competence and ability in his new role as the architect of genocide. For the first time in his murderous career he was to witness the complete process of extermination being carried out. Höss led the company to the railway spur which was adjacent to the main line. Here, the *Reichsführer* watched the selection of a new Jewish transport that had been sent from the Netherlands. Those physically able to work were spared, while those considered unfit were loaded onto trucks and brought directly to the Birkenau gas chamber for 'special treatment'. Himmler and Höss watched the completion of this process take place at Bunker II. The *Reichsführer* looked on in complete silence, but Höss noted that he seemed more interested in observing the reactions of others around him— the officers, the NCOs and Höss himself—than watching the killings being carried out. Afterwards, Himmler and Höss said very little to one another as they left the camp.

During the early evening the guests and camp officers of Auschwitz attended a formal dinner. Höss wrote:

> Himmler asked everyone to introduce themselves before dinner. Those he was interested in, he enquired about their families and various duties they performed. During dinner he questioned me more closely about some of the officers that particularly caught his attention. I took the opportunity and explained my needs concerning staffing. I outlined that there were quite a number of officers unable to run the concentration camp properly and their poor leadership among many of the guard troops. I also asked him to replace many of them and increase the number of guard troops.[69]

Himmler increased the guard units by introducing special guard dog squads. He was very concerned with the number of successful Auschwitz escapees and he categorically insisted that future breaks for freedom be stamped out at all costs.

After the SS dinner, Höss and Hedwig were invited to spend the evening with the *Reichsführer* at *Gauleiter* Bracht's residence. Also present was Schmauser, Kammler and the director of the camp farm, SS-*Obersturmbannführer* Joachim Caesar. According to Höss, Himmler had been in a bad mood all day but by evening time he appeared to be in good spirits again. In between smoking and drinking several glasses of red wine, he engaged in lively conversation with Frau Bracht and Hedwig. He was charming and talkative and discussed various topics of conversation with them, including raising children, new houses, paintings and books. He even recounted stories from his time in the *Waffen*-SS, and spoke of the frontline inspections he had embarked on with the *Führer*. Höss noticed that Himmler deliberately avoided making any reference to the day's events or any other matters concerning official business. Bracht's attempts to steer the conversation in that direction were completely ignored by the *Reichsführer*. Bracht was not a man who could hold his tongue for long though. Back at the villa, Hedwig told Höss that she had found herself alone with Bracht at one stage during the evening and he had taken the opportunity to drop hints to her about the terrible work being carried out in the camp. She conceded that she had already heard rumours from other people, but she wanted '*Rudi*' to confirm whether or not they were true. Höss reluctantly admitted that the rumours were indeed true and that he had received direct orders from the *Reichsführer* to cleanse Europe of Jews by exterminating them in gas chambers. According to Höss, Hedwig 'thought it was cruel, but nothing could be done about it'.[70]

After breakfast the following morning, Höss and Schmauser called to Bracht's house to collect Himmler. The *Reichsführer* informed the men that he wished to revisit the camp but this time he didn't want to be chaperoned. Following a lengthy inspection, he called to Höss's office for a final meeting. Himmler told the commandant that although it was clear that the camp was overcrowded and suffering from various other problems, he would have to struggle on. He informed Höss that he had already authorised a major expansion of the Birkenau camp to allow Eichmann to escalate his Jewish deportation programme. Gypsies would also be shipped to Birkenau, and anyone unfit for labour was to be exterminated along with the Jews. Himmler reassured Höss that work camps near the industrial factories would take large numbers of able-bodied Jews, allowing Höss the time and space to reorganise. He also instructed him that the war-production facilities at Auschwitz were to be completed as soon as possible. Himmler added that Kammler would do his best to support Höss during the construction programme. He concluded the meeting by praising Höss's accomplishments to date, and making the surprise announcement that Höss was being promoted to the rank of *Obersturmbannführer*. Höss was deeply honoured; his promotion was one of the proudest moments of his life.

Before their departure to the nearby I.G. Farben plant, Himmler asked to visit the villa. Höss wrote:

> He [Himmler] made an inspection of my home and its furnishings. He was very enthusiastic about it and talked at length with my wife and the children. He was excited and in high spirits.[71]

Later, as the two men were leaving the villa, they paused for a moment in the garden. Stanislaw Dubiel, the gardener, was standing nearby and he overheard the commandant telling Himmler:

> ...that he was certain that through all his work in Auschwitz he was doing his country a big favour.[72]

Soon afterwards the two men, accompanied by their entourage, set out for Monowitz. The *Reichsführer* seemed thoroughly impressed during the tour of the enormous I.G. Farben site.

After the Buna works, they visited the wastewater-treatment plant. Already tons of untreated sewage was flowing from Birkenau into the Vistula and Sola rivers. Himmler was conscious of the insanitary conditions in the camp and he was growing increasingly concerned that illness and disease would engulf the Auschwitz Zone of Interest. During the tour, Himmler suggested to Höss that a sewage plant should be built at Birkenau. He warned the commandant that sooner or later the problem of pollution in the camp would have to be tackled. Already 107,000 corpses had been buried in Birkenau and they were now decomposing and polluting the ground water. Himmler informed Höss that the only course of action available to him was to disinter these corpses and burn them on specially constructed grills.

Above: Rudolf Höss is interrogated by a member of British Intelligence days after his capture in March 1946. [Courtesy of the Yad Vashem Museum]

Left: Höss is paraded in front of the press following his capture by the British 92 Field Security Section. [Courtesy of the Yad Vashem Museum]

Above: This photograph was taken during the winter of 1943-1944 and shows the prefabricated wooden stable barracks at B II of the Birkenau camp. [Courtesy of the Auschwitz-Birkenau Museum]

Below: The construction of Crematorium IV taken by SS-man Kamann in late 1942. The architects signed off on Crematorium IV on 22 March 1943, without having time to test the incinerators. After two weeks of intensive use, the double four-muffle furnace cracked. The incinerator was decommissioned in May 1943. [Courtesy of the Auschwitz-Birkenau Museum]

Above: The SS held a number of comradeship meetings to try and encourage a sense of solidarity amongst the men. Here, they are singing along to an accordion at Solahuette in the summer of 1944.

Pictured in the front row are Karl Höcker, Otto Moll, Rudolf Höss, Richard Baer, Josef Kramer (standing slightly behind Franz Hössler and partially obscured), Franz Hössler, and Josef Mengele.
[Courtesy of USHMM Archives]

Left: Relaxing among female company and an unidentified officer, Rudolf Höss is pictured wearing a white suit.
[Courtesy of the Yad Vashem Museum]

Above: Hungarian Jews line up on the ramp inside Birkenau in the summer of 1944. The sexes were separated, with men on one side and women on the other, as preparations for the infamous selections began. [Courtesy of the Auschwitz-Birkenau Museum]

A photograph taken by the author at Auschwitz I. A sign reads 'Beware. High-Tension Electric Fence, Danger to Life.' On the left are prisoner block houses.
[Courtesy of the HITM Archive and the Auschwitz-Birkenau Museum]

Above: Pictured left to right at Auschwitz: Dr Eduard Wirths, Dr Enno Lölling, Commandant Richard Baer, Adjutant Karl Höcker and Rudolf Höss, after the formal handing over of the new SS hospital at Auschwitz.
[Courtesy of USHMM Archives]

Left: A decorated Rudolf Höss pictured with Commandant Baer and Karl Höcker after the handing over of the new SS hospital.
[Courtesy of USHMM Archives]

During the summer of 1944, SS officers socialised at an SS retreat at Solahuette, near Auschwitz. Above: Richard Baer, Dr Josef Mengele, and Rudolf Höss.

Right: Rudolf Höss and Josef Kramer. [All pictures on this page courtesy of USHMM Archives]

This photograph was taken at Solahuette, a resort which hosted social functions and formal ceremonies for the SS officers stationed at Auschwitz. It was taken at a pivotal time—the period during which Höss was directing the extermination of the Hungarian Jews.

From left to right: Richard Baer, Dr Josef Mengele, Josef Kramer, Rudolf Höss, and an unidentified officer.

Above: On the afternoon of Saturday, 27 January 1945, soldiers of the 60th Army of the First Ukrainian Front liberated Auschwitz. In total, some 5,800 weak and malnourished prisoners were freed from Birkenau.
[Courtesy of the Auschwitz-Birkenau Museum]

Left: A despondent Rudolf Höss arrives in Auschwitz in May 1946, having been extradited to Poland by the British to stand trial for war crimes. The former commandant was greeted by a flurry of press when he arrived at the airport.
[Courtesy of Yad Vashem Museum]

The Höss family residence as it stands today. On the right of the house is the garden and on the left is the private entrance used by Höss. The commandant's office can be seen behind a tree and a row of conifers. [Courtesy of the HITM Archive and the Auschwitz-Birkenau Museum]

Höss later drove Himmler to the airport, and spent the return journey to Auschwitz consumed by dread at the thought of disinterring all the corpses. June and July had been particularly hot months in Poland and during the first week of July the corpses had begun to putrefy. The smell of rotting flesh gradually rose to the surface and caused a terrible stench to spread across the camp. Plagues of rats had been seen gnawing at the corpse and the first cases of typhus had been diagnosed in the communal camp of the civilian workers who had been deployed to Birkenau.

Back at the camp, Höss decided to visit the burial site. The smell was nauseating, with scattered traces of bodily fluids contributing to the overall stench. Swarms of flies had formed a thick black mist over the area. The commandant was disgusted by the horror that he himself had orchestrated. He decided to call a meeting to discuss the immediate implementation of an open-air cremation pit.

Work on the pit commenced soon after. A massive hole was excavated in the ground and wooden beams, serving as a grill, were laid horizontally at ground level. This makeshift crematorium would suffice until a proper one could be installed at the camp.

The *Sonderkommandos* were given the task of operating both the crematorium and gas chambers, and disinterring the bodies with their bare hands. The group consisted of around 400 inmates. The nauseating stench caused many of them to cover their mouths and noses with handkerchiefs and rags as they unearthed the blood-soaked soil. A fire was ignited using wood and petrol, and the corpses were simply thrown into what became an enormous pyre of burning rags, flesh and bone. It was a horrible sight to behold. Höss wrote:

During the first cremations in the open air we were unable to continue this procedure. During bad weather or when there was a strong wind blowing, the stench from the burning flesh was carried miles into the surrounding area. This noticeably caused many people in the area, in spite of our counter-propaganda, to talk about the burning of the Jews. Although the SS were sworn to secrecy about the exterminations, the deterrent from severe punishments did not stop them talking.[73]

According to Höss, even the anti-aircraft defences protested against the open-air burnings 'because they were easily detected from great distances at night. Nevertheless, the burnings continued, even during the night.'[74]

While the prisoners dug up the bodies and threw them onto the pyre, SS guards watched on, drinking vodka, cognac and other alcoholic beverages, oftentimes in an effort to block out the horror of what they were seeing. However, for many SS guards, their posting to Auschwitz was preferable to having to fight the growing might of the Red Army on the Eastern front. Other guards in the concentration camps had a chip on their shoulders, and felt that they weren't seen as contributing to the war effort to the same degree as the guards in the army. For these men, the tortures and executions at the camp were a way for them to reassert their authority and compensate for their own feelings of inferiority.

Höss disliked the open-air burnings but he saw them as an interim solution to the problem of disposing of corpses. He was aware that Birkenau was still in its infancy but he couldn't help but feel unhappy with the inefficiency from which it still suffered. He believed that the transportation of Jews to Auschwitz had been premature and had taken place long before the necessary arrangements had been made. In his view the system was in chaotic disorder and although his boss had assured him that Auschwitz would play a prominent role in the ultimate destruction of the Jewish race, he was nonetheless deeply troubled about how it was going to be carried out in an organised and efficient manner. The already terrible state of affairs was made worse by the typhus epidemic, which by the second week of July had spread to the prisoners of Birkenau. In early July, Höss received a report informing him that as a result of deteriorating sanitary conditions in the camp, the mortality rate amongst previously able-bodied prisoners was rising dramatically. In spite of all these problems, Jewish transports were still being delivered to the camp on a regular basis. There was a danger that the hygiene levels in the camp would worsen to a catastrophic degree. To make matters even worse, the crematorium in the main camp had not been functioning properly since early June as its chimney was worn out. At the beginning of July, the crematorium had to be shut down altogether to allow the chimney to be removed and relined.

* * * * *

By August, Höss was finding his workload insurmountable. There seemed to be no end in sight to the expansion plans for Auschwitz-Birkenau. Höss was preoccupied with overseeing the construction work and was unable to attend to the various other duties demanding his attention. But as ever, despite all the pressure he was under, he was determined to persevere and to turn Auschwitz-Birkenau into the largest killing centre in history.

SS representatives in Berlin maintained almost daily contact with his office and paid regular visits to the camp. Eichmann was sent to Auschwitz on a number of occasions during the summer to report on the expansion programme at the camp. During one particular visit, Eichmann was present for the arrival of a transport of Jews and he watched the selection process being carried out. He was then driven through Birkenau by a small-tracked motorcycle and taken to one of the bunkers to observe the gassing process. Afterwards, he was taken to the pit to see the corpses being burnt. Eichmann had found the stench unbearable and he later reported that Höss appeared amused by his discomfort.

Despite the horrific scenes Eichmann witnessed at Birkenau, he was impressed with the camp overall, particularly its size. He reminded Höss of the importance of his role in the camp, and warned him to expect numerous more Jewish transports from all over Europe. The gassings were set to mercilessly continue.

On 12 August, an SS guard suffered mild poisoning from hydrocyanic gas during a 'special action', causing Höss to make the following statement.

> [It is]... necessary to warn all those participating in the gassings and all other SS members that in particular opening rooms used for gassing, SS not wearing masks must wait at least 5 hours and keep at a distance of at least 15 metres from the chamber. In addition, particular attention should be paid to the wind direction. The gas being used at present contains less odorous agents and is therefore especially dangerous. The SS garrison doctor declines all responsibility for any accident that should occur in the case where directives have not been complied with by SS members.[75]

Höss and his staff held a number of important discussions on Himmler's plan for the transformation of Auschwitz-Birkenau. They conferred on how best to enlarge Birkenau for the accommodation of 200,000 inmates. Karl Bischoff drew up a plan of the Birkenau site that included two crematoria—numbered II and III. The crematorium at the main camp was renamed Crematorium I. Another crematorium, known as Crematorium IV, was sketched next to Bunker I, and Crematorium V was situated next to Bunker II. The SS intended to build a sixth crematorium in February 1943 but this plan never came to fruition. It was estimated that Crematoria II and III burned an average of 1,440 bodies per day, and Crematoria IV and V burned 768 bodies per day. Höss believed that these figures would be adequate in dealing with the high volumes of prisoners pouring into the camp. From the time of their inception, both Crematorium IV and V were to operate as killing centres. They would have their own gas chambers, a morgue and a furnace hall. The other crematoria would also be adapted to operate as killing machines. Birkenau, it appeared, was finally maturing into a fully fledged factory of death.

Before such facilities were implemented at Auschwitz, Höss decided to visit a fully operational death camp to see how it was run. He settled on Treblinka camp, 50 miles northeast of Warsaw, on the main Warsaw-Bialystok railway line. Construction of the camp had begun in May 1942 and by July the site was up and running, complete with fully operational gas chambers. At Treblinka, Höss was introduced to the commandant, with whom he toured the site. The camp had been divided into three parts. The first section included a reception area, a housing area for German staff, the guard unit, administrative offices, a clinic, storerooms, and a workshop. The second section of the camp had been enclosed by barbed-wire fencing, and Jewish inmates, who had been selected from incoming transports, were housed here. The third section of the camp was the main impetus for Höss's visit—it was home to the killing facility. In accordance with *Aktion Reinhard*, the code-name for the extermination of all Polish Jews in the General Government, Treblinka had started off with an average of six thousand murders a day, but by the time of Höss's visit, this figure had more or less doubled. Höss suspected that the commandant was secretly competing with other camps in a bid to achieve the highest number of exterminations, but it was clear that the camp was struggling to cope with the frequency of transports. Höss observed the camp's gassing process in action but he failed to find the inspiration he had hoped for.

Small gas chambers were used, equipped with pipes to induce the exhaust gas from the engines, coming from old captured transport vehicles and tanks, very often failed to work. Because of that the intakes could not be dealt with according to the plan, which meant to clear the Warsaw ghetto. According to the camp commandant of Treblinka, 80,000 people have been gassed in the course of half a year.[76]

In Höss's opinion, Treblinka was not a very efficient camp. The gas chambers in Auschwitz were much larger, and unlike the commandant of Treblinka, Höss did not waste valuable time and resources killing Jews with exhaust gas. Also, the victims arriving at Treblinka were aware of their impending deaths, whereas at Auschwitz the victims were duped into believing that they were simply going through a delousing process.

At Auschwitz, Bunkers I and II continued gassing thousands of Jews. Jewish men, women and children were now being brought to the camp from all over Europe, including Slovakia, France, Belgium and the Netherlands. Upon arrival, they were herded into the camp like cattle. Auschwitz was not the only camp handling such large volumes of prisoners. Major killing centres had also been established in the forests of Poland—in Belzec, Sobibór and Treblinka.

* * * * *

The final stage in Auschwitz's transformation began on 26 September. Höss received instructions from SS-*Obergruppenführer* Oswald Pohl that all possessions belonging to the prisoners were to be permanently confiscated, labelled and put into storage. Initially, the possessions were stored in Block 26 of the main camp, but there was so much looted property that the Auschwitz authorities were eventually forced to erect six additional barracks close to the main camp. All foreign currency, gold and other precious metals, and any other valuables were to be transported from these special storage facilities to the SS headquarters in Berlin. All usable clothing, shoes, bed linen, blankets, fabrics and household utensils were to be directed to the Ethnic German Liaison Office where they would be distributed amongst German settlers. As for the unusable clothing and other pieces of material, these were to be sent directly to the Reich Ministry of Economy and put to use in the war effort. Höss realised that he could profit enormously from this precious loot, but for the time being he had more pressing matters to take care of.

Höss was still struggling to cope with the continuous stream of transports arriving at the camp. He had witnessed firsthand the chaos that prevailed at Treblinka and he was determined to prevent a similar situation from arising at Auschwitz. However, each new transport added to the backlog of prisoners awaiting 'special treatment', and the gas chambers were buckling under the pressure. Huge numbers of prisoners were also dying from malaria, typhus and dysentery, and all the while the camp still didn't have a proper crematorium in place. With a view to accelerating the rate of cremations in Auschwitz, Höss, SS-*Untersturmführer* Franz Hössler, and the head of the blueprint office, SS-*Obersturmführer* Walter Dejaco, decided to visit the Linzmannstadt ghetto to assess the open-air cremation ditches being managed by SS-*Standartenführer* Blobel. Upon their return, Höss ordered that both exhumations and cremations be escalated. Initially, the pyres had been kept alight through the use of body fat belonging to the corpses, but crude oil, and later methanol, was used as an alternative. Höss wrote:

> I had to oversee everything. I had to watch hour after hour, by day and night, the removal and burning of the bodies... I had to stand for hours in the terrible stench, while the mass graves were being opened and the bodies dragged out and burned.[77]

The sanitary conditions in Birkenau were so bad that it was even dangerous to drink the water. Mingled with the omnipresent smell of burning corpses was the stench of diarrhoea and vomit. On 23 July, Höss placed the camp under quarantine, but this did nothing to impede the rapid spread of disease. In August alone, 14,300 inmates died. Many guards also fell ill. The infection was so contagious that the wife of SS-*Obersturmbannführer* Joachim Caesar contracted typhus and died. Caesar himself fell ill with the disease and was off duty for nearly two weeks. The infection spread to the town of Auschwitz. With the epidemic ravaging Birkenau and its surrounding areas, Höss was eager to install the crematoria as quickly as possible. In fact, work on the crematoria had already begun in earnest, and several hundred labourers had been allocated to the project. Despite having a massive pool of labour at their disposal, the Auschwitz construction office knew that additional help would be needed. The inmates were capable of building wooden barracks and residential buildings and digging drainage systems, but the services of civil engineering firms would be required for the actual construction. In total, 11 construction companies got involved. A civilian firm called Huta, from Kattowitz, was already working on the shell of Crematorium II when it began work on Crematorium IV on Wednesday, 23 September. Approximately 80 men worked on the site—about 60 of these were prisoners, 20 of whom worked on the construction of the chimneys for the Auschwitz contractor Koehler. In total, between 100 and 150 people were employed on the individual work sites. In order to ensure that the various firms worked well together, a *Sonderführer* oversaw the project and made sure that the job was completed to a high standard and in the shortest time possible. Over the following months the *Sonderführer* oversaw the work of such firms as Karl Falck from Gleiwitz, and the Triton Company from Kattowitz, which was handling the drainage work of Crematoria III, IV and V. The Kluge Company from Gleiwitz helped Topf & Sons to build the furnaces for Crematoria IV and V. Huta were contracted to complete the floor and walls of the two underground morgues of Crematorium II, whilst the Vedag Company from Breslau were paid to waterproof the cellars of Crematoria II and III. Höss wrote:

> The crematories were constructed at the end of the two main roads in the Birkenau camp. Firstly, this was undertaken in order to ensure that it did not increase the size of the camp,

and secondly that it was not too far from the camp because there were plans to use gas chambers and undressing rooms as bathhouses when the extermination programme was completed. All the buildings were to be concealed from view by a wall of hedges, but the insufficient materials prevented this from being undertaken. As a temporary measure all the extermination buildings were to be hidden under camouflage netting.[78]

On 23 September, Höss was visited by the WVHA chief, Oswald Pohl. Pohl had come to assess the progress being made at Auschwitz and to inspect the SS factories that he himself had initiated. After first discussing the building projects in the construction headquarters, Höss and Pohl toured the local area, including the armament works. According to Höss, the inspections were extremely thorough. Pohl and his officials were then brought to the Birkenau camp. Pohl inspected the disease-engulfed camp and later observed a gassing procedure being carried out at Bunker II.

In the evening, Höss and other senior personnel enjoyed a beautiful dinner with Pohl in the officer's mess. Baked pike, open sandwiches, real ground coffee and excellent beer were served. Afterwards, Pohl gave a speech on the significance of the mission that had been entrusted to the guards, and reminded them of the importance of maintaining confidentiality. Pohl had carried out numerous inspections at the Auschwitz camp over the preceding months and on each occasion he had been pleased with the progress he observed, noting in particular that the NCOs and the officers seemed to have a very good working relationship. He reminded the guards that although they may not be spilling their blood on the main battlefield, their role in the war was no less demanding and they would be just as influential as the frontline fighters in bringing about Germany's eventual victory. The SS personnel knew that Pohl was referring to the Final Solution to the Jewish Question. Höss was already aware of what this solution would entail and had become increasingly anxious about the situation over the summer. In the presence of his staff and superiors he radiated confidence and determination, but in private he was deeply unhappy and troubled. The increased workload, the mass killings and the disinterment and burning of the corpses all had a profound psychological impact on him. There were evenings when he found it difficult to put it all behind him and go home to his family. He would often wander out to the gas chambers at night, or watch the cremations, simply to avoid returning home. Occasionally he would climb onto his horse and try and outride the haunting sound of prisoners screaming as they took their last breaths in the gas chambers.

> Often at home my mind would suddenly recall some incident at the killing sites. That's when I had to get out because I couldn't stand being in the loving surroundings of my family. When I watched our children happily at play, or saw my wife bubbling with happiness over the baby, this thought often came to me: how long will your happiness continue? My wife never understood my troubled moods and merely blamed them on the problems connected with my work... The married men who worked the crematory or the open-pit burnings often told me that the same thoughts had occurred to them. When they watched the women enter the gas chambers with their children, their thoughts naturally turned to their own families.[79]

Höss became increasingly disgruntled with his heavy workload, the incompetence of his staff and the lack of support and understanding from his superiors. Although his family seemed happy at Auschwitz, Höss felt over-burdened and cut-off from society. On Sundays he would often bundle his family into the car and take them for a drive through the countryside, during which they would stop for a picnic in a field. Other times they would visit the camp's kennels or take a stroll through the stables. Höss often took Klaus riding with him through the agricultural areas of the camp and the farms; he would frequently ride around the perimeter of the base camp to ensure that his son did not enter the cordoned-off areas. Höss also tried to spend more time in the garden of the villa with his family. He would watch contentedly as his children played in the garden. On occasion he would splash around in the pool with them or take them for a swim in the nearby River Sola. Höss thoroughly enjoyed these precious times with his children but the thought of work was never far from his mind. Since they first arrived in the villa, Höss had strived to make life as normal as possible for his family and to shield them from the atrocities that were taking place only a few hundred yards from their door. Klaus, Edeltraut and Brigitte, the eldest of the four children, were aware of the prison camp on the other side of the wall, and of the people incarcerated there. They knew that the staff employed in the villa were prisoners whose crime had been their opposition to the *Führer*, but that was the extent of their knowledge about the reasons for their incarceration. With the exception of Klaus, who probably saw prisoners beaten and whipped whilst riding around the perimeter of the main camp with his father, the rest of the children would rarely have witnessed the inhumane treatment of prisoners. The two older girls, Edeltraut and Brigitte, often begged their father for cigarettes on behalf of the staff. Höss often gave in to their repeated requests and would give them small quantities of Yugoslav cigarettes called Ibar.

By the winter of 1942, in spite of all the changes transpiring around them, life for the Höss family was more or less as it had always been. Höss continued to work long hours, rarely spending any time with his family during the week.

In November Höss was called to a meeting in Eichmann's office in Berlin. Höss chaired the meeting alongside Eichmann, his deputy, and various leaders from Belgium, Holland, France, Slovakia and Hungary, including SS-*Hauptsturmführer* Theodor Dannecker, Alois Brunner, Franz Novak, SS -*Sturmbannführer* Hermann Krumey, Hans Günther, his brother Rolf Günther, and Rudolf Jaenisch. Several important matters were raised; namely the various difficulties involved in transporting the Jews to the camps; the number of Jews that had already been delivered, and how many more were to be expected. The capture and deportation of thousands of Jews to the concentration camps had not been an easy task, the meeting was told. The rail lines and railcars travelling from Europe to the East had encountered many problems and the killing process still needed further refinement. The SS guards gathered around the table and proposed various ways of overcoming these problems and improving the genocide programme. Eichmann made direct references to the Final Solution, stating that those fit for labour were to be spared, while the unfit were to be deported to the extermination camps and killed immediately. Unexpected military set-backs on the Eastern front had generated a number of difficult circumstances for the rolling stock, but Eichmann assured his men that the war would not prevent the successful conclusion of the Final Solution.

Höss sat in silence for most of the meeting, leaving Eichmann, his deputy and several other SS leaders to do most of the talking. The commandant had come to Berlin with the express purpose of ascertaining how many more Jews were to be expected at Auschwitz, and Eichmann informed him that up to one million Jews and Gypsies had been earmarked for the camp. Such a high volume of prisoners made it all the more important that the crematoria be completed post haste. However, at present Bunkers I and II had already exceeded their killing capacity, and the cold weather was preventing the prussic acid from vaporising properly. All in all, the situation looked bleak.

Back at Auschwitz, Höss was busier than ever before and his mood became increasingly irritable and dejected. Those around him were forced to bear the brunt of his despondency—his wife in particular. Hedwig was suspicious that Höss was having an affair with Eleonore Hodys and their relationship had become quite tense as a result. In an effort to dispel Hedwig's suspicions, Höss, while recovering

from a riding accident in hospital, told his wife to dismiss
Eleonore from duty. Days later he issued an order for her
arrest on charges of having committed a violation during
her term of employment at the villa. Eleonore was sent to
a women's penal company, before later being moved to the
special SS prison in the basement of the main administration
building. Whilst under arrest, Eleonore wrote a letter to Höss,
Hedwig and the house cook, Sophie Stippl, proclaiming her
innocence. Her letters were ignored, however, and she soon
found herself confined to a cell.

[The cell had]... a good bed and mattress. I had a table and
stool, could read, write and smoke. I wrote a few times to the
commandant through Grabner and asked for the reason of my
detention. I never got an answer.[80]

Höss, however, was still physically attracted to Eleonore and
he believed that her arrest would somehow force her into his
arms.

On 16 December 1942, about 11.00 p.m., I was already asleep
when suddenly the commandant appeared before me. I had not
heard the cell door open and was very frightened. It was dark
in the cell. I believed at first it was an SS man or a prisoner...
then I heard 'Pst' and a pocket lamp was lit and I saw the face
of the commandant. I broke out, '*Herr Kommandant.*' Then we
were both silent a long time. When I had composed myself, I
thought something evil was afoot and asked: 'What is wrong?'
Then Höss spoke his first words, 'You are coming out.' I asked,
'Now at once?' He replied again, 'Hush be very quiet, we'll talk
it over', and sat at the foot of my bed. I reminded him I had
written to him and why I did not receive an answer, and why I
was under arrest? He did not answer my question, but asked if
I was alright. He had done everything to improve my condition,
and did I need anything? Then he moved slowly from the end
of the bed and tried once more to kiss me. I quickly defended
myself and made some noise. He then warned me to be quiet,

nobody knew he was there. I asked him how he had come in and why no one had seen him. He told me he had come through the garden door and had unlocked the door himself. I was again very irritated and told him that my release from prison had been arranged... He answered that my release was approved, but he did not know that I was supposed to work in the SS hospital. He answered that he would first have to look into it because he had been ill and this was his first time back in the camp where he had the chance to see me. I asked him then why he came at night. I told him that he could see me during the day. I was still very concerned that I would be executed, but Höss told me not to worry. I was under his protection... He asked me why I was always reserved with him. I told him that as commandant he was for me a respectful person who was also married. He said then I should not worry, because he knew what he was doing. He requested for me to be his friend. Then he tried again to kiss me and was somewhat sweeter. During all this time I was very anxious, listening and looking at the door that was open... I could not quite believe that the commandant had walked alone through the camp to see me. I again insisted that he should go away. Finally he went away and told me that I should think about it and that he would come back.[81]

Two days later, shortly after 11.p.m, Höss paid a second visit to Eleonore.

He asked me if I had made a decision. I said 'No, I did not want to... All I wanted was to be released.' He then said that he had prepared everything. He arranged a nice room in a very beautiful house. He said he would see to it very soon regarding my release. Then we had a very long talk for two hours about personal matters. He did not say anything about himself. He asked me about my life and my family situation, which were not in my records. At the end he tried to be friendly. I resisted and made him wait, saying that the door was open and that somebody could come in at any time. He said that I should not worry and that nobody would come in. I did not let that influence me and he went away in nasty mood. The following day was Sunday. In the morning he made a bunker inspection. Then I had to go to another cell that one could open and shut from the inside. It was, if I remember correctly, Cell 6. Some days later, he came during the night. He asked if he should go away. I said 'No'... then he came to me in bed and we had sexual intercourse. Some days later he came again. This time he undressed himself completely. At midnight there was an alarm. I think something was on fire somewhere in the camp. Outside in the hall the light was turned on. One could hear the steps of Gehring. Höss hid himself naked in the corner behind the door and I hid the uniform in bed. Gehring looked through the spy hole and put the light out immediately. When everything was quiet, Höss put his clothes on and went outside, but soon came back and said he could not go out of the camp because there was too much movement. He stayed with me until after one in the morning.[82]

Over the next few weeks Höss, who in the past had vehemently condemned all sexual relationships between female prisoners and SS men, embarked on an affair with Eleonore.

We had four or five nights of sexual intercourse. His interest in me did not wane. We later had some long conversations together. I once again brought up the subject of my release. He said I had to be patient. The next time he came to me I asked what would happen to me if he was discovered. He said I ought to deny it and asked me if I would do it. I swore silence. He then gave me advice that if someone did ask I should say that a prisoner had come to me. I replied that I did not know any prisoners. He thought he knew that more SS men and a nice-looking *Kapo* had interest for me. Then he asked what I had with Fichtinger. I told him that he had written to me and that I had answered him telling him not to bother me. Then he asked if it was an affair, but I replied that he was small and not completely to my taste. His advice was that I should indicate Fichtinger. I did not like to indicate Fichtinger but he thought I could do it quietly. He took a sheet of paper out of his notebook and I had to give him, in the light of his flashlight, a written declaration that I had acquaintance with the prisoner Frans Fichtinger.[83]

Höss promised Eleonore that he would continue to visit her, but he was secretly terrified that their relationship would be exposed. He knew that it was illegal for an SS man to have a relationship with a female prisoner, and that the crime was punishable by death. He didn't trust his staff and he was certain that at least a handful of them bore a grudge against him. He reluctantly decided to stay away from Eleonore. He gave orders for her to be incarcerated in the dark damp cells of Block 11, hoping that their sordid affair would never come to light.*

---

*In February 1943, Eleonore was examined by the bunker doctor and it was confirmed that she was eight weeks' pregnant. During the summer of 1943 she had an abortion. In spite of speculation, there is no credible evidence to suggest that Höss actually knew about the pregnancy during this period, but what is known is that he did order Eleonore's transfer from the SS prison to Block 11, where she was imprisoned in one of the standing cells. Höss hoped that she would quietly die of starvation there. During her incarceration, Eleonore managed to arouse Grabner's interest in her fate. Grabner bore a grudge against Höss and believed that armed with knowledge of the affair he would be able to incriminate the commandant.

Chapter V: Special Treatment

Höss heralded in the year 1943 with his family at Auschwitz, but the festive season was tarnished by news that the bitter and bloody fighting had intensified on the Eastern front. Radio reports of fighting at Stalingrad revealed that brave German legions of the 6th Army were still holding out in the besieged city and were putting up a good fight against their hated Red foe. Yet during the first bitterly cold days of January, it became increasingly apparent that the war in Russia was not going according to plan for Germany.

The set-back on the Eastern Front caused reverberations to be felt in the distant Auschwitz. Plans for the construction of Auschwitz town had been abandoned, and the *Reichsführer's* dreams of resettling millions of ethnic Germans in the East had also run aground. The German Army desperately needed to be able to move both troops and equipment from one area of the front to another as quickly as possible, meaning that the rolling stock, normally used for transporting the Jews by rail, became increasingly less available. In spite of the problems posed by the war, thousands of Jews had been successfully evacuated and transported from all over Europe and the East for the administration of the Final Solution. According to the chief statistician of the SS, Richard Korherr, who compiled a progress report on the Final Solution, approximately 2.7 million Jews were exterminated in 1942 alone. The Operation Reinhard camps, notably Treblinka, Sobibór, Belzec, and a smaller camp called Majdanek, were the main contributors to this figure. Treblinka was still officially the Nazi Party's largest killing centre, but this would soon change. Höss asked to see a copy of the statistical report and he was surprised to discover that Auschwitz had already gassed some 200,000 Jews in Bunkers I and II. He was satisfied with this figure, especially given the array of problems that had beset the camp in recent months.

Bunkers I and II could not claim full responsibility for this death toll, however, as a considerable number of mortalities were attributed to the typhus epidemic that was still claiming lives in Birkenau and the surrounding areas. In January alone, some 4,500 prisoners died from the disease.

* * * * *

On 9 January, Höss received a letter from the district president of Kattowitz proposing that all those who fell sick in the Myslowitz prison should be sent to Auschwitz. It read:

> I do not... fail to recognise that these prisoners, under the circumstances, might cause new cases of disease in the Auschwitz camp. Since, on the other hand, the typhus epidemic has by no means been extinguished in the Auschwitz camp and the comprehensive, protective, sanitary police measures have been taken there, I consider it necessary to make this inquiry.[84]

In his reply, Höss outlined that there were now only isolated cases of typhus in the camp and he feared that the delivery of sick prisoners would increase the threat of a fresh outbreak of the disease. Plans had been drafted to tackle typhus and other infectious diseases but the completion of the water purification plant and the construction of a permanent disinfection facility, known as the Central Sauna, were at the top of the agenda. The Central Sauna's primary role would be to carry out sanitary operations on all incoming transports. Those who entered the facility would be undressed, have their hair cut, undergo a medical examination, be disinfected and showered. However, at present the authorities were preoccupied with refining the killing process and so construction of the Central Sauna was put on the long finger.

Throughout January, Höss was kept up to date on the progress of the four crematoria. Disease in the camp had delayed construction but stringent quarantine measures were finally bringing the situation under control. At the end of January, engineer Kurt Prüfer of Topf & Sons inspected work sites 30, 30a, 30b, and 30c, and reported:

> Crematorium II was structurally completed except for minor secondary work. The three-muffle cremation furnaces are ready and at present are being dry heated. The delivery of the ventilation unit for the corpse cellar was delayed as a result of the suspension on railway cars, so that the installation can take place sooner than 10 days from now. Therefore, the start of operation of Crematorium II will probably be ready by 15 February 1943.[85]

Prüfer was being overly ambitious though as construction had in fact fallen two months behind schedule. In the first half of February, Erfurt received a letter from Topf & Sons regarding an order for Crematorium III. It read:

> We once again confirm receipt of your order for five triple-muffle furnaces, including two electric lifts for the corpses and one provisional hoist for corpses. Also the order for a practical device for charging coal and a device for transporting ashes. You are to deliver the whole installation for Crematorium III. We expect you to take the necessary steps to immediately

dispatch all machines and parts. The complete installation must come into service on 10th April 1943.[86]

Höss made it known to Eichmann that the situation at Birkenau was far from ideal and that the bunkers were struggling to keep up with the incoming transports. Eichmann had been eager to convey Jewish transports to Auschwitz, but he was reluctantly forced to redirect trains to Treblinka and Sobibór. Treblinka, however, was already operating at full capacity. Trains were often backed up for hours at a time while the guards frantically tried to clear the backlog of prisoners. Eichmann realised that the camps were in danger of degenerating into total disorder if the Auschwitz authorities did not complete the crematoria sites soon. Having witnessed the situation at Treblinka, Höss felt that the commandant, Dr Irmfried Eberl, was wholly responsible for the chaos that prevailed and deserved to be prosecuted for not handling the mass killings more efficiently. Höss would not have tolerated Jews being shot out of hand as they were at Treblinka, where officials were simply incapable of managing the gassing facility effectively. Höss also prided Auschwitz's continued deception that prisoners were simply going to be disinfected rather than killed. Transports selected for immediate 'special treatment' were made wait under a cluster of birch trees in the camp until the crematorium became available.

* * * * *

By early February, Birkenau was once again in the grip of a typhus epidemic. On 8 February, Höss, concerned that the disease would further delay the building of the four crematoria and spread to surrounding areas, informed his subordinates that all permissions for leave were to be cancelled until further notice. The high number of civilian workers that were falling ill was also cause for concern. By order of the camp's physician, it was decided that all civilian workers living alongside the ill would be quarantined for three weeks.

The inmates who had already fallen ill or were showing the slightest symptoms of the disease would be disinfected, or in other words sent directly to the gas chamber for 'special treatment'. Afterwards, their bodies were disposed of in open-air cremations in the same manner as the thousands of prisoners who had perished in Bunkers I and II. Pit-burning was still the chief method of corpse disposal in early 1943. Höss wrote:

> Before incineration, gold teeth and rings were removed and the bodies were then placed on layers of wood and a heap of approximately 100 bodies in each hole, and was ignited by means of rags soaked in petrol. After such a heap was properly alight and burning, other bodies were thrown onto it.[87]

Although petrol, methanol, crude oil and alcohol were being used to keep the fires alight, special units tasked with corpse disposal developed a new and more efficient pit design. The pits were dug with indentations at one end which allowed the human fat to be drained off. The stokers could then pour large pails of boiling human fat over the corpses to ensure that they burned as quickly as possible. Höss wrote:

> ...especially during wet weather... the duration of the incineration process was approximately six to seven hours. The smell of the burning bodies could be noticed in the camp proper if there was a west wind.[88]

The fat-burning technique proved very successful but Höss was now faced with the problem of how to dispose of the huge quantities of ashes that were left over. A special squad was assigned the gruesome task of shovelling the ashes out of the pits.

> After clearance of the holes, the remaining ashes were pulverised. This was affected on a concrete plate where prisoners pulverised remains of bones with wooden pounders.[89]

These remains were then piled into heaps and shovelled onto lorries. The lorries transported the ashes to either freshly dug pits, the surrounding marshes and rivers or other secluded spots.

However hideous Höss may have found the open-air cremations, he saw the process as ultimately improving the sanitary conditions in the camp. The bad weather had temporarily contained the epidemic but it had also delayed work on the killing installations. In spite of the delays, at the end of February, Höss received the encouraging news that the five triple-muffle furnaces in Crematorium II were to be finally tested. A few days later, on 4 March, 45 well-fleshed male corpses, which had been specially selected from a group of prisoners who had been gassed in Bunker II, were transported to Crematorium II. The incineration rooms were located on the ground floor, while the gas chamber and mortuary were situated in the cellar. Inside the incineration room, the bodies were cremated under the watchful eyes of Prüfer and several other engineers. Over the next 10 days the furnaces were run in order to dry them out while engineers completed the gas chamber ventilation system. On Saturday, 13 March, it was announced that Crematorium II was officially operational and ready to begin administering 'special treatment'. On the evening of Sunday, 14 March, Höss drove to Birkenau to observe the new crematoria at work. A total of 1,492 women, children, and elderly people from the Krakow ghetto had been selected for the trial run in Crematorium II. That night Jewish prisoners were quietly led to a temporary undressing hut that had been erected next to Crematorium II in the north yard. Höss wrote:

I would never dare admit any doubts. In order to make my subordinates carry out their gruesome tasks, it was emotionally imperative that I should appear if necessary of undertaking such a harsh order. Everyone watched me. They observed my reactions and behaviour. I had to continuously exercise a strong willpower in order to avoid my inner emotions of oppression becoming noticeable. In front of them I had to act cold and indifferent of all human feelings. I even had to look when I was afraid just in case my natural emotions became apparent. I had to observe coldly, while mothers with laughing or crying children went into the gas chambers.[90]

Höss and his subordinates watched as, under the supervision of the *Sonderkommandos*, the Jews were ordered to undress and told to keep their personal effects together so they could find them upon their return. They were then led naked and in single file down the western stairway, with its metal guard rails, and through a doorway to the basement of Crematorium II. A sign hanging over the doorway read 'Bath and Disinfection Room'. On entering the room, huge sieves mounted on pieces of wood or metal, which resembled shower heads, could be seen hanging from the ceiling. Once the prisoners had been crammed inside, the airtight door was slammed shut and secured with two latch bars that had been screwed in tightly. A specially designed peephole, consisting of a double pane of glass, had been fashioned to enable observation of the killing process from the outside.

Depending on the weather conditions, between five and seven kilograms of pale, blue-green granulated Zyklon B was poured into the chamber by SS medical orderlies wearing gasmasks. This quantity of Zyklon B could kill between 1,500 and 2,000 people. The gas entered the room via four metal-meshed hollow columns protruding from the concrete ceiling. The victims started screaming as soon as the gas entered the room, but 40 times the lethal dose of Zyklon B had been used and so their death agonies were not heard for long. Within a few minutes, five at the most, the gas chamber fell silent. When the SS were sure that all the victims were dead the air-extraction system was switched on for 20-30 minutes to suck the poisoned air out of the chamber. The air-tight door was then unbolted and opened, and the *Sonderkommando* immediately began to gather up the corpses of the women, children and the elderly. Many of the dead had their eyes open and their arms wrapped tightly around their neighbour. Some bodies lay crushed near the doorway, covered in scratches and bruises, having been trampled on by other prisoners in their desperate attempts to escape. Others were found lying around the wire-mesh columns. Blood oozed from the noses and mouths of the victims and their faces were blue and bloated; some of the bodies were badly deformed and were no longer identifiable. The chamber was so hot that some of the victims, the children in particular, had probably suffocated from a lack of air rather than from the gas.

Plans for the installation of an electric elevator in the gas chamber had been drawn up, but in the meantime a temporary hoist was used to lift the bodies up to the ground floor. Once all of the victims had been moved into the incinerator room, the *Sonderkommandos* attached leather thongs to the bodies and pulled them along the concrete ground as far as the furnaces. They were then placed face-up and head-to-foot in rows of three on a metal 'corpse board'—this device ran on rollers and rammed into one of the muffles. It was predicted that the incineration process would take from 45 minutes to an hour, but on that particular evening the incinerators were run on only half their capacity to avoid any technical problems. In total, preparation and gassing took just two hours, but the incineration process took nearly 48.

The trial run had been a complete success and a teletype message was duly dispatched from Auschwitz to the SS headquarters to inform them that the new 'bathhouse' had undertaken its first 'special action'. However, believing that all of the camp's crematoria were now fully operational, Eichmann had given orders for a transport of 2,800 Salonika Jews to be dispatched to Auschwitz. Höss's satisfaction with the crematoria trial run was short-lived when he learnt of Eichmann's order. Crematorium II was only in its trial stage, and as for Crematoria III, IV and V, they were still being constructed. Nevertheless, on 20 March, much to the exasperation of Höss, the transport arrived from Salonika. Of the 2,800 Jews who arrived that day, 417 men and 192 women were spared for labour, while the remaining 2,191 deportees were sent directly to the gas chambers. The camp authorities decided to use Crematorium II again for the 'special action', in spite of technical concerns. The selected Jews underwent the same procedure as before, except that this time the ovens were operated at their full capacity. However, it immediately became apparent that the building could not handle such a high volume of cremations and an electrical fire broke out. The ventilation system for extracting the Zyklon B from the chamber also developed a problem. Höss insisted that the crematorium could not be closed down for repair. A second transport of Jews had already been dispatched from Salonika and were *en route* to Auschwitz, and Höss was determined to carry out the 'special treatment' without any disruptions to the schedule. On 22 March, in a desperate attempt to avoid any further damage being done to Crematorium II and to allow engineers to repair the crippled facility, camp authorities insisted that the architects sign off on Crematorium IV. When the Salonika transport arrived the usual selections were carried out and nearly 2,000 Jews were led to their deaths in Crematorium IV. The gassing was carried out in such haste that the camp authorities did not even have time to carry out a trial run on the incinerators.

At the end of the month, Höss received the good news that Crematorium II had been temporarily repaired and returned to the camp. For the next few weeks the crematoria functioned relatively well. Crematorium IV was also run during the Salonika action, but it was overworked and the double four-muffle furnace cracked under the pressure. In a bid to keep the crematorium in working order, engineers were immediately drafted in to repair the incinerator. The situation worsened when days later the internal lining of the chimney and the flue that connected up with the incinerator of Crematorium II began to collapse. Engineers set about rectifying the problem. On 4 April, Crematorium V was officially handed back to the camp authorities, but the airtight doors had yet to be fitted and so the installation was not yet fully operational. Between 16 and 17 April, work on the doors was completed by a civilian firm working for Huta.

Crematorias II and IV were back in working order by mid-April. That same month, Höss was visited by SS-*Sturmbannführer* Alfred Franke-Gricksch, adjutant to SS-*Obergruppenführer* Maximilian von Herff, who was head of the SS Central Personnel Office in Berlin. Franke-Gricksch was accompanying Herff on an inspection tour of the General Government. During their visit to Auschwitz, Franke-Gricksch was brought to Birkenau camp to witness the gassing of 2,930 Salonika Jews in Crematorium II. Although the process went smoothly, Höss was still perturbed by the recent crematoria breakdowns. But in spite of the various set-backs and the almost constant bickering between the architects and engineers, Höss was surprised to learn that in just two months some 30,000 victims from the Salonika action, as well as 7,000 German, Polish and Yugoslavian Jews, had been exterminated. Although these figures were considered impressive, any hope of increasing the killing capacity was quickly dashed when both crematoria were shut down in May. Crematorium II was temporarily taken out of commission so that engineers could reline the chimney, while Crematorium IV's incinerator was decommissioned. There was now an increased urgency for the other two crematoria to be completed. Discussions between Höss and Eichmann revealed that more transports would be arriving at Auschwitz in the coming weeks.

During Eichmann's visit, Höss repeatedly tried to get him to open up, but according to the commandant, even on the occasions when they drank together, Eichmann still kept his emotions well guarded. Höss considered Eichmann a model SS soldier. He was hard and callous and completely focused on the Final Solution. He showed no pity towards his victims and had made it his mission to exterminate the Jewish race in the shortest time possible. Höss was equally guarded in Eichmann's presence and was careful to hide any occasional flickering of sympathy he felt for his victims. Any sign of weakness would be interpreted as a betrayal of the *Führer* himself. Höss would have to persevere with the extermination process and leave his emotions behind him at the camp gate. 'There was no escape from this difficulty',[91] Höss wrote.

* * * * *

Eichmann ignored the reported problems with the camp's crematoria and continued to send transports to Auschwitz, telling Höss that he would just have to improvise. The situation worsened yet again when Crematoria II and IV were pronounced out of service. The incineration capacity of the camp had dropped considerably, and in order to cope with the incoming transports, Höss was grudgingly obliged to revert to the open-air burnings. Only Crematorium I in the main camp and Crematorium V were capable of offering limited support in the disposal of the mounting corpses.

Although the camp was primarily a killing centre, Höss was also under pressure from the authorities in Berlin to contribute prisoners to the pool of slave labour. But the warmer weather exacerbated the insanitary conditions and caused the mortality rate to soar. The severely malnourished prisoners were dying in large numbers. Höss broached the importance of maintaining the prisoners' health in a number of staff meetings. He noted the poor latrines, the unsatisfactory sewer system and the need for more sick bays. He was also opposed to the system of pits, as the high water table would lead to further infection of the ground water. The head of the Central Construction Office indicated that a large disinfestation unit for Birkenau was under construction and it was agreed that it would serve as a permanent solution for the delousing of all able-bodied prisoners. On 22 May, in a speech to Hans Kammler and other functionaries, Höss clarified the primary objective of the Auschwitz-Birkenau camp. Those who had not been selected for 'special treatment' were to be kept as healthy as possible and used for labour in the various armament firms. In one of his few inspiring speeches, Höss spoke about the evolution of Auschwitz.

[The camp was]... originally intended as a quarantine camp. This later became a Reich camp and thereby destined for a new purpose. As the situation developed evermore critical, its position on the frontier of the Reich and G.G. [General Government] proved especially opportune, since the filling of the camp, and with workers, was guaranteed. Recently to that came matters concerning the Jewish question, which required means to accommodate 60,000 prisoners at first, which has increased to 100,000 within a short period. The prisoners of the camp are predominately planned for the industries which are locating in the vicinity. The camp contains within its sphere of interest various armament firms, for which the works are continuously provided.[92]

A few days later the Auschwitz authorities set about improving the sanitary conditions in the camp. They resolved to reconstruct the sewage system, change the structure of the latrines, dig a main drainage ditch leading to the Vistula, and complete the Central Sauna disinfestation facility.

Alongside the high rate of disease amongst the prisoners, there was also a growing concern over the number of SS personnel who had contracted typhus and other debilitating diseases. The Auschwitz garrison physician, SS-*Untersturmführer* Dr Bruno Kitt, and his assistant, SS-*Hauptsturmführer* Dr Horst Paul Sylvester Fischer, took particular interest in the spread of disease at the camp. Höss noted in Kitt's file that due to his hard work the number of disease-related deaths had actually fallen at the camp.

During Kitt's service he developed the skills of a surgeon by operating on prisoners in the SS hospital. Although scores of his patients died, he boasted that he saved the lives of many SS men as a result. For his efforts, Höss later awarded

Kitt the War Service Cross 2nd Class with Swords. The terrible suffering Kitt wreaked on his human guinea pigs was only outdone by his successor SS-*Hauptsturmführer* Dr Josef Mengele. Höss was hugely impressed by the handsome 32-year-old combat veteran. Mengele went on to become the most highly decorated SS officer at Auschwitz to win the Iron Cross 1st Class. He had originally volunteered to come to Auschwitz in order to establish an experimental physiological and pathological department in the camp. He hadn't been in the camp very long before his sinister and merciless nature came to light. Like Kitt, Mengele was interested in eradicating cases of typhus at the camp but his practices were much more extreme. On 25 May 1943, with Höss's approval, Mengele sent some 1,000 Gypsies, suspected of having typhus, to the gas chambers. As camp physician, Mengele had a never-ending supply of human specimens on whom to experiment. Wearing his white doctor's coat and gloves, he was usually present at the selection ramps in order to single out those unfit for work. Mengele was obsessed with genetics and the theory of a Nazi master race, and he availed of the selections to hand-pick victims for participation in his own sadistic medical trials. He experimented on twins, dwarves and prisoners who had developed a form of gangrene known as noma—this condition was common in the Gypsy camp in Birkenau on account of the terrible living conditions. Mengele also carried out an array of other experiments, including the agonising injection of methylene dye directly into children's eyes to see if it would turn them blue.

* * * * *

Throughout the month of June, the camp's crematoria experienced a host of technical problems. Finally, on 24 June, the run of bad luck ended with the return of Crematorium III. Within a week Crematorium II was also back in operation. By the end of June, Auschwitz-Birkenau had an official daily incineration output of 4,756 corpses.

Yet, despite the engineers' repeated warnings not to overload the crematoria, the Auschwitz authorities continued to operate the installations at their absolute capacity. According to engineers' reports, the furnaces were being operated incorrectly and were constantly overheated. It was suggested that the *Sonderkommandos* were deliberately damaging the internal lining of the furnaces with their fire irons.

By early July, transports to Auschwitz-Birkenau had increased in size and there was a corresponding increase in the number of prisoners being selected for 'special treatment'. Throughout the summer, Höss regularly oversaw the arrival of new transports. He would stand for long periods of time, either alone or in the company of his subordinates, watching as the new victims were loaded onto trucks and driven into the camp, with a fake Red Cross vehicle in close pursuit. Once the trucks had finished unloading the victims in the crematorium yard, several camp doctors would congregate nearby and watch as the procession of people filed down the concrete steps and into the changing rooms. Minutes later cans of Zyklon B would be removed from the 'Red Cross' vehicle and placed alongside the gas chamber's small chimneys. Soon afterwards, a signal would be given to the SS medical orderlies standing on the roof, and they would put on their gas masks, open the cans of Zyklon B and pour the granules through the openings in the roof. Höss wrote:

> I had to look through the peep-hole of the gas chambers and observe those inside being killed, because the doctors wanted me to see the process of extermination.[93]

Höss found the sights he beheld appalling, but he remained calm and composed in the presence of the doctors and his subordinates. Many SS officials were made witness the gassing process in operation. On a number of occasions, the *Reichsführer* sent 'various high-ranking party leaders and SS officers to Auschwitz to see for themselves the extermination process of the Jews.'[94] The dignitaries would listen intently as the commandant explained the procedure in detail. They would then be led into the crematorium, and instructed to peer through the small, thick observation window at the multitudes of prisoners inside. An order would be given to commence the operation, and as the men, women and children began screaming and writhing in panic, the dignitaries would be politely asked to once again peer through the peep-hole. Some of the dignitaries would calmly ask questions of the SS men during the gassing process, while others would compliment the guards on the efficiency of the process. Many, however, were visibly upset by the scenes and were rendered speechless. Occasionally they would ask Höss how he could bear to carry out such a harrowing assignment on a regular basis, adding that they did not envy his job. But generally, most visitors to Auschwitz observed the procedure with interest, and like Höss, outwardly appeared unmoved by the victims' suffering.

At home, Höss continued to conceal his emotions. He would retire to his study and try to block out the day's events with several glasses of vodka followed by a cigar. By the summer of 1943, the villa no longer served as the refuge from camp life it had once been for him. The rumours of his affair with Eleonore Hodys had caused a rift in his marriage, and Hedwig, who was six months pregnant with their fifth child, could rarely bring herself to be intimate with her estranged husband. Outwardly, however, the couple appeared as happy as ever and neither the house servants nor the children's governess were aware of any marital problems.

Life in the villa continued more or less unchanged. Whilst war rationing greatly affected most families, the Höss's gardener, Stanislaw Dubiel, secretly supplied the household with various types of food.

The food warehouse was well stocked at that time because they stored food taken from Jews who came to Auschwitz in mass transports, and who in most cases were then led straight to the gas chambers... Frau Höss explicitly stated that no SS man should find out about it. I assured her I was doing it with a friend. For Höss's private household I used to take sugar, flour, margarine, various kinds of baking powder, soup seasoning, pasta, oatmeal, cocoa, cinnamon, semolina, peas and other products. Frau Höss was never satisfied, she kept on informing me about what she didn't have at home and wanted me to see if I could get it for her. She didn't use all those products in her own household, she sent some of them to her relatives in Germany. Their second supplier was the director of the canteen and camp abattoir [SS-*Untersturmführer* Friedrich] Engelbrecht... He delivered meat, smoked meat and cigarettes from the canteen. I saw Höss's house boxes containing 10,000 Yugoslav cigarettes called 'Ibar'. You could only get them in the prison canteen. Frau Höss offered me these cigarettes for the illegal work she made me do.[95]

According to Dubiel, it was not just food and cigarettes that were regularly smuggled into the Höss household.

A former prisoner and professional criminal Erich Grönke would come to the Höss's house everyday and bring fancy leather goods and all types of shoes for men, women and children. All the clothes that the commandant and his sons used to wear were made in Grönke's leather factory. The best tailors were assigned for this purpose, first the Poles and later well-known Jewish specialists from France, Belgium and other countries. Two Jewish women tailors worked in the Höss house for about a year and a half. They sewed outfits for Höss's wife and daughters from the fabrics that Grönke delivered from the supplies stolen from Jews... clothes and other things that had previously belonged to gassed Jews were later checked in the leather factory warehouses in search for hidden valuables, especially gold, diamonds and money. Grönke himself told me that they found a lot of these valuables.[96]

The prisoners' valuables were originally stored in the camp's Zone of Interest, but during the first half of 1942 a special storage facility was opened, which the inmates nicknamed 'Canada', and in time this name was adopted by the guards. Canada consisted of six barracks and was situated about 500 metres from the main camp. Some 1,500 prisoners were responsible for sorting through the looted property in shifts. In December 1943, a much bigger warehouse, known as Canada II, was opened on a site between Crematoria II and III and Crematoria IV and V at Birkenau. Canada II comprised 30 permanently overflowing wooden barracks. For the SS guards, Canada I and II were a veritable treasure trove. Supervision was surprisingly remiss and as a result many SS men regularly filled their pockets. Höss was aware of the corruption at the camp and the thriving black market that his guards were fuelling. Diamonds, gold, coins, dollars, foreign currency, food and alcohol were all being sold on to the market at huge profits. Many items of clothing and furniture were also being pilfered. However, Höss was also actively lining his pockets and profiting from the dead. Dubiel stated that he often saw Hedwig and the children wearing clothes stolen from Canada.

> Frau Höss swapped lingerie that was delivered occasionally for the women prisoners working in her household. It came from the Canada warehouse where they kept things stolen from the gassed Jews. Höss's house was furnished in the same way— everything was made by prisoners from the materials that were in the camp. The house had the most wonderful furniture, the desk drawers were upholstered in leather, which were all stolen from Jews... by taking advantage both of the prisoners' work and the camps supplies, Höss created such a wonderful well-equipped home that his wife declared: 'I want to live and die here'. They didn't lack anything thanks to the huge supplies of all types of goods accumulated in the camp.[97]

Höss was aware that SS policy dictated that all valuables taken from prisoners were the exclusive property of the Nazi state and that individual profit was forbidden. He also knew that as commandant he should be leading by example. He had already broken the rules by starting a relationship with a prisoner and he was now guilty of further exploitation by stealing from the dead. He tried to divert attention from his own wrongdoings by highlighting the unlawful activities of others. Höss accused the commander of the Auschwitz sentry battalion, SS-*Sturmbannführer* Max Gebhardt, of regularly bringing female prisoners back to his barracks. He ordered Gebhardt to stand before a court martial. Höss's actions saw Gebhardt removed from Auschwitz and sent to the front. Another officer whom Höss targeted that summer was *Lagerführer* SS-*Hauptsturmführer* Hans Aumeier. Aumeier had earned a lot of respect at Auschwitz on account of the brutal tortures and executions he carried out at Block 11. But he and Höss had their differences. The commandant tried to have him removed from his post on several different occasions, and he eventually succeeded when Aumeier was found guilty of corruption charges and transferred on Höss's personal order. Aumeier was replaced by SS-*Hauptsturmführer* Heinrich Schwarz, who was officially appointed *Lagerführer*—deputy to the commandant.

* * * * *

During July and August recurring problems with the crematoria continued to hamper operations. If all five crematoria were running simultaneously, Auschwitz had an enormous killing potential, yet only two were currently in operation. Crematorium IV was out of service, as was Crematorium II while it was being repaired; Crematorium I had been closed down altogether at the request of the Political Department; and as for Crematoria III and V, these installations were being overworked as they were running at their absolute capacity. Höss desperately tried to accelerate the killing process. Reports reveal that between April and September in 1943, Crematoria II, III, IV and V worked for only two months at full capacity. Only a quarter of their maximum capacity was utilised. Nonetheless, in the midst of all these technical problems an enormous amount of people were still sent to their deaths in all four crematoria. In total, 'special treatment' was administered to between 160,000 and 210,000 victims.

By October, the average transport arriving at Birkenau had increased in size yet again. Although prisoners were usually transferred to the 'bathhouses' without incident, riots would occasionally break out amongst larger groups. One such episode occurred on 23 October, when 1,800 Polish Jews arrived from Bergen-Belsen. The prisoners in this transport had bought exorbitantly priced passports, having been promised by the *Gestapo* that they would send them to Portugal, and from there on to South America. At the railway station in Oswiecim, between the Auschwitz and Birkenau camps, the prisoners were greeted by SS-*Obersturmführer* Hössler, who introduced himself as a representative of the Foreign Ministry. He assured the prisoners that they would soon be continuing on their journey but first they had to be disinfected. To avoid delaying their train, which was scheduled to leave at 7.00 a.m., they were ordered to go immediately to the undressing room. Höss wrote:

> After approximately two thirds had been brought into the undressing room, mutiny started as the other third entered. In the course of this the lighting installation was torn down, the SS men were attacked and one stabbed to death, and the prisoners succeeded in disarming the SS guards who had been sent to reinforce the employed prisoners when the situation looked like getting out of hand. Chaotic shooting occurred between the prisoners and the sentries posted at the entrance. When I arrived there I gave immediate orders to close all doors and continue with the gassing process of the two thirds which had entered the chamber. After all this was finished I proceeded together with the sentries into the undressing room, using searchlights into a corner and then let them out individually.

They were then shot in another room of the crematorium with small arms ammunition on my orders.[98]

One young woman, realising she was being led to her death, managed to grab a pistol from SS man Schilinger as she was entering the gas chamber. She shot Schilinger several times before turning the gun on a second SS man, Emmerich. Countless other women joined in the revolt and began hurling themselves at the guards. The rebellion was eventually put down and those involved were shot dead. Schilinger died from his wounds and Emmerich was left permanently crippled.

* * * * *

Höss was very unhappy with the conditions in the camp and the attitude of a number of SS guards. He believed that many of them were guilty of a careless, inefficient manner, only undertaking the duties that were absolutely necessary of them. In fact, a number of guards regularly turned up for their shifts drunk and were unable to perform their tasks to the satisfaction of the commanding officers. Höss was outraged by this unruliness. He was determined to stamp out any insubordination and was prepared to reshuffle the camp personnel if necessary. He believed that the blind allegiance demanded by the SS should be strictly adhered to and any guard who fell foul of this deserved to be severely punished. Höss regularly lectured the guards on the importance of the SS code of conduct, yet he himself was guilty of breaking many of the rules he claimed to support. Höss's greed for wealth had driven him so far as to rip gold fillings out of the mouths of corpses in the camp's crematoria. Rumours of the corruption at Auschwitz eventually filtered back to the SS headquarters in Berlin, and an investigation was ordered. Höss was deeply worried that he would be implicated during the inquiry.

In late October, SS-*Obersturmführer* Konrad Morgan arrived unannounced at Auschwitz. Morgan introduced himself to Höss as an investigative judge of the SS reserve and an examining magistrate of the State Criminal Police. He told the anxious commandant that he had been sent as part of a concerted effort by the higher authorities of the SS in Berlin to investigate allegations of corruption in the camp. According to Morgan, the SS headquarters had uncovered evidence of financial corruption and sexual wrongdoings in the camp and he had been granted unrestricted access to both Auschwitz I and II, including the SS garrisons.

Morgan immediately launched the investigation, touring both camps with his colleagues and raiding the non-commissioned officers' barracks. The investigation was swift and it caught all of the guards by surprise. Luckily for Höss, the villa was not searched. However, Morgan discovered a wealth of gold, pearls, rings and money in all different currencies, in the possession of the SS staff, confirming that corruption was indeed rife at Auschwitz. Morgan told Höss that he was deeply disappointed with the conduct of the SS soldiers and that a full investigation into his findings would be undertaken and individual SS soldiers would be prosecuted. Those found guilty would be either shamefully expelled from the SS or sent to the Eastern front. An inquiry would also be made into the running of the camp. Guards suspected of carrying out executions in Block 11 without first seeking permission from headquarters in Berlin would also be targeted. One such officer who was implicated in the unlawful killings at Block 11 was SS-*Untersturmführer* Maximilian Grabner. Morgan had unearthed large quantities of valuables, including money and gold, in Grabner's quarters. They had been secretly stowed away in the barracks of the Political Department, which he had been in charge of directing since June 1940. Under suspicion of theft, corruption and the unauthorised shooting of prisoners, Grabner was arrested and removed from the camp to stand trial in a Weimar court.*

Over the next few days, news of the corruption charges at Auschwitz spread throughout the SS. On 10 November, SS-*Obergruppenführer* Oswald Pohl travelled to Auschwitz from the WVHA in Berlin for an important meeting with the commandant. During their meeting, Pohl outlined the future plans for Auschwitz-Birkenau. He informed the commandant that he had been negotiating with numerous businesses in a bid to develop Auschwitz into a system of satellite camps located on industrial sites. Already, some 50 camps were located in the area, including the Buna camp at Monowitz, the Jawischowitz camp near the mines at Brzeszcze, a small shoe factory camp in Chelmek, and a number of other camps were in the process of being erected. In total, there were 33,000 prisoners working in the satellite camps.

The SS enterprises were proving very lucrative indeed, bringing in an average of two million Reichsmarks every month. Due to the vast size of the enterprise, Pohl explained that command of the Auschwitz-Birkenau complex and its satellite camps would have to be subdivided into three individual command groups. On account of the unavoidable changes to the system at Auschwitz, and the fact that the responsibility would be too great for any one person, it was with reluctance that the SS had decided to remove Höss from his post as commandant. However, in view of his service and his accomplishments at the camp he was offered a choice of either becoming the commandant of Sachsenhausen

---

* On the night of 8 December, after Höss had left Auschwitz to begin his new job in Berlin, he received word of a fire in the stores of the Political Department. The fire had been deliberately started by Grabner and others in a desperate attempt to destroy the evidence the commission had gathered against them. The investigation team unearthed a bank account that had been set up by Grabner and others containing a balance of several hundred thousand Reichsmarks. Grabner was convicted and sentenced to 12 years imprisonment.

concentration camp or being promoted to the staff of Pohl's Economic Office.* Pohl allowed the commandant 24 hours to consider the offer. Höss had no desire to command another concentration camp so the following day he was left with little choice but to accept Pohl's offer and join the staff of the Economic Office. He told his superiors that he was happy with his promotion but he was secretly distraught over his removal from Auschwitz after having invested so much energy in the camp. He confided in Hedwig over his disappointment. According to Dubiel:

> From what Frau Höss said I understood that Höss really wanted to stay in Auschwitz, and that even though the transfer to the headquarters meant a promotion, he wasn't happy about it. He thought the transfer was the result of plots against him by the boss of the camp agricultural economy, Dr Joachim Caesar, who he didn't get on with.[99]

Hedwig and the children were to remain behind at the villa in Auschwitz.** Prior to Höss's departure for Berlin, he invited some of his close associates to toast his future success at a dinner party in his house. A few days later he made his last inspection of the main camp and Birkenau, accompanied by his new 31-year-old adjutant, SS-*Hauptsturmführer* Viktor Zoller. One of the last duties he undertook at Auschwitz was to promote the camp's head of pharmacy, SS-*Hauptsturmführer* Adolf Krömer. Höss wrote in Krömer's file that he was a very able man who was highly respected by both the guards and doctors under his command.

---

* In a bid to save Höss's post at Auschwitz, his old party comrade and fellow convict, Martin Bormann, who was now head of the Party Chancellery, wrote to Himmler and requested that he be lenient with Höss. However, the *Reichsführer* insisted that Höss would have to be removed on account of the widespread allegations of corruption at Auschwitz.
** On 30 September 1943, the Höss's fifth child, Annemäusl, was born. Rudolf and Hedwig nicknamed her 'Mäusl'.

* * * * *

On 1 December, Höss took up office as the newly appointed chief of Department DI—the central office of the political section within the WVHA. He succeeded SS-*Obersturmbannführer* Artur Liebehenschel, who took over his post as commandant of Auschwitz. Höss's deputy was SS-*Obersturmführer* Johannes Otto and both men worked closely with the deputy of concentration camps, SS-*Standartenführer* Gerhard Maurer. Höss wrote:

> My area of responsibility was the Political Department; communications, weapons and the control of all the concentration camps in the area. In the Political Department, the work consisted of processing the legal proceedings; applications for death sentences, for example in cases involving sabotage...[100]

Höss's main responsibility in his new role was to improve the overall concentration camp system and he enjoyed much more power and authority than he'd ever had at Auschwitz. Armed with a detailed knowledge of the entire system, Höss ardently believed that he could find solutions for overcrowding, bad sanitary conditions, a lack of building materials, and any other problems that might arise. Although he didn't enjoy office duties, he knew his job would involve a lot of travel between the various camps. He would also have the opportunity to revisit Auschwitz and share with the new commandants his proficiency in administering 'special treatment'.

Chapter VI: *Aktion* Höss

At the beginning of 1944, the German war machine suffered a series of devastating military set-backs. On the Eastern front, the Red Army had made considerable advances and was driving its enemy back towards the Reich frontier. Newspapers reported on heroic German legions sacrificing their lives to secure victory for the German nation, but throughout the Reich, and indeed across all of the occupied countries, the reality was very bleak.

Slave labour was desperately needed in order to increase armament production. During early 1944 the labour shortage had become so acute that it looked likely that there would be a temporary change in policy towards the Jews. Although those unfit for work would still be killed, the process of 'special treatment' would become more selective. It was reported that some officers were keen to send as many prisoners as possible to the 'bathhouses' but this was deemed counterproductive. Death camps such as Kulmhof, Sobibór, Belzec and Treblinka had been closed down, leaving other camps, Auschwitz-Birkenau in particular, to bear the full weight of responsibility for the remnants of the Jewish communities of Poland, France, the Netherlands, Italy and the rest of occupied Europe. More flexible selections would have to be implemented. But even the WVHA had its doubts. Höss anticipated that many new arrivals, if not most, would be unfit for work in German industry. He was deeply concerned by the overcrowding of the concentration camps, the primitive conditions of the sub-camps, and the fact that many prisoners were too malnourished to be of any use to the war effort. He wrote:

> The camps are becoming very overcrowded, causing countless problems. Many thousands of Jews are transported to Auschwitz to be used in the new arms industry, and conditions have gone from bad to worse. These camps [sub-camps] have been simply thrown together and improvised by those in charge of the camp construction in such difficult circumstances that they are too primitive to work effectively. The hard work, which most prisoners were not adapted to, and the continual lack of food and other supplies has presented an awful state of affairs. If they had been gassed at Auschwitz, then at least they would have been saved from all this anguish. Most, however, died anyway in only a short time, not having ever contributed to the war effort. In my reports I raised this problem continually, but Himmler's need for more prisoners in the arms industry only highlighted the pressure he was under. Week by week the *Reichsführer* became fixated by the increasing numbers that showed the deployment of prisoners.[101]

The demand for labour had become so intense that, according to Höss, Himmler would 'no longer pay attention to the death rates'.[102] The *Reichsführer* couldn't understand how so many prisoners were arriving at the camps every week and yet so few were actually spared for slave labour. 'In reality', wrote Höss, 'a high amount were totally worthless'.[103] Transports often arrived with most of their passengers already half dead. Attempts to save the lives of these prisoners 'only put a large strain on the camps, and took away essential space and food from fit workers'.[104] Höss tried to improve the situation with the help of the deputy inspector of concentration camps, SS-*Standartenführer* Gerhard Maurer, and Pohl. Over the course of several months measures were put in place to ensure that as many prisoners as possible were put to work in the armament factories rather than being sent to extermination camps. But while the offices of the WVHA took various administrative routes in an effort to claim the transports for the armament industry, the RSHA seemed determined to exterminate the majority of those arriving at the camps.

Höss repeatedly sent communications to the RSHA offices, in which he outlined the deplorable conditions in the camps, but they simply ignored him. His frequent tours of the camps did little to alleviate the overcrowding and disease that was claiming the lives of so many otherwise able-bodied prisoners. Albert Speer, the Minister of Armaments, was particularly insistent that for Germany to be victorious in the war, the armament factories needed to be adequately staffed. By the end of February the labour shortage was so acute that the *Führer* himself intervened, instructing Himmler to deport 100,000 Jewish slave workers from the sole remaining Jewish community in Europe—Hungary.

For some time now, the German Foreign Office had been putting pressure on the Hungarian government to enforce stricter anti-Jewish laws. According to reports from Eichmann's office, there were almost 725,000 Jews living on Hungarian territory. When the German occupation forces rolled into Hungary on 19 March 1944 they were accompanied by an advance party of the *Sonder Einsatzkommando* (Special Operation Unit), followed by Eichmann and a band of 140 trucks and command cars. On 21 March, Eichmann was assigned temporary living quarters in the Hotel Majestic in the Schwabenberg district of Budapest. It was from this base that he would direct the fate of thousands of Hungarian Jews.

Himmler instructed that the Hungarian Jews be transported to Auschwitz-Birkenau for selections to be carried out. The able-bodied prisoners would then be dispersed amongst the various concentration camps serving German industry. Those selected for labour would be held in quarantine until transport became available for them. In effect, the *Reichsführer* was planning to turn Birkenau into a huge labour exchange, just as he had done with the main camp in 1940, albeit on a smaller scale. The Auschwitz authorities were instructed to prepare for a large consignment of Hungarians Jews. They were also told that a more discerning effort was to be made in selecting those fit to serve the Reich. Eichmann was in charge of transporting the Hungarian Jews directly to Auschwitz. He personally commenced negotiations with the Hungarian police and helped to organise the ghettoisation of the Jewish population in Hungary.

As preparations got underway for the transportation of the Hungarian Jews, Höss received a new commission from Pohl—he was charged with ascertaining the number of Jews the armament industry could expect. In late April, Höss visited the chief of the RSHA, Heinrich Müller, in the hope that he might be able to help him. During their meeting they spoke at length about pending operations in Hungary, but Müller was unable to answer Höss's question regarding the Jews. He advised him to journey to Budapest to personally meet with Eichmann. A couple of days later Höss left Berlin by train and travelled to the Hungarian capital, and met Eichmann in his Schwabenberg office. Höss listened attentively as Eichmann outlined his plans to uproot and deport nearly one million Jews from Hungary. He told Höss that the Hungarian authorities had agreed to the deportations and that these Jews would refresh the dwindling supply of slave labour. It was crucial that no able-bodied prisoner be accidentally overlooked and sent to the gas chambers. Eichmann told Höss that his mammoth task had been made that bit easier by the willingness of the Hungarian authorities to cast out their Jewish compatriots.

But despite the government's compliance, the operation still faced a mountain of difficulties. Eichmann told Höss that it would take a considerable amount of time to organise the deportation so it was crucial that the Jews didn't suspect that they were in any kind of danger. Deportation plans had already been put in place and trains carrying more than 3,000 Jews a day would begin arriving in Auschwitz some time in May. A large amount of rolling stock would be required but every effort had been made to ensure that its use would not affect the war effort. For this reason, Jews from Budapest would not be included in the first wave of transports to Auschwitz. Eichmann hoped to deliver more than 760,000 Jews, nearly five per cent of Hungary's population, to Auschwitz during the summer, but he realistically predicted that the figure would be slightly lower.

Höss had dinner with Eichmann that evening and the following day he returned to Berlin, satisfied that he had gathered all the information required by Pohl. Once Pohl had a clear picture of the events transpiring in Hungary, he informed Höss that he was to be responsible for making arrangements for the massive influx of Hungarian Jews to Auschwitz. During late April and early May, Höss made two more visits to Budapest to consult with Eichmann in preparation for the shipments to Auschwitz. During Höss's visits to Hungary he always made sure he sent food and luxury goods home to his family. According to Dubiel:

> Whenever he [Höss] went to Hungary, he sent home big cases of wine. He travelled to Hungary as a special plenipotentiary for the extermination of the Jews in Europe. That's how his wife officially called him.[105]

Höss spent his time in Hungary carefully observing Eichmann's negotiations with the Hungarian government departments and the army. During their private meetings, Höss found Eichmann's devotion to the SS invigorating and he became more convinced than ever before that the extermination of the Jews was an absolute necessity.

When Höss returned to Berlin he spoke at length with Pohl about the developments in Hungary and stressed that a lot of work needed to be done at Auschwitz to prepare it for the transports. The new commandant had already made complaints about the running of the camp and Höss was keen to pay a visit. However, his visit was to be much more long-term as on 7 May the *Reichsführer* appointed him commander of the overall SS garrison at Auschwitz. Ever since his departure in November 1943 he had been reluctant to sever ties with the camp and had hoped that he might one day be given the opportunity to return. He would now be returning to spearhead a major operation—the scale of which had never before been witnessed at Auschwitz. Höss relished the challenge his new post represented.

On 8 May, the new SS garrison commander Rudolf Höss arrived in the main camp, where he was greeted by Hedwig and the children. They had not seen him for six long months. It had been a difficult time for all of them but Höss had felt better about them remaining behind in Auschwitz as it was a lot safer than Berlin. The Allied raids on Germany had intensified during the first half of 1944 and the Reich capital had been badly damaged by the daily aerial attacks.

It did not take long for Höss to become reacquainted with his old camp. On the day of his arrival, SS-*Obersturmbannführer* Artur Liebehenschel, the commandant of Auschwitz I, was relieved of his post and replaced by SS-*Hauptsturmführer* Richard Baer. Höss described Liebehenschel as a quiet, good-natured man, who unfortunately had no idea how to run a concentration camp. Höss had received reports through his office in Oranienburg alleging that the commandant had been promising prisoners that he would put a stop to the gassings. He had forbidden guards to shoot anyone attempting to escape, and any *Kapo* caught beating an inmate was punished. All arbitrary executions had also been stopped and the small standing cells in Block 11 were removed. The commandant had also squandered his time in needlessly long meetings while the general condition of the camp was neglected. The RSHA had complained to Glücks and requested that Liebehenschel be transferred to the Lublin-Majdanek camp.

* * * * *

A lot had changed at Auschwitz-Birkenau since Höss's departure. Liebehenschel had divided the camp into three independent camps, assigning the largest section, that of Birkenau, to the command of SS-*Sturmbannführer* Friedrich Wilhelm Heinrich Hartjenstein. Both men worked well together, but like Liebehenschel, Hartjenstein lacked the brutal disposition necessary in a commandant. During Höss's inspection of Birkenau he found himself dissatisfied with the general running of the camp and filed a report to the RSHA in Berlin. When Eichmann arrived from Budapest to make a formal inspection of Birkenau he was incensed to discover that Hartjenstein had not carried out his orders.

The incineration installations at Crematorium V were not fully operational because the ovens were being filled with special fireclay paste; the open-air cremation ditches, which had been hastily dug behind the gas chamber to compensate for the low incineration output, were standing idle. As a result, corpses were piled outside awaiting disposal. Hartjenstein was immediately relieved of his command and transferred to the Natzweiler concentration camp in the Alsace region of France. His replacement was none other than Höss's first ever adjutant, and an old veteran of the concentration camp system, SS-*Hauptsturmführer* Josef Kramer. Kramer arrived at Auschwitz on 8 May and took up office as the new *Lagerführer* of Auschwitz II-Birkenau. Birkenau was still suffering from overwhelming overcrowding and severe shortages of food, with hundreds of prisoners perishing daily. But for the time being Höss's priority was to make preparations for the arrival of the Hungarian Jews.

The first transport, consisting of 1,800 people, arrived at Birkenau in early May. Höss expected many more convoys in the weeks ahead. To prepare for their arrival he ordered that Crematorium V be put into operation again. An engineer's report, however, confirmed that Crematorium V's furnaces were still damaged and because of their slow incineration rate they had been replaced with five small incineration ditches. It was suggested that Bunker II be reactivated instead and that it be designated Bunker 2/V. Höss agreed as past experience had taught him that it was generally not the process of killing that proved problematic, but rather how to dispose of the bodies afterwards. To ensure the process went as smoothly as possible, Höss put SS-*Hauptscharführer* Otto Moll in charge of all four crematoria and assigned a special squad to the task of expanding the inside of the crematoria. A track was laid between Crematorium V and the pits so that the corpses could be loaded onto trolleys and transported quickly. The other killing installations were also overhauled, including Crematoria II and III, which received new elevators that connected the gas chambers to the incineration rooms. Even the walls of the changing rooms and the gas chambers were given a fresh coat of paint.

In order to establish a direct link between the Auschwitz station and the crematoria, the train lines were extended through the main entrance of Birkenau, with plans in place for them to eventually run as far as Crematoria II and III. Hundreds of prisoners worked day and night laying the three-way railway track through the camp and constructing the loading and unloading ramps. By the second week of May the railway line was complete and the finishing touches were applied to the ramps. At these ramps, Höss would coordinate the destruction of the Hungarian Jews, an operation which had been given the codename '*Aktion* Höss'.

The first major Hungarian transport arrived at Auschwitz on 15 May. The trains pulled over the new spur bringing them through the gate and into Birkenau, where they halted at the ramps. Here, *Aktion* Höss was put into operation. The prisoners, the majority of whom were pre-war citizens of Romania and Czechoslovakia, were unloaded from the overcrowded cattle trains and separated into two columns: one for women and children, the other for men. One or two SS medical doctors then carried out the selection and subdivided the columns. Those unfit for labour were directed to the crematoria, while all able-bodied workers were either interned in Auschwitz or transferred to other camps in the Reich. The number of prisoners selected for labour from each transport varied daily; it could be as low as 10% of the total transport, or as high as 50%. But the majority of prisoners who passed through the gates of Birkenau were immediately sent to their deaths. Roughly 3,300 Jews arrived in the camp every day, but this figure rose as high as 4,300 on occasion. On 20 May, for instance, a convoy arrived carrying approximately 3,000 people, of whom 2,000 were unfit for work. The following day, on 21 May, two convoys reportedly arrived from Hungary carrying 6,000 people, of whom only 2,000 were fit for work, and the remainder were sent straight to the gas chambers. On that particular day both the incinerators of Crematoria II and III were being serviced so the corpses had to be disposed of in the three incineration ditches next to Crematorium V. Although the specially built track from the crematorium to the pits had been laid, it was never used because it was considered an inconvenience. Instead, the *Sonderkommandos* were forced to drag the corpses directly from the gas chamber to the pits.

* * * * *

New Hungarian convoys were arriving at Birkenau every day. Höss visited the camp on a regular basis to oversee the selections; he also occasionally visited the open-air ditches to ensure that the corpses were disposed of in time for the arrival of the next transport. Within just two weeks of the *Aktion* commencing, approximately 122,700 prisoners had been sent to their deaths. Birkenau alone was gassing between 5,000 and 6,000 Jews every day. The *Aktion* was the most sustained mass killing so far in the history of the Auschwitz camp, and was comparable to the scale of murders carried out at Treblinka during July and August of 1942.

In order to ensure the camp didn't descend into chaos, Höss increased the number of *Sonderkommandos* working in shifts in the four crematoria. The whole of the horrific operation was supervised by only a handful of SS men. The sight of women and children walking to their deaths had become so commonplace at Auschwitz that the SS men often stood around, chatting and joking amongst themselves, while the prisoners filed into the small chambers. No reports were ever filed of an SS guard suffering from any kind of psychological breakdown as a result of the killings. The majority of SS guards carried out their duties with an unflinching ruthlessness. Höss was aware of the brutality that prevailed in both camps, including the illegal shootings, but he didn't intervene. He could seek refuge in his office if he ever needed to close the doors on camp life and when he embarked on his regular walks around the main camp or around Birkenau he had developed the ability of averting his eyes from the suffering of the prisoners. Any moments of pity he may have felt were overridden by his staunch belief that all those who passed through the gates of the camp were subhuman adversaries of the state. He was determined to wipe out the Jewish race by systematic brutality

Throughout June new transports continued to be sent from Hungary. Although on the whole the operation was a success, the number of prisoners being sent to the gas chambers began to exceed the official incineration capacity and, as before, the crematoria began to overflow with corpses. Many victims were burned in the nearby pits to cope with the high volume of corpses.

Over the coming weeks the crisis escalated. Thousands of Hungarian Jews continued their one-way passage to the gas chambers and a great deal of valuable labour was lost in the process. At countless selection processes, Höss witnessed families desperately clinging to one another and beseeching the authorities not to separate them. But Höss found that it was often easier to send young and healthy women to the gas chambers along with their offspring than to try and pry them apart.

During the summer of 1944, all four crematoria were working more or less simultaneously, killing thousands of prisoners every day. Höss's killing factory was at its peak. The ovens were working at full capacity and the incineration ditches were being used day and night. The frenzied gassings and burnings went on for weeks, irrespective of Germany's deteriorating military situation. During July an average of 3,500 prisoners were arriving at the ramps every day and more than three quarters of these new arrivals were sent directly to the gas chambers. This phenomenal figure was a testament to Höss's brutal organisational skills. In just eight weeks he had masterminded the killing of more than 320,000 Hungarian Jews. However, towards the end of July reports from Budapest announced that deportations were to be suspended. The number of transports quickly petered out and the Hungarian operation came to an end, prompting Höss to leave Auschwitz on 29 July and return to Berlin.

Command of the garrison was handed over to Baer in his wake. Höss believed that Auschwitz had finally fulfilled its potential, and he felt confident that Baer would successfully exterminate whole sections of the camp. Before Höss's departure, discussions were held regarding the future of the Gypsy camp. At its peak, there was an estimated 23,000 Gypsy men and women in the camp. However, owing to overcrowding and a shortage of food and water, disease had quickly spread through the camp, killing 21,000 Gypsies. The remaining 2,897 men, women and children were rounded up on the night of 2 August and marched to the gas chambers. Höss was not present at the mass murder but he was informed by SS-*Obersturmführer* Johann Schwarzhuber, the commandant of the men's camp at Birkenau, that the procedure had not gone smoothly as many of the Gypsies had suspected their fate and had refused to go quietly.

In Oranienburg, Höss resumed his duties as the inspector of concentration camps. However, by August the situation in Germany had changed dramatically. Although the camps continued mercilessly killing their prisoners, Germany was struggling to stave off its enemies on both the Eastern and Western fronts. In the East, German troops were desperately trying to defend against the Russian onslaught, and through incredible effort they had succeeded in slowing down their enemy. But cracks were beginning to appear in Germany's position in the East and any hope of repairing the situation was rendered impossible by a crippling shortage of troops. To make matters worse, the Russians were now fighting on Polish soil, east of Warsaw. On 6 September, as battles in Poland intensified, Himmler gave orders for the liquidation of Auschwitz; to include the complete destruction of all four crematoria as well as Bunkers I and II. The order stressed that all personal effects from the warehouses, as well as building materials and equipment, were to be transported by motor vehicle and train back to the Reich. Half of the 150,000 prisoners incarcerated in Auschwitz, most of them Poles and Russians, were to be relocated to concentration camps in the West. Höss was informed that Buchenwald, Bergen-Belsen, Dachau, Flossenbürg, Gross-Rosen, Mauthausen, Natzweiler, and Ravensbrück were to receive the Auschwitz prisoners, and he quickly set about preparing these camps for their new arrivals.

* * * * *

In October, Grabner stood trial in a Weimar court. The presiding judge proposed the death sentence, but due to a lack of evidence the trial had to be postponed.

However, during Grabner's pre-trial hearing, which Höss attended, he stated that both Commandant Höss and SS-*Obersturmbannführer* Dr Rudolf Mildner had supported the various executions he had carried out. He also stated that Hans Aumeier, SS-*Obersturmführer* Franz Johann Hofmann and SS-*Hauptsturmführer* Heinrich Schwarz had helped him to carry out the executions.

Höss denied all allegations and managed to evade prosecution for war crimes, but Grabner was determined to exact revenge on him. He decided to inform the investigating SS judges of Höss's affair with Eleonore Hodys. The SS judge *Untersturmführer* Wiebeck proceeded to interview Höss, telling him that a woman called Eleonore Hodys had been questioned in a prison hospital in Munich and had admitted to having had sexual relations with him. Höss denied the allegations, insisting that he had always strongly disapproved of sexual relationships between female prisoners and SS men. He maintained that he would never sink so low as to be intimate with a prisoner. He accused Eleonore of conjuring up their relationship and subsequently being locked in a cell for her errant behaviour. Wiebeck could not prove that any sexual wrongdoing had taken place, but SS-*Obersturmführer* Konrad Morgan, who had been pursuing allegations against Höss for over a year, believed Eleonore's statement. Luckily for Höss, by the time the interview was conducted with Wiebeck, the Soviet Army was bearing down on Auschwitz and the whole of the Nazi state was under threat.

* * * * *

During the final months of 1944, Höss's office in Oranienburg was a hive of activity, with his department struggling to cope with the mounting problems caused by the advancing enemy. Conditions in many of the concentration camps had deteriorated to such an extent that Höss was compelled to personally inspect them. One particular camp that he visited was Bergen-Belsen in Lower Saxony. The camp had originally opened in April 1943 with a capacity of 500 inmates. Unlike other camps, the families incarcerated here were allowed to stay together and to wear their own clothes. By the summer of 1944 the camp was overcrowded with Hungarian Jews and conditions were steadily worsening. The camp's commandant, SS-*Sturmbannführer* Adolf Hass, had also been accused of negligence and it was decided to relieve him of his command. In early December, Höss journeyed to Bergen-Belsen to meet with Hass and the commandant of Auschwitz II-Birkenau, Josef Kramer.

On 1 December, Kramer was transferred from Birkenau to Bergen-Belsen. He arrived at the camp with a large number of prisoners who had been part of the evacuation order. The march to the camp had been horrific, with long columns of prisoners trudging for miles through the rain and cold. Hundreds had collapsed from exhaustion and died by the roadside, whilst others who were too weak to go on were shot by the guards. Those who had survived the march were in a terrible state. Virtually all of them were weak and severely malnourished.

Höss learnt that Kramer had been incredibly callous and negligent during the march, making little effort to ensure that the prisoners had adequate supplies and shelter along the way. In spite of this, Höss considered Kramer the ideal candidate to take over Bergen-Belsen as he hoped that his brutal approach would put an end to rumours that the camp was for so-called pampered Jews. Kramer's appointment as commandant was an enormous undertaking. According to Höss, sanitary conditions were far worse in Bergen-Belsen than at Auschwitz and the prisoner barracks were very run down. Overcrowding was a huge problem and it was exacerbated by the arrival of the first batch of Auschwitz evacuees.

When Höss returned to Berlin he found the city ravaged by daily and nightly assaults. Fires raged across the bombed and battered capital. In the wilderness of this devastation, the city continued to function as best it could. On occasions when Höss was forced to take to the air-raid shelters, his thoughts would inevitably turn to the safety and welfare of his family. It was for this reason that he instructed Hedwig to evacuate the villa and return to Germany with the children. According to Dubiel, the family had accumulated so much property that four railway carriages were required to transport everything. The cellar was filled with expensive wine and champagne that had to be carefully packaged before being loaded onto the awaiting trucks. Other SS families, in the vicinity of Auschwitz, were also packing up their belongings, eager to escape Poland before the arrival of the Red Army.

Höss spent Christmas with his family near Ravensbrück. Despite the strict food rations, Hedwig was determined to celebrate as best she could with her husband and five children. But the mood in Germany had changed considerably since the previous year. The atmosphere was one of impending defeat and no amount of festive cheer could dispel the increasing sense of despondency in the Höss household. The *Führer's* New Year speech, which was broadcast from the *Grossdeutscher Rundfunk*, did nothing to alleviate the sense of hopelessness that hung over Germany. The speech made no mention of the vicious fighting going on in the West, where thousands of German soldiers had died on the Reich's borders. The *Führer* assured his listeners that there would be a dramatic reversal of fortunes, with Germany rising up once more and achieving victory. Höss hoped for his sake, and for the future well-being of his family, that a triumphant conclusion to the war was indeed in sight.

The New Year holiday ended on 3 January 1945 and Höss returned to Berlin. The capital was buried under snowdrifts but it was still clear that the city had suffered further bombings. Many businesses and factories were severely disrupted by shortages of raw materials, but people could still be seen shuffling through the snow, on foot or by public transport, going about their business. The only industry that appeared relatively unaffected by the deteriorating situation was that of armament production. This very lucrative enterprise was still relying heavily on the pool of slave labour being procured by the SS. It was therefore paramount to Germany's continued war effort that the slave labour system be sustained. By the end of 1944, some half a million prisoners were working in German factories. At Auschwitz and the surrounding sub-camps, the able-bodied were marched back to Germany to be used as slave labour. Only two months earlier the *Reichsführer* had ordered the cessation of extermination operations across the Reich. At Birkenau, the *Sonderkommando* had dismantled the killing facilities. The incineration ditches had also been levelled, and the pits, which had been filled with the ashes and crushed bones of murdered prisoners, were emptied and covered over with fresh turf and other vegetation.

Crematorium I in the main camp was turned into an air-raid shelter and the chimney and holes in the ceiling, through which the Zyklon B had been inserted, were removed. The furnaces in Crematoria I, II, III and IV were also dismantled and the usable parts were transported to other camps. On the night of 17 January, some 58,000 prisoners were evacuated from Monowitz and the Auschwitz sub-camps; about 20,000 prisoners were evacuated from the Auschwitz-Birkenau camp alone. The majority of the inmates were forced out into the snow and made march west, towards Germany, in freezing night-time temperatures. As they shuffled along the icy road, the night sky occasionally lit up with the flashes of Russian gunfire in the distance. Any prisoner, children included, who was unable to keep pace with the mass exodus was shot on the spot and their lifeless body thrown by the roadside.

The small number of SS guards who had been left behind at Auschwitz were given instructions for the demolition of the crematoria, to include Bunkers I and II. Having blown up the remaining shells of Crematorium II and III in the early afternoon of 20 January, Crematorium V was rigged with dynamite six days later. Crematorium IV had already been demolished after it had been damaged by a fire during a *Sonderkommando* revolt in October 1944. During the demolition of the crematoria, special SS units murdered approximately 700 prisoners at Birkenau and nearby sub-camps. When news arrived that the Red Army were advancing along the main road from Krakow, the guards were ordered to destroy the remaining camp records, set fire to the Canada stores and exterminate the remaining prisoners. However, fearing for their lives, the SS guards fled the camp, leaving the soldiers of the First Ukrainian Front to liberate Auschwitz and its sub-camps.

* * * * *

Just days before Auschwitz was captured, Höss had driven to Poland to personally ensure that everything was destroyed in the camps as ordered. But due to advancing Russian forces he only made it as far as the Oder River near Ratibor. In spite of his fears of the advancing Red Army, Höss helped transport some of the Auschwitz prisoners west into Sudetenland. According to Höss, he met officers travelling in cars from Auschwitz and he used their vehicles to evacuate as many prisoners westwards as possible. He even considered using the railway but it was simply too chaotic. During the frantic evacuations many railroad cars had been abandoned by guards; the prisoners had been left locked inside the carriages and had frozen to death in the sub-zero temperatures. Conditions on the roads were equally unfavourable. With scarcely any means of transport available, thousands of prisoners were forced to travel on foot. Countless people died in the arctic conditions, with many more being shot by guards because they were unable to keep up with the march. Near the town of Glubczyce in Poland, Höss stopped his car and watched as a *Luftwaffe* motorcyclist shot a prisoner dead against a tree. When he angrily enquired why he had executed the man, the *Unteroffizier* arrogantly retorted that it was none of his business. Höss pulled out his pistol and shot the man dead in the snow. He had killed him not because he felt any compassion for the murdered prisoner but because the prisoner had been able-bodied and was therefore of value to the slave labour industry.

Over the coming weeks the confusion and devastation of the evacuations was exacerbated by the fact that *Volksdeutsch* refugees were frantically trying to escape from the clutches of the Red Army. Stories leaked back to Höss of Russians raping and murdering the women and children who fell into their clutches. Innocent people had been burned to death with flamethrowers; some victims were forced to walk naked through the streets whilst others had their tongues nailed to tables or were hung from lamp posts. Anyone suspected of aiding the Nazis was subjected to brutal reprisals at the hands of the Soviet troops. Some commanders reportedly ordered their men to murder the entire population of *Volksdeutsch*-occupied villages.

Whilst the terrified exodus of refugees streamed westward, Höss continued to oversee the running of the concentration camp system, ensuring that all evacuation orders were carried out. One of the last and most important tours of inspection that he undertook was in March 1945, in the company of Pohl and Dr Lölling.

We visited the camps in Neuengamme, Bergen-Belsen, Buchenwald, Dachau and Flossenbürg. I then parted from *Obergruppenführer* Pohl and, together with Dr Lölling, visited Leitmeritz on the River Elbe, one of the largest labour camps. The reason for the visit was as a result of an order from the *Reichsführer* which Pohl had to convey to all of the camp commandants, that no more Jews were to be killed and that the mortality rate of the prisoners was to be reduced by whatever means were available. A similar instruction was given to the commandants regarding possible evacuation of the camps. The camp at Belsen, in particular, was in a state of chaos. Millions of bodies still lay in the neighbourhood of the temporary crematorium [exaggerated figure]. Effluent could not be cleared, and a start was made in building emergency latrines and extending the sludge traps. Pohl ordered Kramer to send work parties into the surrounding woods and collect whatever edible materials they could find and to add them to the rations. It was not possible to increase supplies as the Provincial Ration Office refused to contribute to the camp at Belsen. Because he was unable to proceed with incinerations due to the lack of timber, I personally told Kramer to fell trees in the nearest forest. I was subsequently able to confirm that accommodation and water supply was improved, but that the basic complaint, the lack of rations, could not be improved upon.[106]

Approximately 60,000 inmates desperately needed to be fed, but the huge influx of new arrivals at the camp only exacerbated the situation. Not only were the prisoners dying of starvation, but typhoid and other deadly diseases were raging through the camp. The overcrowding also meant that there was a chronic shortage of accommodation, but in spite of Höss's best efforts to provide Kramer with new huts, there weren't enough materials available with which to repair the half-built buildings. Conditions inside the camp were atrocious. Höss feared that all sense of organisation was dissipating. Roll-calls were no longer being properly carried out as too many of the inmates lacked the strength to even stand up. Many of the prisoners were so badly emaciated that their arms and legs were like matchsticks, the bones protruding through what remained of their flesh. The evacuees from Auschwitz had been herded into one corner of the camp and left to die. After their death, their corpses were left lying around, often for days at a time, awaiting incineration. The stench of disintegrating bodies filled the camp.

Yet despite these horrific living conditions, the camp officials, under Höss's supervision, were determined to uphold order. The guards weren't concerned for the welfare of the prisoners; their only concern was for the loss of slave labour their deaths signified. As the war was drawing to a close, Höss's abhorrence of the Jews and the other incarcerated prisoners intensified. Where once Höss had felt sympathy for the prisoners' suffering, he was now void of all compassion. He was consumed by a determination to oversee the running of the concentration camps to the bitter end.

Chapter VII: Retribution

By April 1945, the German military were retreating across a scarred and devastated wasteland. On both the Eastern and Western fronts the last agonising moments of the war were being played out. In early April, less than 100 miles east of Berlin, German infantries and Panzer *truppen* were struggling to hold the front against the superior Soviet artillery and aviation defence. As the Red Army gathered momentum, more towns and villages were left reeling in their wake. The German Army was forced into retreat across the country. In the Reich capital, the government awaited the final Soviet onslaught along the River Oder. The air was heavy with a sense of foreboding and despair. It was only a matter of time before the Russians reached Berlin.

Höss had few illusions about what the future held in store for Germany, yet he continued to listen to the endless radio propaganda broadcasts in the vain hope that his fears might be quelled. Although he was still a loyal member of the SS, he couldn't quite buy the Party line that everything was going to be alright. In spite of the deteriorating military situation, and his own doubts and fears, Höss continued to use every means available to him, orthodox and unorthodox, to ensure that his department ran smoothly. However, on 16 April, whilst Höss was overseeing the evacuation of Sachsenhausen and Ravensbrück, the offices of the WVHA were attacked by the Allies. The headquarters' personnel, along with the office typewriters, safes, decoding machines, and any documents that had been salvaged from the ruins, were loaded onto busses and trucks, and on Himmler's orders, were moved temporarily to Ravensbrück concentration camp.

Höss was ordered to prepare a motorcade to transport SS officials and their families to Barth in Pomerania. Although they were protected by a squad of SS troops, the threat of low-flying enemy aircraft meant the journey had to be undertaken at night. The main road was very congested due to the thousands of civilians fleeing the capital in the same direction, and Höss was concerned that the group might get split up. They hurriedly moved from one forest to another in an effort to avoid Russian aircraft. Everywhere they looked they were greeted by scenes of chaos and disorder. The roads and forest tracks were littered with corpses, burned-out vehicles, abandoned prams, handcarts and suitcases. The prisoners who had collapsed from their injuries were moved to the side of the road and left to suffer where they lay. Höss's column progressed pitifully slowly. Glücks and Gerhard Maurer decided to take a different route and they drove to Warnemünde, while Höss's group continued on its perilous journey to Barth.

The rest of the group was accommodated in the former munitions factory in Barth. We remained there for two days; an order then came to move to Rendsburg in Holstein where we were to meet up with *Gruppenführer* Glücks and Maurer— who had left us—at the *Waffen*-SS Logistic headquarters. The families of the group's personnel accompanied us with the main transport, which I had to lead. In Rendsburg we were joined by the following people: *Gruppenführer* Glücks with his wife and driver; Frau Eicke, the wife of Glück's predecessor, with her daughter and her two children; Lölling, with his wife and son; Sommer with his wife; Kiener with a women and child; Frau Dr Salpeter, whose husband remained in Berlin [Salpeter was a deputy to *Obergruppenführer* Pohl in the Main Office]; myself with my wife and children; Burger with Frau Kleinheisterkamp; the wife of a commander of a *Waffen*-SS division. She was Swedish and made her way to a Swedish consulate and was not seen again; *Obersturmführer* Biemann from Amt 2 of Amtsgruppe D; Maurer with his driver. Two lorries with luggage and all the intelligence material went missing in Rostock... I found accommodation in a stable for one night in Klein Benecke, 20 km north of Rendsburg, for the column. The following day Kiener was able to find accommodation for the women and children in a school building. On 1 May, following a discussion between *Obergruppenführer* Glücks and *Obergruppenführer* Prutzman, we travelled on to Flensburg.[107]

During the journey to Flensburg, Höss was told that the *Führer* had been killed while leading his troops in a last-ditch defence in Berlin.* News of his death shocked both Höss and Hedwig. Without his protection they feared it was only a matter of time before they were hunted down by the Russians. They considered taking poison to avoid being captured but decided against it for the sake of their children.

During the night of 1 May, Höss and his family arrived in St Michaelisdonn in Holstein. Here, Hedwig and the family were accommodated by Frau Thomsen's mother, whose daughter had been the children's teacher at Auschwitz. Höss's driver, *Oberscharführer* Hager, and a prisoner had accompanied them there, and they brought all of their luggage to Frau Thomsen in St Michaelisdonn. The next morning Höss returned to Rendsburg, taking his eldest son Klaus with him.

---

* Although Adolf Hitler had committed suicide whilst hiding in the Reichskanzlei *führerbunker* on 30 April 1945, Nazi radio broadcast that the *Führer* was killed whilst leading his troops in a last-ditch defence.

Klaus had persistently pleaded with his father to allow him to take part in the final battles in northern Germany. During the course of the morning they drove to Flensburg.

> We were supposed to meet with *Polizeipräsident, Oberführer* Hinz. Hinz was unable to accommodate us. On his advice, we travelled to a wood on the road to Apenrade, 2 km north of Flensburg, where we changed our clothes. That evening Glücks, Maurer and I visited Hinz once again in order to hear what the *Reichsführer's* decision was. Hinz told us he had been unable to contact Himmler. We were to look for him at the Naval School in Mirwick. There we found Himmler.[108]

Höss found the *Reichsführer* in a strangely effusive mood. 'Well gentlemen', he exclaimed, 'Now it's over, you know what to do.'[109] Himmler calmly issued his last order and told them to try to hide themselves in the army. With no further duties left for them to perform, Höss, Glücks and Maurer prepared to leave.

> This was the goodbye from the man I respected so highly, in whom I had placed such tremendous confidence, whose orders and sayings were gospel to me. Maurer and I just looked at each other in silence thinking the same thought. We were both old Nazis and SS officers who lived for our ideology.[110]

For Höss, the prospect of carrying on without a leader was daunting. He had spent his entire life following orders from various authorities and now the very structure upon which he had built his life was giving way. In his determination to be a good bureaucrat to the very end, Höss began preparing for the events that lay ahead. The group discussed their limited options and decided that their only real chance of evading capture was to disguise themselves as members of the *Wehrmacht* and to cross the border into Denmark.

The other members of the staff were to scatter and try to get through as best they could. The women and children were taken care of by *Gruppenführer* Gebhardt, head of the SS field hospital in Hohenluchen. The following morning, Maurer and I went once again to *Oberführer* Hinz who told us that our last chance was for him to arrange for *Kapitän* zur See Luth to accommodate us. The following morning we were given paybooks with false names and clothing. I took the name of Franz Lang, Petty Officer. As far as I recall the others took the following names: *Sturmbannführer* Burger—Wolff; Maurer—a maiden name [presumably his wife's] which I no longer remember; Glücks—Sonnemann; Lölling—Dr Gerla II. The rest of the group were not to take false names as they were not in so much danger. Maurer, Burger and I received instructions to proceed to Rantum on the island of Sylt. The paybooks and instructions for others were not yet ready and were not expected to be completed until 5 May. During the morning of Sunday 3 May, Maurer, Burger and myself set off for Rantum. It was my intention to break the journey at Bredstedt, and visit the Torbers. [Frau Torber is a sister-in-law of Frau Thomsen in St Michaelisdonn]. I parted from Maurer and Burger at a crossroads near Walsbull, on my route to Bredstedt, and agreed to meet up with them the following day at Niebull. When I arrived there the next day, I met nobody. From Niebull I then travelled to Rantum and reported to the HQ of the Naval Intelligence School.[111]

At the naval school, Höss heard a radio announcement that the *Reichsführer* had been arrested near a British checkpoint close to Lüneburg, but had committed suicide by ingesting poison. Himmler's fate prompted Höss to also carry a vial of poison with him to ensure that he would not fall into the hands of his enemies alive.

Days later, still disguised as a member of the German navy, Höss was captured by the British. Confident that he could outwit the guards he decided not to commit suicide. He was briefly interrogated before being moved to a prison camp. His guards were completely unaware of his status and, since he was a member of the German navy, they never thought to look for an SS tattoo. During his imprisonment, Klaus was allowed to visit his father once every few days. After nearly four weeks in jail, Höss was released early. He managed to secure a job through the employment office with a farmer in Gottrupel, called Peter Hansen. A few days later, Höss decided to visit St Michaelisdonn.

> I asked Frau Thomsen to inform my wife of my presence... I took the opportunity to remain at Frau Thomsen's overnight. I left again the following day. During the day we met at a sandy area behind St Michaelisdonn, near the sugar factory. In the evening I met my wife in Frau Thomsen's house. Towards the end of June I made a second visit to St Michaelisdonn where once again I met my wife alone in the sandy area.[112]

Like many other Nazi fugitives, Höss was shrewd enough to go into hiding in the British zone of Germany. He maintained contact with Hedwig through her brother Fritz Hensel, who was working in Flensburg. Hensel often brought Höss food and various home comforts. Although Höss missed his family he enjoyed working as a labourer. Those who met 'Franz Lang' thought him a quiet, practical man, who worked hard to earn his money. Yet, behind the disguise was a man harbouring a dark secret. Although he had gone unnoticed by the British authorities, he was in constant danger of arrest and prosecution. He tried to carry on with his life in spite of this threat, working on the land and making contact with his family whenever he could.

> In September, I travelled to Frau Torber in Bredstedt, remained there for a day and returned to Gottrupel in the evening. Whilst I was at Frau Torbel's I wrote a detailed letter to my wife. My wife's reply was sent on to me in Gottrupel, without any covering letter, by Frau Torbel.[113]

Over the coming weeks Höss remained in hiding, working diligently on the land and rarely mixing with his colleagues. In 1945, shortly before Christmas, he met up with Hensel once more in Flensburg. Höss wrote, 'We had a meal in a local pub, where he brought me up to date on a variety of matters'.[114] Hensel revealed that Allied military police forces and military intelligence units were searching for Nazi criminals with the intention of bringing them to justice. The Allied armies were joining forces with survivors of the concentration camps to form hunting parties which were targeting specific SS officials. Hensel told Höss that the British Field Security Police were also looking for him. These intelligence units, he said, had been tracking down the perpetrators' wives and children as they suspected that familial attachments would keep them living nearby. They were right. In November, soldiers from an intelligence unit located Hedwig and interrogated her. She told the officers that she had last seen her husband in Rendsburg on 30 April 1945, but the British soldiers were unconvinced.

* * * * *

Since the autumn of 1945, the War Crimes Investigation Section 21 Army Group and the British Intelligence Corps had been looking for Höss. Following the British liberation of Bergen-Belsen in April 1945, Commandant Kramer and a number of survivors were questioned and Höss's name was repeatedly mentioned. Kramer spoke at length about Höss, and former prisoners willingly divulged details of their encounters with him in Auschwitz. Over the coming weeks, the 92 Field Security Section picked up on the trail of the former commandant of Auschwitz. After questioning a number of Nazis and guards who had accompanied the Höss family to northern Germany, they finally received information that the family were living in a flat in the sections area, near a sugar factory in St Michaelisdonn. The Höss family home was immediately put under surveillance, and one dark, cold November evening, members of the 92 Field Security raided the property. According to Captain William Victor Cross, an officer with the 92 Field Security Section:

> [Frau Höss] was asked where her husband was and she replied that he was dead... We knew from experience that widows usually had a photograph of their late husband... Searching the flat we could not find a photograph, and felt that he was alive.[115]

The officers left the property and after 'assessing various aspects of Frau Höss's story, members of the section gained the firm impression that she was lying'.[116] While the intelligence corps prepared to arrest Hedwig and her children, Hensel paid his final visit to Höss on 3 March 1946. He had brought with him a parcel from Hedwig that contained food and clothing. Höss wrote:

> At that time he showed me two letters which my wife wrote to him from which I was able to tell how my family was.[117]

On the night of 5 March, members of the 92 Field Security Section, consisting of Captain Victor Cross, Sergeant Bernard Clarke and four other soldiers, arrested Hedwig and imprisoned her. She was separated from the children and locked in a cell on her own. The eldest children were questioned, whilst the youngest were cared for by a specially trained team. For the next five days Hedwig was interrogated. She was repeatedly asked to disclose the whereabouts of her husband but each time she stubbornly insisted that he was dead. The guards finally decided to trick her into revealing the truth. Officers organised for a train to be shunted along a railway line, directly behind Hedwig's cell, making as much noise as possible. Captain Cross wrote:

We informed Frau Höss that the train outside was to take her three sons [In fact she only had two sons—Klaus and Burling] to Siberia, unless she told us where her husband was, and his aliases; if she did not do this then she could have two minutes to say goodbye to her sons, or tell us what we wanted to know. We left her for ten minutes or so with paper and pencil to write down the information we required. Fortunately our bluff worked; she wrote down the information and she and her sons were sent home.[118]

Hedwig revealed her husband's whereabouts at 4.00 p.m. on Monday, 11 March 1946; she also admitted that Höss had paid her a visit in St Michaelisdonn. She told her interrogators that he was living under the alias Franz Lang on a farm owned by Peter Hansen, in Gottrupel near Flensburg. The entire 92 Field Security Section assembled almost immediately and made preparations for its men to journey to Flensburg to capture the commandant. When they arrived in the area that evening, they liaised locally with the 93 and 318 Field Security Section, and made plans to surround the farm and surprise the Nazi fugitive.

At 11.00 p.m. that evening the intelligence section arrived at Gottrupel and located the farm. Trucks carrying soldiers, a medical officer, and Captain Cross, slowly advanced towards the farm and surrounded a stable block that was also used as a slaughter house. Breaking through the front door they came face to face with a frightened man in his pyjamas, gaunt and shabby in appearance, who had evidently been awoken by the disturbance. A medical officer of the 5 Royal Horse Artillery, 7 Armoured Division, immediately lunged at the man and prised open his mouth, examining him for any hidden poison. The section had obtained information that all members of *Amtsgruppe* D had been issued with the same poison with which Himmler had succeeded in killing himself following his capture. But unfortunately for Höss the two vials of poison he always carried had been accidentally broken two days earlier. The bewildered man was pulled upright and Captain Cross demanded to know his identity. 'Franz Lang', came the defiant reply. He was asked a second time, this time more aggressively, to admit his real identity. The man repeated that his name was Franz Lang, prompting Sergeant Clarke to attack him; he punched him four times in the face before Höss finally surrendered and admitted his real name. Clarke angrily dragged Höss out to one of the slaughterhouse tables, where he ripped his pyjamas off his body and began punching him violently, knocking him to the ground in the process. Another soldier from the party began repeatedly kicking Höss. According to Clarke, the blows dealt and the screams elicited were endless.

Fearing that Höss would be beaten to death, Captain Cross intervened and told his men to stop unless they wanted a corpse on their hands. Blood-soaked and badly bruised, Höss was yanked back to his feet, handcuffed, and covered in a blanket, before being shoved into a waiting car and driven back to the Field Security Headquarters at Heide. During the car journey, Clarke forced a substantial amount of whisky down Höss's throat. The drunken Höss tried to sleep, but Clarke kept aggressively poking his service stick under his eyelids and warning him to keep his eyes open.

They arrived at Heide in the early hours of the morning. Höss's blanket was taken from him and he was ordered to walk naked through the snow, across the barracks courtyard to his cell. For three days he was subjected to regular beatings and denied sleep. According to Private Ken Jones of the 5th Royal Horse Artillery stationed at Heide, 'They brought him to us when he refused to cooperate over questioning'.[119] Two other soldiers were detailed to join Private Jones in Höss's cell 'to help break him down for interrogation'.[120] Night and day, guards surrounded him, armed with axe handles. Their job was to ensure that he didn't fall asleep, and if he showed any signs of doing so they were to prod him with the handle of the axe. When Höss was taken outside for exercise he was allowed to wear only a thin cotton shirt and jeans in the snow. 'During the first interrogation', wrote Höss, 'they beat me to obtain evidence'.[121] After preliminary questioning, the interrogators decided to submit a report in the form of a statement in Höss's own words. It was to be signed by him and witnessed by two NCOs from the section, Sergeant Kudisch and Sergeant Roberts. Throughout the proceedings, Höss was subjected to further physical abuse and was force-fed alcohol. In fact, Höss's own riding crop was used to whip him. Only semi-conscious and barely able to keep his eyes open after three nights of sleep deprivation, Höss gave his statement and was ordered to sign an eight-page confession at 2.30 a.m. on Thursday, 14 March. 'I do not know what was in the statement', Höss wrote, 'or what I said, despite the fact I signed it'.[122]

In the statement, numbered N10-1210, he wrote about his formative years, his ascension through the ranks of the SS, his duties and tasks as commandant of Auschwitz, and the horrific process of exterminating the Jews. The last pages were devoted to his promotion in the WVHA and his subsequent escape to northern Germany with his family. Captain Victor Cross wrote a section report on the interrogation and noted:

> Höss gave his statement in a very matter of fact way and it appears he is quite willing to give information.[123]

The following day, on 15 March, after having been forced to make a full confession to the authorities, a weary and dishevelled Höss was handed over to Captain Alexander, of the No.1 War Crimes Investigation Team. He was taken to the Rhine Army at Minden-on-the-Weser, where he was interrogated and beaten yet again. On 16 March, his interrogators obtained a second signature from him, this time at the bottom of an English text. A broken and emotionally drained Höss was returned to his cell. Four days later, on 20

March, Höss was once again frogmarched out of his cell and interrogated for hours on end.

During his weeks of imprisonment in Minden-on-the-Weser, Höss became deeply depressed. Since his arrest he had neither washed nor shaved and was forced to wear handcuffs at all times, even while locked in his cell. Despite his utter dejection and isolation, he never considered his imprisonment unjust. He never exhibited any signs of remorse, but he seemed to have accepted responsibility for his actions and knew that he would face the death sentence.

> After three weeks I was shaved, my hair was cut, and I was allowed to wash myself. My handcuffs had not been removed since my arrest. The next day I was taken by car to Nuremberg together with a prisoner of war who had been sent from London to stand as a witness in Fritzsche's defence.[124]

The POW Höss refers to was Moritz von Schirmeister. He had been the personal press attaché of Josef Goebbels. At the end of the war he was arrested by the British and interned in a POW camp in England. During the car journey, they spoke freely to one another. Höss told Schirmeister that he was being brought to Nuremberg because SS-*Obergruppenführer* Ernst Kaltenbrunner's defence attorney had summoned him as a witness for his defence.* The conversation then turned to their respective arrests and interrogations by the British. According to Schirmeister, the former commandant of Auschwitz confided in him that he had signed a statement admitting to the murder of two and a half million Jews.

---

* Since June 1942, SS-*Obergruppenführer* Dr Ernst Kaltenbrunner had been the director of the RSHA. He oversaw the *Einsatzgruppen* death squads that followed the invasion forces of the German Army into the Eastern territories. At the Nuremberg trials he was charged with war crimes, crimes against humanity and conspiring to commit crimes against peace. The most notable witness in this trial was Rudolf Höss.

But I could just as well have said that it was five million Jews. There are certain methods by which any confession can be obtained, whether it is true or not.[125]

When Höss and Schirmeister arrived in Nuremberg on 1 April, the city still bore the undeniable signs of war, with many of the buildings gutted and flattened. In the 1930s, Nuremberg had been home to the mass Nazi Party rallies; now the Americans had designated it the stage for the international military tribunal. At Nuremberg Prison, Höss was surprised to be housed amongst the chief Nazi criminals, including Hermann Göring, Rudolf Hess, Albert Speer, and Julius Streicher. During his first few days there he was left alone in a dark cell. He saw no one other than the mess attendants who brought him a tray of food three times a day. The food was basic but good. Höss spent hours on end every day either sitting on his bed or pacing back and forth in his small cell. Eventually he was moved to another cell, which had a clean bed, a table, a chair, and most importantly, a window. Wearing dyed-black army fatigues, he was permitted to walk around the prison courtyard with the other prisoners, so long as they walked one behind the other and maintained a distance of four feet at all times. On the whole, Höss's quality of life improved at Nuremberg, but he was still interrogated daily and subjected to a variety of psychological tests.

* * * * *

Höss was questioned at length by the Americans between 1 April and 4 April. He recounted his life story, from his childhood onwards; his decision to join the Nazi Party; his entry into the SS, and his career as the commandant of Auschwitz. He spoke openly about all of these events and gave precise answers to questions put to him by the judges, the defence counsel and the prosecution. He even corrected various statements and figures he thought were untrue. He protected no one—Kaltenbrunner included. Throughout the interrogations, he spoke calmly and candidly about what he had done, repeatedly stating that he had considered the mass murders administrative procedures.

On 5 April, Höss was interrogated yet again. On this occasion, he revealed that, judging by the figures he had obtained from Eichmann, he had ordered the deaths of some 2,500,000 victims, while at least another 500,000 prisoners had died from illness and exhaustion during his time in command. The American officers produced a three-page affidavit, which they had typed themselves, and Höss was instructed to sign it. The affidavit was written in English, a language Höss didn't speak, so he insisted that it be translated into German. On 8 April, the prosecutors grudgingly handed him a translated document to sign. The prosecution decided against calling the former commandant to the witness stand. However, Höss was called to the stand by the defence lawyer acting on behalf of SS-*Obergruppenführer* Ernst Kaltenbrunner, who was hoping to shift some of the blame onto Himmler.

A week later Höss was asked to repeat his testimony concerning the estimated death toll at Auschwitz. During cross-examination by Colonel Amen, Höss stated that all the killings had been ordered by *Reichsführer* Himmler, yet at no time did he try to deny his own role in the murderous hierarchy of the SS. He knew that he had subjected hundreds of thousands of Jews to living conditions likely to bring about their physical demise and he conceded that he had enslaved them and deported them to Auschwitz under inhumane conditions, only to starve, beat and gas many of them. Despite being aware of his terrible deeds, Höss seemed unable to piece them all together and recognise the sheer enormity of his crime. Those who questioned him were surprised by his character. They anticipated meeting a monster but instead they were greeted by a calm and composed individual, who appeared on the surface to be quite ordinary. The American psychologist, G.M. Gilbert, who was given the arduous task of maintaining a psychological surveillance of the Nuremberg prisoners, reported that Höss's personality appeared to have been split in two by the Nazi regime. Even Sergeant Bernard Clark of the 92 Field Security Section, who was in charge of censoring letters sent by Höss to his wife and children, remarked:

> There were two different men in that one man. One was brutal with no regard for human life. The other was soft and affectionate.[126]

On 16 April, Höss was subjected to a secret interrogation and to his surprise he was brought face to face with Otto Moll. Höss had told his interrogators that Moll had been responsible for the exhumation of over 100,000 corpses at Auschwitz and had overseen their cremation in specially adapted pits. Later on in the war, Höss had made Moll responsible for all four crematoria, marking the birth of the 'Moll Plan'.*

On 5 May, Höss was forced to watch a concentration camp newsreel. He was monitored closely for any evidence of an emotional reaction during scenes of emaciated corpses being dragged into pits and piled on top of countless other murdered men, women and children. But Höss was determined not to give his captors the satisfaction of breaking him and he maintained a stony expression for the duration of the newsreel.

* * * * *

Höss's deepest fears were confirmed when the British and American authorities agreed to extradite him to Poland to stand trial there. Just before he left for Poland, Höss attempted to smuggle a letter out to his wife, in which he apologised to

---

* The 'Moll Plan' was the liquidation of Auschwitz and the evacuation of its prisoners.

her for confessing to the atrocities at Auschwitz. Although he admitted to the crimes, he claimed that he had been tortured into making false admissions. The letter never found Hedwig, however, as it was confiscated by one of the jailers.

Höss left Nuremberg on 25 May—the same date as his and Hedwig's wedding anniversary. With his wrists weighed down by heavy-duty handcuffs, he was driven to the airport, accompanied by Dr von Burgsdorff and Josef Bühler. An American aircraft flew them to Warsaw via Berlin. Höss was greeted by a flurry of press when he arrived at the airport and armed guards had to form a protective circle around him. Under the glaring spotlight of the press, and a torrent of abuse from a crowd of angry onlookers, Höss was handed over to the Polish authorities. He was brought to a Warsaw prison under heavy escort. For the first time since his arrest in the British zone, Höss was filled with a deep sense of foreboding. He knew that he was more reviled in the East than anywhere else in Europe. He wrote of his arrival at the prison:

> Several officials approached me immediately and showed me their Auschwitz tattoo numbers. I could not understand them.[127]

In Höss's eyes he had not committed a crime—he had merely been doing his job as a member of the SS. He still harboured a deep hatred for the Jews and the Polish and he continued to adopt a hard and callous attitude towards the former prisoners of the camp.

Höss spent almost the entire next two months of his incarceration locked inside a dark, cold, musty cell. His endless hours of confinement were rendered all the more difficult by the fact that he was not allowed to read or write anything to make the time pass more quickly. He knew that such isolation was intended to mentally break him, and it wasn't long before he became restless, agitated and depressed. He would pace back and forth across his cell for hours on end, or lie on his black, iron bed, staring up at the ceiling. His thoughts frequently turned to his family and he worried about their welfare. He wasn't allowed to write letters home or receive visitors and his sense of isolation intensified by the day. The lack of exercise and the insufficient rations of food also became a problem.

On 30 July, Höss was driven to the Warsaw railway station, along with seven other Nazi prisoners, including the notorious SS-*Sturmbannführer* Amon Göth, the former commandant of Plaszow labour camp. Here, under heavy armed guard, they were informed that they were being taken to Krakow to stand trial before a Supreme Polish National Tribunal. When they finally pulled into Krakow they had to wait at the station for a car to arrive. During this time a crowd began to gather. According to Höss:

> They angrily cursed us. *Sturmbannführer* Göth was recognised almost straight away, and if the car had not arrived when it did, we would have been attacked with stones.[128]

Höss found his first few weeks of imprisonment in Montelupich Prison in Krakow intolerable. Initially, he was deprived of all external stimuli and he began to experience prison psychosis. A young Polish guard took to beating him regularly, making his imprisonment all the more unbearable. Occasionally, the monotony of prison life was broken by pre-trial interrogations or visiting officials enquiring how he was being treated, but he never uttered a word about his ill-treatment. He had resigned himself to the fact that he would end his days in Poland. He had no delusions about what the future held for him: he knew that the death sentence was a certainty. He didn't expect the Poles to treat him kindly. Almost all of the guards were mourning someone close to them who had died either while fighting in the war or during their incarceration in a concentration camp. Höss became the target of a great deal of anger and recrimination.

On a regular basis I received only the smallest amount of bread
and not even a ladleful of their soup.[129]

Höss knew that if the guards had their way, 'they would
finish me off'.[130]

In October, Höss's prison life suddenly changed for
the better. The prosecutor's office decided that he should
be forced to write a detailed explanation of his crimes.
Psychology professor, Stanislaw Batawia, and Professor
Jan Sehn, the prosecuting attorney for the Polish War
Crimes Commission in Warsaw, ordered that the former
commandant of Auschwitz write about the evolvement of
the camp, the process of extermination, his impressions of
the various SS men he came into contact with, and most of
all, that he should give a frank and honest description of
his thoughts on the events that led him to become a mass
murderer. Even though the words Höss was poised to write
would be used against him during his trial, he was quite
willing to put his memoirs down on paper. He was astute
enough to know that this document would take many
weeks to complete and would thereby prolong his life.

Sitting at a wooden table affixed to a wall, he began to
document his life. Scribbling with a pencil on low-grade
paper he tried to recall the various dates and events as best
he could. Although on one level he saw his writings as a
fatalistic submission, on another level he was happy to
reveal the difficulties he had experienced as a commandant.
Throughout his writings he was very honest about the extent
of his involvement in the entire course of events. Under Jan
Sehn's direction, with whom he became quite close over
time, he wrote about the early concentration camps, his
experiences at Sachsenhausen and Dachau, Russian POWs
and the types of guards he had encountered. He went on
to write about the Jews, the Gypsies, the women's camp
and the gassing procedures. He was even asked to give

descriptions of those responsible for planning and ordering the construction of Auschwitz.

Over the ensuing months, Höss wrote on a daily basis, re-reading his work and correcting words and phrases in an effort to perfect the narrative. He was not allowed to keep a knife to sharpen his pencil so he regularly made alterations to the clarity of the pencilled writings to make them more legible. Once he had completed each section, which was numbered in the margins of each page, he scrawled the year and month and either signed his name with the letter 'H' or simply wrote 'Höss'.

When he had finally completed the various chapters, Sehn suggested that it might serve as a further refuge from the monotony of prison life if he undertook to write about himself. Höss wrote his memoirs over the course of just two months. In early March 1947, whilst still applying the finishing touches to his autobiography, he was informed that proceedings against him were underway in Warsaw, and he would stand trial in a matter of days. The indictment drafted by the prosecution charged him with membership of criminal organisations, the SS and the Nazi Party, serving as commandant of Auschwitz concentration camp, chief of Department DI of the SS-WVHA, and as commander of the Auschwitz garrison during the Hungarian deportations to the camp. He was also charged with physically and mentally abusing prisoners, as well as overseeing the theft of property and valuables that included removing valuable dental work from the mouths of the dead.

The proceedings commenced in Warsaw on 11 March. The journey from Krakow to the Polish capital was undertaken under heavy security but by the time Höss arrived in Warsaw his case had attracted considerable international interest. On the morning of his trial he was transferred to the court's detention cell; from there he was escorted through a door that opened directly onto the dock. As he entered the packed courtroom, hundreds of pairs of eyes turned in his direction. The crowd had expected to be faced with a monster, but at first glance the man before them seemed perfectly ordinary and there was no visible indication of his potential to commit unspeakable evil. But as soon as he took to the stand his cold manner came to light. He was emotionally detached and repressed. In spite of this, he answered most of the questions put to him openly and honestly. At no point did he deny the charges levied against him. He spoke calmly about the challenge of building Auschwitz and transforming Birkenau into a killing factory. Throughout the court case, Höss listened impassively to the testimony of experts, former prisoners, and members of the Auschwitz personnel who had also been extradited to Poland to face war crimes. Sometimes their words seemed to almost weary him, and occasionally he showed signs of irritation. Whenever the prosecutor submitted evidence, Höss would lean forward and listen intently to the details of his crimes being listed. A mounting tension could be detected between him and the former prisoners, but unlike other SS men, he kept his prejudices in check and remained outwardly composed.

Höss conceded that he had sent hundreds of thousands of Jews to the gas chambers and admitted that he had been a main accomplice in the implementation of the Final Solution. From the comforts of his office he had instructed others to torture and murder hundreds of thousands of prisoners. He was the creator of Auschwitz and had become an arbiter of life and death. However, he refused to repent during his trial, insisting that he had believed at the time that his actions were justified. He claimed that he had simply been a cog in the SS wheel and that he'd had no choice but to carry out the orders issued to him from Berlin. He believed that he had been a victim of the state and that his loyalty and obedience had been exploited. He also accused the state of thwarting his efforts to lead an ethical life. Finally, he said he did not wish to seek leniency from the court, but merely requested permission to send a final letter to his family and return his wedding ring to his wife. The proceedings were completed on 29 March and Höss was returned to his cell under heavy guard to await sentencing.

* * * * *

On 2 April, Höss was led into a packed courtroom for the final time. The judges filed in and the crowd took their seats. Höss was instructed to stand as his sentence and its terms were read aloud. As he stood there listening to his litany of crimes, which included membership of hostile organisations and offences against both the Jewish people and humanity, his face registered no emotion. After he was sentenced to death by hanging he made a brief statement before the court; he thanked his defence counsel for all their hard work during the case and defiantly declared to the courtroom that he would not seek clemency. He was then escorted back to his cell.

The following day, under armed guard, Höss was escorted back to Wadowice Prison near Krakow to await his execution.

He was to be hung at Auschwitz—the scene of the majority of his crimes. On 11 April, he wrote his final letters to Hedwig and the children. In his first letter, which he addressed to 'my dear good Mutz',[131] he wrote that his life was now coming to end. He tried to justify his actions and said that it was tragic that although he believed himself to be a kind, gentle, good-natured and very helpful person, he had somehow become the greatest mass murderer of all time. He said that his name had been disgraced throughout the world. He went on to say:

And you, my poor ones, have suffered unnecessary problems because of my name, especially the children.[132]

He concluded his letter by saying:

For the last time I send you loved ones my regards, to you all my
dear good children, my Annemäusl, my Burling, my Püppi, my
Kindi and my Klaus, and you, my darling and best Mutz.[133]

He then wrote a final letter to all of his children:

You, my dear, good children! Your daddy has to leave you
now. For you, poor ones, there remains only your dear, good
mummy. May she remain with you for a long time. You do not
understand what your good mummy really means to you, and
what a loved possession she is to you. The affection and care of
a mother is the most beautiful and valuable thing that exists on
this earth. I have understood this for some time, and now regret
it because it's all too late. To you, my dear children, I address
therefore my last plea: Never forget your dear good mother!
She has constantly taken care of you with such sacrificing love.
How much of the good things in life has she sacrificed for you?
How she feared for you when you were ill and how painfully
and tirelessly did she nurse all of you. Only for your sake must
she suffer now all of the despair and poverty. Don't ever forget
this through life. Help her now in her fate. Love and be good
to her always. Help her with your limited strength. In this way
forfeit her thanks for your love and care she sacrificed for you
during the days and nights. Klaus, my dear boy! You are the
oldest. You are now going out into the world. You now have to
make your own way through life. You have good abilities. Use
them! Retain your good heart. Become a person who is guided
principally by warmth and compassion. Learn to think and to
judge for yourself, dutifully. Don't accept everything without
criticism. Learn from life.

The biggest mistake I made in my life was that I believed
everything devotedly which came from the top, and I didn't
dare to have the least bit of misgiving about the truth of that
which was presented to me. Walk through life with your eyes
open. Don't become biased; examine the pros and cons in all
matters. In all your accomplishments, don't just let your mind

speak, but listen above all to the voice in your heart. Much, my dear boy, which I say at the moment, will not be understood by you. But always remember my last advice. I wish you, my dear Klaus, all the luck in your life. Become a capable, uncomplicated person who has his heart in the right place

Kindi and Püppi, you my big girls! You are still much too young to learn the degree of the hard fate metered out to us. But you especially, my dear good girls, are especially duty-bound to stand at your poor unfortunate mother's side and with love help her in every conceivable way. Surround her with all your childlike love from your heart and show her how much you love her. I can only implore you, listen to your dear good mother! She will show and care for you in her own devoted way and give those lessons you will require for life in order to become good and able human beings.

As basically different as you two are in your character, you both, my dear, and you my dear Hausmütterle, have, however, a kind nature and good hearts. Keep these throughout your later life. This is very important. Only later will you understand that and will you remember my last words.

My Burling, you dear little boy! Retain your happy child nature. The cruel life will tear you, my dear boy, soon enough away from your child's world. I was happy to hear from your dear mother that you are making good progress in school. Your dear father is powerless to tell you anything more. You poor little boy have now only your dear good mummy left who will care for you. Listen to her with love and kindness and so remain Daddy's dear Burling.

My dear Annemäusl. How little did I get the chance to familiarise your dear little personality. Your dear good mummy will have to take you, my dear Mäusl, for us into her arms and tell you of your daddy, and how very much he loved you. May you be for a long time mummy's little ray of sun and continue to give her much joy. May you, with your sunny ways, help your poor dear mummy through all the dull hours. Once more from my heart I ask you all, my dear good children, take to heart my last words. Think of them again and again. Keep in loving memory, your Dad.[134]

Höss enclosed his wedding ring with the letters, and he asked the prison authorities that it 'be delivered officially to my wife'.[135]

* * * * *

On 15 April, Höss was escorted by heavy guard to Auschwitz, to the same building in which he had presided over the fate of thousands of people. A sombre, heavy silence prevailed during the 30-minute journey. The convoy of vehicles arrived at 8.00 a.m. Höss was handcuffed and led to the basement of his former office. He was kept in the same basement in which he had conducted his affair with Eleonore Hodys.

On the day originally scheduled for his execution, an angry mob, many of whom were former inmates, gathered to witness the hanging. The crowd began shouting abuse and pushing against the wooden fence built to hold the people back. Fearing the spectators would surge forward and kill Höss with their bare hands, the Polish authorities decided to divert the crowd with a hoax. Soldiers pretended to escort Höss away in a car, only to secretly return him to his cell. His execution was then scheduled for the following morning, when only a handful of people would be present.

The morning of 16 April was grey and overcast. To his jailers, Höss's manner was passive. He remarked that he wasn't feeling well and was unable to eat very much so he requested a coffee instead. His last request was that the soldiers send his kindest regards to his wife and children and that they ask the Polish people to forgive him for what he had done. When the time finally came for Höss to be led to the gallows, he wearily clambered to his feet. As he was passing by the officials he paused and repeated his regret over what he had done to the Polish people. He then asked the officials for their forgiveness. The guards handcuffed him and led him out of his cell.

Flanked by four Polish soldiers, he was escorted from the entrance of the former SS administration building to the gallows, which were situated on a grassy tract of land near the former *Gestapo* offices and Crematorium I. There was no angry mob baying for Höss's blood this time; only a handful of people would witness his execution. As he walked over to the gallows, which had been erected by German POWs, his face was a blank canvas. His hands were handcuffed behind his back, and with the help of the executioner, whose face was concealed by a black hood, Höss climbed onto a stool placed on top of the trapdoor. A priest named Tadeusz Zaremba, who had been personally requested by Höss, approached the gallows. A prosecutor read out the sentence and asked Höss if he had any last words, but he had nothing to say. The executioner then placed a lined rope in one loop over Höss's head and adjusted it accordingly around his neck. The executioner returned to his station, and with a nod of the head from one of the officials he pulled the stool out from beneath Höss's feet.

The commandant's body struck the trapdoor, which immediately burst open, leaving his body hanging limply in mid-air. For a few moments nobody moved or made a sound—the swaying of the rope was the only movement. The silence was finally broken by the priest's recital of the prayer for the dying. It was eight minutes past ten o'clock. Höss's body was taken down from the rope, and at 21 minutes past ten the prison doctor pronounced him dead. His corpse was then wrapped in a blanket and loaded onto a truck. He was cremated at a secret location and his ashes were disposed of in a nearby river.

Epilogue

Rudolf Höss had finally been avenged for all his heinous crimes. He went to his grave without making a public statement about his offences, nor did he utter a single word about the Nazi ideology for which he had sacrificed both his own life and the lives of so many others. Ultimately, his biggest regret as he ascended the steps to the gallows was not that he had committed so many appalling crimes against humanity but rather that his fatherland had lost the war. In his mind he had been following orders and his actions in the camp did not detract from his life outside of it where he was a loving husband and father.

Höss had no idea of the indelible mark his deeds would have on the twentieth century. He tried to shift responsibility for the deaths of 1.2 million people onto the German state. While writing his autobiography in the confines of his cell, he conceded that the extermination of the Jews had been a mistake, but argued that the murders had not been premeditated. In a desperate attempt to justify the gassings, Höss claimed that the children who had been gassed to death had suffered considerably less than the children who had died in the great fire storms the Allied bombings had given rise to in the German cities. The air crews had purposely killed innocent German women and children using phosphorus bombs and yet they hadn't been brought to justice for their crimes. The SS on the other hand had used the more humane Zyklon B to deliver a quick and painless death to their victims and yet they were being depicted as the monsters. What Höss fails to mention is that the extermination of the Jews was a policy of ideology that was in no way connected to the war.

Every country in Europe was affected by the Final Solution, and Höss and the SS hierarchy left a legacy of pain and loss in their wake. Höss was rendered all the more sinister in the public consciousness by his outwardly normal appearance. Yet in front of his subordinates he was a colourless administrator who ordered the deaths of millions from the comfort of his office. He was absorbed in his work and constantly strived for the approval and recognition of his superiors. The peak of his career was his innovative introduction of the gas chambers to Auschwitz and the consequent evolvement of the camp. Although Höss claimed to struggle daily with the murderous duties assigned to him, he was propelled onwards by a blind allegiance to the Nazi state.

At Auschwitz, Höss was neither chiefly ideologically motivated, nor was he a Nazi fanatic perverted by torture and death. His driving force was a desire to succeed in the realms of the SS order, irrespective of the heinous tasks assigned to him. Like so many of his fellow perpetrators, he was not a natural-born killer, but a process of gradual desensitisation helped him to excel in the field. It was Höss's innovation that set him apart from the other robot-like guards. As commandant he frequently used his own initiative to bolster the camp and develop it into a more efficient killing centre. On a number of occasions he even dared to criticise the SS hierarchy and voice his own views, including those concerning the system of murder within the camp. When Höss was offered the dressed-up promotion to concentration camp administration in Berlin, he accepted the position with some reluctance. It was clear he did not want to leave Auschwitz. Not only was he emotionally attached to the camp but he also felt that he had worked hard to implement a system that no successor would be capable of sustaining. He believed that no other commandant could possibly emulate his level of competence.

Throughout his time at Auschwitz, Höss was a diligent worker who took great pride in the outcome his efforts produced. Like so many other SS men, he managed to suppress any revulsion his work gave rise to by seeing Jews as 'the enemy'—a deplorable race with no intrinsic claim to life. In order to unravel the complex motivations of a man like Höss, one must also look outside of the man himself and to the ideology that possessed him. Auschwitz developed Höss into a mass murderer but he had been a willing accomplice from the very beginning. He chose to put the education he received into practice. The day he carried out his first murder he unknowingly knotted the hangman's noose that would avenge the 1.2 million murders he committed, and the devastation he caused to the lives of countless friends and family members in the process.

Summary of Rudolf Höss's Career

Dates of Rank

SS-*Anwärter*: 20 September 1933

SS-*Mann*: 1 April 1934

SS-*Sturmmann*: 20 April 1934

SS-*Unterscharführer*: 28 November 1934

SS-*Scharführer*: 1 April 1935

SS-*Oberscharführer*: 1 July 1935

SS-*Hauptscharführer*: 1 March 1936

SS-*Untersturmführer*: 13 September 1936

SS-*Obersturmführer*: 11 September 1938

SS-*Hauptsturmführer*: 9 November 1938

SS-*Sturmbannführer*: 30 January 1941

SS-*Obersturmbannführer*: 18 July 1942

Rudolf Höss's Significant Awards

Iron Cross 1st Class (WWI)

Iron Cross 2nd Class (WWI)

Baden Military Bravery Medal (WWI)

Honor Cross for Combatants 1914-1918

Hungarian War Service Medal for Combatants 1914-1918

Turkish War Medal (WWI)

Silver Wound Badge (WWI)

Baltic Cross 1st Class (*Freikorps*)

Baltic Cross 2nd Class (*Freikorps*)

SS 8 year Long Service Decoration

War Merit Cross (2nd Class with Swords)

SS Honor Ring

SS Honor Sword

List of the Officers Appointed to Auschwitz-Birkenau from 1940-1945

Adolph, Benno
Albert, Roland
Arnold, August Christian
Aumeier, Hans
Baer, Richard
Bartels, Johann-Detlef
Baumgatner, Ludwig
Bayer, Wilhelm
Beer, Rudolf
Beger, Bruno
Bischoff, Karl
Blaschke, Otto
Bodmann, Franz
Böhne, Ludwig
Brauning, Edmund
Brossmann, Otto
Burger, Wilhelm
Caesar, Joachim
Capesius, Victor
Conrad, Hans
Dejaco, Walter
Desch, Johann
Dienstbach, Oskar
Drees, Eduard
Eggeling, Karl
Ehrenberger, Raimond
Ehser, Max

Engelbrecht, Friedrich
Entress, Friedrich
Ertl, Fritz
Fischer, Horst
Fischer, Karl-Josef
Frank, Willy
Fritzsch, Karl
Frommhagen, Erich
Ganninger, Heinrich
Gebhardt, Max
Gerber, Gerhard
Goebel, Walter
Grabner, Maximilian
Grunberg, Georg Dietrich
Gussregen, Georg
Halblieb, Franz
Hartjenstein, Friedrich
Heidl, Otto
Heimann, Karl
Höcker, Karl
Hoffmann, Karl
Hofmann, Franz Johann
Horstmann, Rudolf
Höss, Rudolf
Hössler, Franz
Jobst, Willibald
Josten, Heinrich

Jothan, Werner
Kirschneck, Hans
Kitt, Bruno
Klein, Fritz
Klipp, Kurt
Koenig, Hans Wilhelm
Kollmer, Josef
Kramer, Herbert-
Gunther
Kramer, Josef
Kratzer, Theodor
Kraus, Franz Xaver
Krebsbach, Eduard
Kremer, Hans Hermann
Kreuzmann, Paul
Krömer, Adolf
Kudriawtzow, Armand
Kudriawtzow, Georg
Kühler, Heinz
Kurz, Alois
Lange, Theodor
Langermann, Armand
Liebehenschel, Artur
Lucas, Franz
Maier, Franz Xaver
Meimeth, Alfred
Mengele, Josef
Merbach, Hans Erich
Meyer, Georg Franz
Meyer, Valentin
Meyr, Max
Möckel, Karl Ernest
Moehlmann, Arie
Moser, Hans Karl
Mulka, Robert
Muller, Max

Muller, Paul
Münch, Hans
Muslow, Hans
Neumann, Robert
Orlich, Rudolf
Paulsen, Thomas
Pflaum, Guntrum
Pfütze, Bruno
Pinnow, Willy
Plaza, Heinrich
Plorin, Artur
Polenz, Walter
Pollok, Josef
Popiersch, Max
Precht, Elimer Luder
Reinicke, Otto Emil
Reischenbeck, Wilhelm
Rieck, Andreas
Rieck, Willi
Ritzheimer, Heinz
Rohde, Werner
Sauer, Julius
Sautter, Erich
Schattenberg, Heinz
Schatz, Willi
Schemmel, Alfred
Schindler, Hans
Schippel, Helmet
Schlachter, August
Schluter, Friedrich
Schmidetzki, Walter
Schneier, Reinhold
Schöttl, Vincenz
Schulte, Wilhelm
Schulz, Otto Ludwig
Schurz, Hans

Schütz, Walter
Schwarz, Heinrich
Schwarzhuber, Johann
Schwela, Siegfried
Seidler, Friedrich
Sell, Max
Siegmann, Wilhelm
Simon, Josef
Stark, Hans
Stenger, Franz
Stocker, Emil
Stoppel, Otto
Storch, Henry
Storde, Karl
Tager, Heinrich
Teuber, Karl Heinz
Thilo, Heinz
Thomsen, Reinhard
Trzebinski, Alfred
Turek, Friedrich
Uhlenbrook, Kurt
Urbanczyk, Walter
Verbruggen, Alfons
Vetter, Helmet
Von Helmersen, Erwin
Von Sauberzweig,
Georg
Wagner, Rudolf
Weber, Bruno
Weymann, Hans
Wiegand, Konrad
Wirths, Eduard
Wolter, Fritz
Wotke, Karl
Wuttke, Herbert
Ziemssen, Wilhelm

Zoller, Victor
Zorn, Werner

Glossary and Abbreviations

Einsatzgruppen: Mobile killing units of the SS, Sipo-SD.

Führer: German word for 'leader'. This was Adolf Hitler's title.

Gau: One of the 42 Nazi Party administrative districts into which Nazi Germany was divided.

Gauleiter: Nazi Party boss in a *gau*.

General Government: Part of eastern Poland occupied by the German military.

Gestapo: *Geheime Staatspolizei*—secret state police.

Kapo: A prisoner placed in charge of his fellow inmates by the SS.

Kapp Putsch: The 1920 *Freikorps* revolt led by Wolfgang Kapp that attempted to overthrow the Weimar Republic.

Political prisoner: A person who has been imprisoned for their nonconformist political views.

POWs (prisoners of war): Members of armed forces who are captured and imprisoned by an enemy during a conflict.

Reich: German word for 'empire'. Adolf Hitler's reign, which lasted from 1933 to 1945, is often referred to as the Third Reich.

Reichsführer-SS: Reich chief of the SS and German police.

RSHA: *Reichssicherheitshauptamt*—Reich Main Security Office, formed in late 1939, uniting the *Gestapo*, criminal police, SIPO and SD.

SD: *Sicherheitsdienst*—security service of the Nazi Party.

Sonderkommando: Special unit of the SS which consisted of camp prisoners whose primary responsibility was to dispose of corpses.

SS: *Schutzstaffel*—guard detachment created in 1925 as an elite Nazi Party bodyguard that evolved into a security and intelligence service with a military arm.

Totenkopf: *Totenkopfverbände*—Death's Head, a unit of the SS deployed to guard concentration camps.

Waffen-SS: Weapon SS—military arm of the SS from 1939 onwards.

Wehrmacht: Armed German forces.

WVHA: *Wirtschafts und Verwaltungshauptamt*—SS Economic and Administrative Head Office responsible for SS economic enterprises and concentration camps from 1942, under the command of Oswald Pohl.

Rank Equivalents

German Army	Waffen-SS	British Army
Gemeiner, Landser	*Schütze Oberschütze*	Private
Grenadier	*Sturmmann*	Lance Corporal
Obergrenadier		
Gefreiter	*Rottenführer*	Corporal
Obergefreiter	*Unterscharführer*	
Stabsgefreiter		
Unteroffizier	*Scharführer*	Sergeant
Unterfeldwebel	*Oberscharführer*	Colour Sergeant
Feldwebel		
Oberfeldwebel	*Hauptscharführer*	Sergeant Major
Stabsfeldwebel	*Hauptbereitschaftsleiter*	Warrant Officer
	Sturmscharführer	
Leutnant	*Untersturmführer*	Second Lieutenant
Oberleutnant	*Obersturmführer*	First Lieutenant
Hauptmann	*Hauptsturmführer*	Captain
Major	*Sturmbannführer*	Major
Oberstleutnant	*Obersturmbannführer*	Lieutenant Colonel
Oberst	*Standartenführer*	Colonel
	Oberführer	Brigadier General
Generalmajor	*Brigadeführer*	Major General
Generalleutnant	*Gruppenführer*	Lieutenant General
General	*Obergruppenführer*	General
Generaloberst	*Oberstgruppenführer*	
Generalfeldmarschall	*Reichsführer-SS*	

Endnotes

* Whilst translating sections of the handwritten memoirs of Rudolf Höss, the author also consulted and compared for accuracy the published material of Steven Paskuly, *The Memoirs of the SS Kommandant at Auschwitz*, Prometheus Books, Buffalo, NY, 1992, and *The Commandant of Auschwitz*, Phoenix Press.

1. Laurence Rees, Auschwitz: *The Nazis and the Final Solution*. BBC Books, 2005.

2. Taken from the handwritten memoirs of Rudolf Höss— (Reminiscences)/96, volume 1-5, inventory number 49757 [Auschwitz-Birkenau Museum].

3. Taken from the handwritten memoirs of Rudolf Höss— (Reminiscences)/96, volume 1-5, inventory number 49757 [Auschwitz-Birkenau Museum].

4. Taken from the handwritten memoirs of Rudolf Höss— (Reminiscences)/96, volume 1-5, inventory number 49757 [Auschwitz-Birkenau Museum].

5. Taken from the handwritten memoirs of Rudolf Höss—(Reminiscences)/96, volume 1-5, inventory number 49757 [Auschwitz-Birkenau Museum].

6. Taken from the handwritten memoirs of Rudolf Höss—(Reminiscences)/96, volume 1-5, inventory number 49757 [Auschwitz-Birkenau Museum].

7. Taken from the handwritten memoirs of Rudolf Höss—(Reminiscences)/96, volume 1-5, inventory number 49757 [Auschwitz-Birkenau Museum].

8. Taken from the handwritten memoirs of Rudolf Höss—(Reminiscences)/96, volume 1-5, inventory number 49757 [Auschwitz-Birkenau Museum] and also supported due to clarity of writing by the publication *Death Dealer* [Da Capo Press] and *Commandant of Auschwitz* [Phoenix Press].

9. *Commandant of Auschwitz*. Phoenix Press. Pages 106/107.

10. *Commandant of Auschwitz*. Phoenix Press. Pages 106/107.

11. Steven Paskuly, Death Dealer: *The Memoirs of the SS Kommandant at Auschwitz*. Prometheus Books, Buffalo, NY, 1992. Page 261.

12. Steven Paskuly, *Death Dealer. The Memoirs of the SS Kommandant at Auschwitz*. Prometheus Books, Buffalo, NY, 1992. Page 251.

13. Steven Paskuly, *Death Dealer. The Memoirs of the SS Kommandant at Auschwitz*. Prometheus Books, Buffalo, NY, 1992. Page 309.

14. Testimony by Aniela Bednarska on 29 December 1962. Obtained from Auschwitz-Birkenau Museum and translated from Polish into English.

15. Account by Aniela Bednarska on 29 December 1962. Obtained from Auschwitz-Birkenau Museum and translated from Polish into English.

16. Steven Paskuly, *Death Dealer. The Memoirs of the SS Kommandant at Auschwitz*. Prometheus Books, Buffalo, NY, 1992. **Page 122.**

17. Steven Paskuly, *Death Dealer. The Memoirs of the SS Kommandant at Auschwitz*. Prometheus Books, Buffalo, NY, 1992. Page 123.

18. Taken from the handwritten memoirs of Rudolf Höss—(Reminiscences)/96, volume 1-5, inventory number 49757 [Auschwitz-Birkenau Museum].

19. Taken from the handwritten memoirs of Rudolf Höss—(Reminiscences)/96, volume 1-5, inventory number 49757 [Auschwitz-Birkenau Museum].

20. Taken from the handwritten memoirs of Rudolf Höss—(Reminiscences)/96, volume 1-5, inventory number 49757 [Auschwitz-Birkenau Museum].

21. Taken from the handwritten memoirs of Rudolf Höss—(Reminiscences)/96, volume 1-5, inventory number 49757 [Auschwitz-Birkenau Museum].

22. Taken from the handwritten memoirs of Rudolf Höss—(Reminiscences)/96, volume 1-5, inventory number 49757 [Auschwitz-Birkenau Museum].

23. Steven Paskuly, *Death Dealer. The Memoirs of the SS Kommandant at Auschwitz*. Prometheus Books, Buffalo, NY, 1992. Page 285.

24. Steven Paskuly, *Death Dealer. The Memoirs of the SS Kommandant at Auschwitz*. Prometheus Books, Buffalo, NY, 1992. Page 285.

25. Account taken by Stanislaw Dubiel who worked as a general gardener in the Höss villa and carried out various duties in the house between 6 November 1940 and 18 November 1945. Testimony obtained in Polish and translated into English.

26. Laurence Rees, *Auschwitz*. BBC Books, 2005. Page 66.

27. Laurence Rees, *Auschwitz*. BBC Books, 2005. Page 66.

28. *Commandant of Auschwitz*. Phoenix Press. Pages 106/107.

29. Account by the housekeeper of SS-*Untersturmführer* Georg Gussregen, who visited Auschwitz and the Höss villa during the summer of 1941.

30. Irena Strzelecka, 'Hospitals', in Yisrael Gutman and Michael Berenbaum—*Anatomy of the Auschwitz Death Camp*. Bloomington and Indianapolis: Indiana University Press, 1994. Page 389.

31. Obtained from the [IMW] Imperial War Museum London. Rudolf Höss Interrogation Papers from the C.S. Mackay report Ref: 05/14/1. Page 5.

32. Obtained from the [IMW] Imperial War Museum London. Rudolf Höss Interrogation Papers from the C.S. Mackay report Ref: 05/14/1. Page 5.

33. Steven Paskuly, *Death Dealer. The Memoirs of the SS Kommandant at Auschwitz*. Prometheus Books, Buffalo, NY, 1992. Page 156.

34. Taken from the handwritten memoirs of Rudolf Höss— (Reminiscences)/96, volume 1-5, inventory number 49757 [Auschwitz-Birkenau Museum].

35. Taken from the handwritten memoirs of Rudolf Höss— (Reminiscences)/96, volume 1-5, inventory number 49757 [Auschwitz-Birkenau Museum].

36. Taken from the handwritten memoirs of Rudolf Höss— (Reminiscences)/96, volume 1-5, inventory number 49757 [Auschwitz-Birkenau Museum].

37. Steven Paskuly, *Death Dealer. The Memoirs of the SS Kommandant at Auschwitz*. Prometheus Books, Buffalo, NY, 1992. Page 133.

38. *Commandant of Auschwitz*. Phoenix Press. Pages 106/107.

39. Taken from the handwritten memoirs of Rudolf Höss— (Reminiscences)/96, volume 1-5, inventory number 49757 [Auschwitz-Birkenau Museum] and also supported due to clarity of writing by the publication *Death Dealer* [Prometheus Books] Page 133.

40. These figures were taken from the published extract; *Auschwitz 1270 to the Present*. Deborah Dwork & Robert Jan Van Pelt. Norton, 1996.

41. Taken from the handwritten memoirs of Rudolf Höss— (Reminiscences)/96, volume 1-5, inventory number 49757 [Auschwitz-Birkenau Museum] and also supported due to clarity of writing by the publication *Death Dealer* [Prometheus Books] Page 157.

42. Testimony by Aniela Bednarska on 29 December 1962. Obtained from Auschwitz-Birkenau Museum and translated from Polish into English.

43. Account by the housekeeper of SS-*Untersturmführer* Georg Gussregen, who visited Auschwitz and the Höss villa during the summer of 1941.

44. Testimony by Aniela Bednarska on 29 December 1962. Obtained from Auschwitz-Birkenau Museum and translated from Polish into English.

45. Testimony by Aniela Bednarska on 29 December 1962. Obtained from Auschwitz-Birkenau Museum and translated from Polish into English.

46. Testimony by Aniela Bednarska on 29 December 1962. Obtained from Auschwitz-Birkenau Museum and translated from Polish into English.

47. Testimony by Aniela Bednarska on 29 December 1962. Obtained from Auschwitz-Birkenau Museum and translated from Polish into English.

48. Account taken from Stanislaw Dubiel who worked as a general gardener in the Höss villa and carried out various other duties in

the house between 6 November 1940 and 18 November 1945. Testimony obtained in Polish and translated into English.

49. Account taken from Stanislaw Dubiel who worked as a general gardener in the Höss villa and carried out various other duties in the house between 6 November 1940 and 18 November 1945. Testimony obtained in Polish and translated into English.

50. Account taken from Stanislaw Dubiel who worked as a general gardener in the Höss villa and carried out various other duties in the house between 6 November 1940 and 18 November 1945. Testimony obtained in Polish and translated into English.

51. Account taken from Stanislaw Dubiel who worked as a general gardener in the Höss villa and carried out various other duties in the house between 6 November 1940 and 18 November 1945. Testimony obtained in Polish and translated into English.

52. Account taken from Stanislaw Dubiel who worked as a general gardener in the Höss villa and carried out various other duties in the house between 6 November 1940 and 18 November 1945. Testimony obtained in Polish and translated into English.

53. Testimony by Aniela Bednarska on 29 December 1962. Obtained from Auschwitz-Birkenau Museum and translated from Polish into English.

54. Testimony by Aniela Bednarska on 29 December 1962. Obtained from Auschwitz-Birkenau Museum and translated from Polish into English.

55. Account given in January 1963 by Janina Szczurak, Hedwig Höss's dressmaker. Account obtained from Auschwitz-Birkenau Museum and translated from Polish into English.

56. Account given in January 1963 by Janina Szczurak, Hedwig Höss's dressmaker. Account obtained from Auschwitz-Birkenau Museum and translated from Polish into English.

57. Account by Eleonore Hodys resulting from interrogation by Konrad Morgan, investigative office of the RKPA SS HAG— winter 1944. English edition published by the US Army from a

copy supplied by former SS officer Gerhard Wiebeck in SS Dachau, published in 1945. Statement provided by Charles Provan to author in April 2007.

58. Account given by Eleonore Hodys, resulting from interrogation by Konrad Morgan, investigative office of the RKPA SS HAG— winter 1944. English edition published by the US Army from a copy supplied by former SS officer Gerhard Wiebeck in SS Dachau, published in 1945. Statement provided by Charles Provan to author in April 2007.

59. Testimony by Aniela Bednarska on 29 December 1962. Obtained from Auschwitz-Birkenau Museum and translated from Polish into English.

60. Richard Breitmann, *The Architect of Genocide*. The Bodley Head: London, 1991. Page 189.

61. *Commandant of Auschwitz*. Phoenix Press, 2000. Pages 144/145.

62. Account by SS-*Sturmbannführer* Hans Aumeier whilst under interrogation on 25 July 1945. Handwritten notes supplied by David Irving to the author and translated by the author.

63. Obtained from the [IWM] Imperial War Museum London from the Rudolf Höss interrogation papers of C.S. Mackay: Ref: 05/141/1. Page 4.

64. Steven Paskuly, *Death Dealer. The Memoirs of the SS Kommandant at Auschwitz*. Prometheus Books, Buffalo, NY, 1992. Pages 158/159.

65. Steven Paskuly, *Death Dealer. The Memoirs of the SS Kommandant at Auschwitz*. Prometheus Books, Buffalo, NY, 1992. Page 159.

66. Steven Paskuly, *Death Dealer. The Memoirs of the SS Kommandant at Auschwitz*. Prometheus Books, Buffalo, NY, 1992. Page 159.

67. Extract from the [NA] National Archives microfilm T/1270—interrogation of Rudolf Höss [1946].

68. Taken from the handwritten memoirs of Rudolf Höss— (Reminiscences)/96, volume 1-5, inventory number 49757 [Auschwitz-Birkenau Museum].

69. Taken from the handwritten memoirs of Rudolf Höss— (Reminiscences)/96, volume 1-5, inventory number 49757 [Auschwitz-Birkenau Museum].

70. Evidence that Rudolf Höss told his wife about the exterminations was obtained from the [NA] National Archives microfilm T/ 1270—interrogation of Rudolf Höss [1946].

71. Steven Paskuly, *Death Dealer. The Memoirs of the SS Kommandant at Auschwitz.* Prometheus Books, Buffalo, NY, 1992. Pages 286/290.

72. Taken from the handwritten memoirs of Rudolf Höss— (Reminiscences)/96, volume 1-5, inventory number 49757 [Auschwitz-Birkenau Museum].

73. Taken from the handwritten memoirs of Rudolf Höss— (Reminiscences)/96, volume 1-5, inventory number 49757 [Auschwitz-Birkenau Museum].

74. Taken from the handwritten memoirs of Rudolf Höss— (Reminiscences)/96, volume 1-5, inventory number 49757 [Auschwitz-Birkenau Museum].

75. Extracted document from the PMO Archives, dated 12 August 1942.

76. Taken from the handwritten memoirs of Rudolf Höss— (Reminiscences)/96, volume 1-5, inventory number 49757 [Auschwitz-Birkenau Museum].

77. Taken from the handwritten memoirs of Rudolf Höss— (Reminiscences)/96, volume 1-5, inventory number 49757 [Auschwitz-Birkenau Museum] and also supported due to clarity of writing by the publications *Death Dealer* [Prometheus Books] and *Commandant of Auschwitz* [Phoenix Press].

78. Steven Paskuly, *Death Dealer. The Memoirs of the SS Kommandant at Auschwitz*. Prometheus Books, Buffalo, NY, 1992. Page 163.

79. Steven Paskuly, *Death Dealer. The Memoirs of the SS Kommandant at Auschwitz*. Prometheus Books, Buffalo, NY, 1992. Page 163.

80. Account by Eleonore Hodys resulting from interrogation by Konrad Morgan, investigative office of the RKPA SS HAG— winter 1944. English edition published by the US Army from a copy supplied by former SS officer Gerhard Wiebeck in SS Dachau, published in 1945. Statement provided by Charles Provan to author in April 2007.

81. Account by Eleonore Hodys resulting from interrogation by Konrad Morgan, investigative office of the RKPA SS HAG— winter 1944. English edition published by the US Army from a copy supplied by former SS officer Gerhard Wiebeck in SS Dachau, published in 1945. Statement provided by Charles Provan to author in April 2007.

82. Account by Eleonore Hodys resulting from interrogation by Konrad Morgan, investigative office of the RKPA SS HAG— winter 1944. English edition published by the US Army from a copy supplied by former SS officer Gerhard Wiebeck in SS Dachau, published in 1945. Statement provided by Charles Provan to author in April 2007.

83. Account by Eleonore Hodys resulting from interrogation by Konrad Morgan, investigative office of the RKPA SS HAG— winter 1944. English edition published by the US Army from a copy supplied by former SS officer Gerhard Wiebeck in SS Dachau, published in 1945. Statement provided by Charles Provan to author in April 2007.

84. Letter of 9 January 1943, APK, RK 2903, page 10, to Rudolf Höss from the District President in Kattowitz.

85. Report from engineer Prüfer, 29 January 1943. APMO, BW 30/34. Page 101.

86. Translated from Document BW30/25, obtained from the Auschwitz-Birkenau Museum. Dated 6 March 1943.

87. Obtained from the [IWM] Imperial War Museum London from the Rudolf Höss interrogation papers of C.S. Mackay: Ref: 05/141/1. Page 3.

88. Obtained from the [IWM] Imperial War Museum London from the Rudolf Höss interrogation papers of C.S. Mackay: Ref: 05/141/1.

89. Obtained from the [IWM] Imperial War Museum London from the Rudolf Höss interrogation papers of C.S. Mackay: Ref: 05/141/1.

90. Taken from the handwritten memoirs of Rudolf Höss—(Reminiscences)/96, volume 1-5, inventory number 49757 [Auschwitz-Birkenau Museum].

91. Taken from the handwritten memoirs of Rudolf Höss—(Reminiscences)/96, volume 1-5, inventory number 49757 [Auschwitz-Birkenau Museum].

92. Typed extract of a document showing Höss's speech reference number AFZ234211 - supplied to author from Polish researcher Marcin Bratkrajc.

93. Taken from the handwritten memoirs of Rudolf Höss—(Reminiscences)/96, volume 1-5, inventory number 49757 [Auschwitz-Birkenau Museum].

94. Taken from the handwritten memoirs of Rudolf Höss—(Reminiscences)/96, volume 1-5, inventory number 49757 [Auschwitz-Birkenau Museum].

95. Account taken from Stanislaw Dubiel who worked as a general gardener in the Höss villa and carried out various other duties in the house between 6 November 1940 and 18 November 1945. Testimony obtained in Polish and translated into English.

96. Account taken from Stanislaw Dubiel who worked as a general gardener in the Höss villa and carried out various other duties in

the house between 6 November 1940 and 18 November 1945. Testimony obtained in Polish and translated into English.

97. Account taken from Stanislaw Dubiel who worked as a general gardener in the Höss villa and carried out various other duties in the house between 6 November 1940 and 18 November 1945. Testimony obtained in Polish and translated into English.

98. Obtained from the [IWM] Imperial War Museum London from the Rudolf Höss interrogation papers of C.S. Mackay: Ref: 05/141/1. Page 4.

99. Account taken from Stanislaw Dubiel who worked as a general gardener in the Höss villa and carried out various other duties in the house between 6 November 1940 and 18 November 1945. Testimony obtained in Polish and translated into English.

100. Account taken from the written confession of Rudolf Höss by British Intelligence officers of the 92 [FSS] Field Security Section on 14 March 1946. Pages 4/5. [Military Intelligence Corps Museum, Chicksands, Bedfordshire].

101. Taken from the handwritten memoirs of Rudolf Höss— (Reminiscences)/96, volume 1-5, inventory number 49757 [Auschwitz-Birkenau Museum].

102. Taken from the handwritten memoirs of Rudolf Höss— (Reminiscences)/96, volume 1-5, inventory number 49757 [Auschwitz-Birkenau Museum].

103. Taken from the handwritten memoirs of Rudolf Höss— (Reminiscences)/96, volume 1-5, inventory number 49757 [Auschwitz-Birkenau Museum].

104. Taken from the handwritten memoirs of Rudolf Höss— (Reminiscences)/96, volume 1-5, inventory number 49757 [Auschwitz-Birkenau Museum] and also supported due to clarity of pages by using the publications *Death Dealer* [Da Capo Press] and Steven Paskuly, *Death Dealer. The Memoirs of the SS Kommandant at Auschwitz*. Prometheus Books, Buffalo, NY, 1992.

105. Account taken from Stanislaw Dubiel who worked as a general gardener in the Höss villa and carried out various other

duties in the house between 6 November 1940 and 18 November 1945. Testimony obtained in Polish and translated into English.

106. Account taken from the written confession of Rudolf Höss by British Intelligence officers of the 92 [FSS] Field Security Section on 14 March 1946. [Military Intelligence Corps Museum, Chicksands, Bedfordshire].

107. Account taken from the written confession of Rudolf Höss by British Intelligence officers of the 92 [FSS] Field Security Section on 14 March 1946. [Military Intelligence Corps Museum, Chicksands, Bedfordshire].

108. Taken from the handwritten memoirs of Rudolf Höss— (Reminiscences)/96, volume 1-5, inventory number 49757 [Auschwitz-Birkenau Museum].

109. Taken from the handwritten memoirs of Rudolf Höss— (Reminiscences)/96, volume 1-5, inventory number 49757 [Auschwitz-Birkenau Museum].

110. Steven Paskuly, *Death Dealer. The Memoirs of the SS Kommandant at Auschwitz*. Prometheus Books, Buffalo, NY, 1992. Page 178.

111. Account taken from the written confession of Rudolf Höss by British Intelligence officers of the 92 [FSS] Field Security Section on 14 March 1946. [Military Intelligence Corps Museum, Chicksands, Bedfordshire].

112. Account taken from the written confession of Rudolf Höss by British Intelligence officers of the 92 [FSS] Field Security Section on 14 March 1946. [Military Intelligence Corps Museum, Chicksands, Bedfordshire].

113. Account taken from the written confession of Rudolf Höss by British Intelligence officers of the 92 [FSS] Field Security Section on 14 March 1946. [Military Intelligence Corps Museum, Chicksands, Bedfordshire].

114. Account taken from the written confession of Rudolf Höss by British Intelligence officers of the 92 [FSS] Field Security Section on

14 March 1946. [Military Intelligence Corps Museum, Chicksands, Bedfordshire].

115. A letter obtained from the Military Intelligence Museum, written by Captain Cross of the 92 [FSS] Field Security Section to Colonel Robson on 27 March 1985 to the Intelligence Corps Museum regarding his memories of the surveillance and subsequent arrest of Hedwig Höss and her children.

116. Report by the 92 [FSS] Field Security Section Ref = 92/010/15 March 1946 to: - GS196) 8 Corps District. [Military Intelligence Corps, Chicksands].

117. Account taken from the written confession of Rudolf Höss by British Intelligence officers of the 92 [FSS] Field Security Section on 14 March 1946. [Military Intelligence Corps Museum, Chicksands, Bedfordshire].

118. Report by the 92 [FSS] Field Security Section Ref = 92/010/15 March 1946 to: - GS196) 8 Corps District. [Military Intelligence Corps, Chicksands].

119. Report by the 92 [FSS] Field Security Section Ref = 92/010/15 March 1946 to: - GS196) 8 Corps District. [Military Intelligence Corps, Chicksands].

120. Report by the 92 [FSS] Field Security Section Ref = 92/010/15 March 1946 to: - GS196) 8 Corps District. [Military Intelligence Corps, Chicksands].

121. Taken from the handwritten memoirs of Rudolf Höss— (Reminiscences)/96, volume 1-5, inventory number 49757 [Auschwitz-Birkenau Museum].

122. Taken from the handwritten memoirs of Rudolf Höss— (Reminiscences)/96, volume 1-5, inventory number 49757 [Auschwitz-Birkenau Museum].

123. A letter obtained from the Military Intelligence Museum, written by Captain Cross of the 92 [FSS] Field Security Section to Colonel Robson on 27 March 1985 to the Intelligence Corps Museum regarding his memories of the surveillance and subsequent arrest of Hedwig Höss and her children.

124. Taken from the handwritten memoirs of Rudolf Höss—(Reminiscences)/96, volume 1-5, inventory number 49757 [Auschwitz-Birkenau Museum].

125. From the testimony of Moritz von Schirmeister.

126. Rupert Butler, *Black Angels*. Pen & Sword Books. Page 238.

127. Taken from the handwritten memoirs of Rudolf Höss—(Reminiscences)/96, volume 1-5, inventory number 49757 [Auschwitz-Birkenau Museum].

128. Taken from the handwritten memoirs of Rudolf Höss—(Reminiscences)/96, volume 1-5, inventory number 49757 [Auschwitz-Birkenau Museum].

129. Taken from the handwritten memoirs of Rudolf Höss—(Reminiscences)/96, volume 1-5, inventory number 49757 [Auschwitz-Birkenau Museum].

130. Taken from the handwritten letter by Rudolf Höss to his children—(Reminiscences)/96, volume 1-5, inventory number 49757 [Auschwitz-Birkenau Museum].

131. Taken from the handwritten letter by Rudolf Höss to his children—(Reminiscences)/96, volume 1-5, inventory number 49757 [Auschwitz-Birkenau Museum].

132. Taken from the handwritten letter by Rudolf Höss to his children—(Reminiscences)/96, volume 1-5, inventory number 49757 [Auschwitz-Birkenau Museum].

133. Taken from the handwritten letter by Rudolf Höss to his children—(Reminiscences)/96, volume 1-5, inventory number 49757 [Auschwitz-Birkenau Museum].

134. Taken from the handwritten letter by Rudolf Höss to his children—(Reminiscences)/96, volume 1-5, inventory number 49757 [Auschwitz-Birkenau Museum].

135. Taken from the handwritten letter by Rudolf Höss to his children—(Reminiscences)/96, volume 1-5, inventory number 49757 [Auschwitz-Birkenau Museum].

Bibliography

Books

Berenbaum, Michael, and Gutman, Yisrael, *The Anatomy of the Auschwitz Death Camp.* United States Holocaust Memorial Museum, Indiana University Press, 1994.

Breitman, Richard, *The Architect of Genocide.* The Bodley Head, London, 1991.

Broad, Perry, *Auschwitz State Museum: KL Auschwitz Seen by the SS.* 1998.

Buchheim, Hans, *SS und Polizei im Nationalsozialistischen Staat.* Duisdorf bei Bonn: Selbstverlag der Studiengesellschaft fur Zietprobleme, 1964.

Butler, Rupert, *Black Angels.* Pen & Sword Books, 1978.

Cesarani, David, *Eichmann.* Vintage, 2005.

Dicks, Henry, *Licensed Mass Murder: A Socio-Psychological Study of Some SS Killers.* London, Chatto Heinemann, 1972.

'Dienstaltersliste der Schutzstaffel der NSDAP'. Stand vom 1. Oktober, 1934. Berlin, Personalkanzlei der Reichsführer-SS, 1935.

'Dienstaltersliste der Schutzstaffel der NSDAP'. Stand vom 1. Dezember, 1936. Berlin, Personalkanzlei der Reichsführer-SS, 1937.

'Dienstaltersliste der Schutzstaffel der NSDAP (SS)'. Stand vom 1. Dezember, 1938. Mit Berichtigungsheft, Stand vom 15 Juni 1939. Biblio Verlag, Osnabruck, 1987.

'Dienstaltersliste der Schutzstaffel der NSDAP' (SS-*Oberstgruppenführer* und SS-*Standartenführer*). Stand vom 9 November 1944. Berlin, 1944.

'Dienstaltersliste der Schutzstaffel der NSDAP' (SS-*Oberststurmbannführer* und SS-*Sturmbannführer*). Stand vom 1. Oktober, 1944. Berlin, 1944.

'Dienstaltersliste der Waffen-SS'. (SS-*Obergruppenführer* bis SS Hauptsturmfuhrer). Stand vom 1. Juli 1944. Biblio Verlag, Osnabruck, 1987.

Dixon, Jeremy, *Commanders of Auschwitz*, Schiffer Military History, Atglen, PA, 2005.

Dwork, Deborah and Jan Van Pelt, Robert, *Auschwitz: 1270 to the Present*. Norton, 1996.

Eisenbach, Artur, *Operation Reinhard: Mass Extermination of the Jewish Population in Poland*. Polish Western Affairs, 3 January 1962, 80-124.

FitzGibbon, Constantine, *The Commandant of Auschwitz*. London, Phoenix Press, 2000.

Friedrich, Otto, *The Kingdom of Auschwitz*. New York, Harper Collins, 1982.

Harris, Whitney R., *Tyranny on Trial: The Evidence at Nuremberg*. Dallas, Southern Methodist University Press, 1954.

Hilberg, Paul, *The Destruction of the European Jews*. Chicago, Quadrangle Books, 1960.

Hohne, Heinz, *Der Orden Unter dem Totenkopf: Die Geschichte der SS*. Gutersloh: Sigbert Mohn Verlag, 1967.

Höss, Rudolf, Auschwitz State Museum, *KL Auschwitz Seen by the SS*. 1998.

Kogon, Eugen, Lanbein, Herman and Ruckerl, Adalbert, *Nazi Mass Murder*. Yale University Press, New Haven, 1993.

Kommandant in Auschwitz, Deutsche Verlags-Anstalt, 1958.

Kremer, Johann Paul, *Auschwitz State Museum: KL Auschwitz Seen by the SS.* 1998.

MacLean, L. French, *The Camp Men: The SS Officers who Ran the Nazi Concentration Camp System.* Schiffer Publishing, 1999, Atglen, Pa.

Mattogno, Carlo, *Die Deportation Ungarischer Jeden von Mai bis Juli 1944*, Viertel—Jahreshefte fur freie Geschichichtsforschung, 2001.

Mattogno, Carlo, *The Gassing of the Gypsies in Auschwitz on 2 August, 1944.*

Mattogno, Carlo, *La, Zentralbauleitung der Waffen-SS und Polizei Auschwitz.*

Neufert, Ernst, *Bau-Entwurfslehre*, Bauwelt-Verlag, Berlin 1938.

Paskuly, Steven, *Death Dealer. The Memoirs of the SS Kommandant at Auschwitz.* Prometheus Books, Buffalo, NY, 1992.

Pressac, Jean-Claude, *Auschwitz: Technique and Operation of the Gas Chambers.* The Beate Klarsfeld Foundation, New York, 1989.

Pressac, Jean-Claude, *Die Krematorien von Auschwitz. Die Technik des Massenmordes.* Piper Verlag, Munchen/Zurich, 1994.

Rees, Laurence, *Auschwitz: The Nazis and the Final Solution.* BBC Books, 2005.

Reitlinger, Gerald, *The Final Solution: The Attempt to Exterminate the Jews of Europe, 1939-1945.* New York: Beechhurst Press, 1953.

Reitlinger, Gerald, *The SS Alibi of a Nation 1922-1945.* Arms & Armour Press, 1981.

Rothkirchen, Livia, *The Final Solution in its Last Stages.* Yad Vashem Studies on the European Jewish Catastrophe and Resistance, 8, Jerusalem, 1970, 7-29.

Sehn, Jan, 'Oboz Koncentacyjny i zaglady Oswiecim' in *Biuletyn Glownej Komisji badania zbrodni niemieckich w Polsce.* Vol. I, Warsaw, 1946.

State Museum-Auschwitz-Birkenau, Auschwitz in den Augen der SS, Staatliches Museum Auschwitz, Auschwitz 1997.

Steinbacher, Sybille, *Auschwitz*, Penguin Books, 2005.

Sydnor, Charles W., *Soldiers of Destruction: The SS Death's Head Division 1933-1945*. Guild Publishing, London, 1977.

Tenenbaum, Joseph, *Auschwitz in Retrospect: The Self-Portrait of Rudolf Höss, Commandant of Auschwitz*. Jewish Social Studies, 15, July-October 1953, 203-36.

Van Pelt, Robert Jan, *The Case for Auschwitz: Evidence from the Irving Trial*. Indiana University Press, Bloomington/Indianapolis, 2002.

Journals

A copy report submitted by Captain Victor Cross following the arrest and interrogation of Höss by 92 Field Security Section and covering the statement by Höss. Reference—92/010. Dated 15 March 1946. [Military Intelligence Museum, Chicksands]

A letter to Rudolf Höss from Kammler, 18 June 1940, box BW ½, file 1/9. [Auschwitz Museum]

A Letter written by Schlachter to Rudolf Höss, 30 August 1940. [Osobyi Archive, Moscow] 502/1. File 214, 91f. [United States Holocaust Research Institute, Washington D.C, microfilm RG 11.001M.03, reel 34]

Affidavit by Rudolf Höss, 5 April 1946, at Nuremberg (ND: 3868—PS, NA Microfilm M.1270, Reel.7)

Document relating to the interrogation by Konrad Morgan, investigative office of the RKPA SS HAG—winter 1944. English edition published by the US Army from a copy supplied by former SS officer Gerhard Wiebeck in SS Dachau, published in 1945. Statement provided by Charles Provan to author.

Excerpted from a memorandum dated 27 April 1942 by Dr Erhard Wetzel (a lawyer), who was serving as desk officer in the Reich Ministry for the Eastern territories.

Extracts from the papers of C.S. Mackay, Ref: 05/141/1—Interrogation of Rudolf Höss. [Imperial War Museum—London]

Institute für Zeitgeschichte, Munich: Akten der Parteikanzlei [microfiche] Rudolf Höss Aufzeichnungen.

Memorandum from *Gestapo* Headquarters, 15 June 1944.

National Archives of the United States, Washington DC Microfilm T-1270.

National Archives of the United States, Washington DC Microfilm A3343 Series SO.

National Archives of the United States, Washington DC, Captured German Record Group 242 (RG 242) Microfilm Series T-74, T-81, T-120, T-354, T-501, T-580, T-581: War Crimes, RG 238 N1 Series (Microfilm T-301) NG Series (Microfilm T-1139).

'Nazism: A History in Documents and Eyewitness Accounts, 1919-1945', Volume II, J. Noakes and G. Pridham, editors. Schocken Books, New York, (c) 1988 by the Dept. of History and Archaeology, University of Exeter. ISBN 0-8053-0973-5 (vol. 1), 0-8052-0972-7 (vol. 2). Document #690 on p.979.

Office of US Chief Counsel for the prosecution of axis criminality APO 124A, US Army Interrogation Division. Translation Document No.3868-PS. Affidavit of Rudolf Höss—5 April 1946. [Reproduced from the holdings of the US Holocaust Memorial Museum Archives]

Papers supplied by the Auschwitz-Birkenau State Museum, based on the testimony of Aniela Bednarska, dated 29 December 1962. Translated from Polish into English.

Papers supplied by Charles Provan. Originally published by the US Army from a copy supplied by former SS officer, General Gebhard Wiebeck in SS Dachau. Published in 1945. .

Papers supplied by the Auschwitz-Birkenau State Museum, based on the testimony of Janina Szczurak, dated January 1963. Translated from Polish into English.

Papers supplied by the Auschwitz-Birkenau State Museum, based on the testimony of Stanislaw Dubiel. Translated from Polish into English.

Plan of Auschwitz-Birkenau, 6 January 1942, box BW 2/6. [Auschwitz Museum]

[PRO] UK Public Records Office documents Ref: F0371/57649. Dated March 1946. Relating to Foreign Office communiqués to the Polish delegate on the War Crimes Commission to hand over Rudolf Höss to the Polish authorities to face trial.

Records created and inherited by Government Communications Headquarters (GCHQ). Division within HW General Records of the Government Code and Cypher School. HW 16 Government Code and Cypher School: German Police Section Decrypts of German Police Communications during WWII. [Public Records Office]

Records of the SS officers from the Berlin Document Centre, Oswiecim, and Brzezinka. Microfilm A.0132 Reels 1-10. [Research & correspondence relating to specific parts of the history of Auschwitz-Birkenau verified and obtained from the Head of Archives at the Auschwitz State Museum, Dr Piotr Setkiewicz.]

Reference Section Report 92/C10/359. Dated 13 November 1945. Relating to the interrogation reports of Hedwig Höss and later Rudolf Höss. [Military Intelligence Museum, Chicksands]

RSHA Statistical Tables, coll. NS 19, file 3979, 3, 11. [Federal Archive Koblenz]

Rudolf Höss disposition, 14/15 March 1946 (ND: NO-1210).

Rudolf Höss written statement whilst under interrogation by British intelligence officers of the 92 Field Security Section. Dated 14 March 1946. [Military Intelligence Museum, Chicksands]

The Rudolf Höss manuscript registered under signature: Wspomnienia (Reminiscences)/96, volume 1-5, inventory number 49757—Auschwitz-Birkenau State Museum.

Trials of War Criminals before the Nuremberg Military Tribunals—Washington, U.S Govt. Print. Off., 1949-1953, Vol. IV, p. 1166.

Index